Football Confidential 2

FOOTBALL CONFIDENTIAL
2

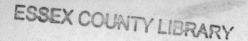
For Julie-Anne, Pandora, Teresa, Nicholas, Sarah, Isobel, Emily and Sarah. Thanks for your love, joy and forbearance.

First published 2003
© David Conn, Chris Green, Richard McIlroy and Kevin Mousley 2003
The moral right of the authors has been asserted

ISBN 0 563 48858 1

Published by BBC Worldwide Limited
Woodlands, 80 Wood Lane, London W12 0TT

Commisssioning editor: Ben Dunn
Project editor: Barnaby Harsent
Production controller: Kenneth McKay

Printed and bound in Great Britain by Mackays of Chatham
Cover printed by Belmont Press Ltd, Northampton

Contents

Foreword

When we wrote the first *Football Confidential* in the autumn of 1999, football was a pretty self-satisfied place.

The new Wembley Stadium was apparently on schedule to throw open its doors in 2002. Our professional football clubs were quaking with avarice at the prospect of previously undreamed-of wealth from a new television rights agreement. There was rampant optimism surrounding Kevin Keegan's ultimately comical Euro 2000 campaign.

During the next three years all these expectations unravelled. The realization that football was hopelessly suited to dealing with the large sums of money pouring into the game from television, or that it was largely incapable of rising above petty rivalries for the sake of collective interest, soon became obvious in the City – whose investors fled the sport within months of a batch of clubs going for public listing in 1997.

At the time of writing, (Autumn 2002) the Wembley project – three ministers of sport, three chairmen and two secretaries of state later – is a crumbling and ghostly ruin, although the deal has apparently been struck to secure the place. The rights cash pledged by ITV Digital disappeared when the notion that there was money in selling armchair subscriptions to the likes of Tranmere versus Crewe on a wet Thursday evening was exposed for what it was: nonsense. And the English national team was rescued by Kevin Keegan electing to fall on his sword, thus paving the way for Sven-Goran Eriksson's appointment. (Even the FA don't get everything wrong!)

As four football fans (of West Ham, Halifax, Manchester City and West Brom) we followed these developments with the same mixture of alarm, dismay and nervous expectation as the millions of other devotees of the national game. The difference, perhaps, is that so little of it was much of a surprise to us. In *Football Confidential* we had probed some of the back rooms of soccer and we like to think we exposed the rank amateurism of much of the infrastructure that has supported our game over the years: the stubborn resistance to blindingly obvious necessities such as employing fully qualified physiotherapists to look after expensive players, and the spurning of this type of sports science by a supposedly highly professional sport awash with money – even when much of the expertise was home grown and had to go abroad for an audience. Or the dreadful hassle, pitfalls and cost of following your team, or even England, on official trips.

This new collection of investigations will, we hope, further contribute in a small way to the process of bringing a little clarity to the world of football behind closed doors. It contains more of the same kind of exposure you may have read about in *Football Confidential* but what you will find is a greater scrutiny of the individuals who exploit the loose disciplines of the football business – individuals such as Michael Knighton at Carlisle in 'The Juggler' or Terry Smith and his eccentric and disastrous spell as chairman of Chester City in 'Patriot Games'. Elsewhere there is focus on clear conflicts of interest such as that found in 'Take Your Seats', the story of a firm, well connected to the Football Association at the time, which cashed in on the recommendations of the Taylor Report investigating the Hillsborough disaster.

The range of investigations is as broad, featuring stories from your local park to table-toppers in the professional leagues. It has required guile, obviously, to put these together and stamina, especially when dealing with the FA's press office or the nation's rail and motorway networks.

When some of these investigations were broadcast they did not make us very popular in some quarters, even within the BBC. Two investigations in particular – 'Swansong', which looked at Ken Bates's business past and present stewardship of Chelsea, and 'Double Agents', which exposed Celtic manager Martin O'Neill's shareholding in a company controlled by one of our biggest football agents – caused some problems for our colleagues elsewhere in *Five Live* and *BBC Sport*.

Of particular surprise to us was the reaction of O'Neill himself, a man highly regarded and respected in football, who showed a less well-known aspect of his personality by turning to his lawyers in an attempt to stop us broadcasting facts he knew to be true. We ended the foreword to our first book reprising the old saying that 'news is something somewhere someone does not want you to know'. This story is a prime example.

Bad news is something the FA must have become used to over the years, particularly of late, with such debacles as the Wembley stadium saga, the 2006 World Cup bid and clubs continuing to play the guardians of the national team for fools. Our efforts have not been received with much enthusiasm by them, despite many of the investigations in this book exposing people and practices that you imagine a governing body would welcome being brought into the light. But not a bit of it.

There were some people who were helpful and forthcoming, Howard Wilkinson for example, and one or two others who, for their sake, we will not name. On other occasions it was a complete drag, as in the chapter 'Sorted!', a probe into the use of drugs in football, where they refused to cooperate at all and, in the case of our investigation into the FA disciplinary process, 'Another Fine Mess', where the press office largely spent their time querying our right to ask questions on the issue.

All successful businesses are driven by their customers. Without fans, professional football would be just an amateur kickabout in a park. Football fans differ from customers in that they can claim to have an emotional, if not a financial share, in the business. Long after the players, managers and board have died or moved on, it is the fans who embody the identity of the club and pass it from one generation to the next. In any other business they would be cherished and served instead of, as is too often the case, being treated as a dumb herd to be milked, dumped on at will or used as a stepping stone to personal wealth.

With such flaws in the relationship between those who run the game and those who pay for it, is it any wonder, for all its slick and burgeoning media presence, that football can produce the kind of financial crisis that is facing many of our smaller clubs, or the notion that you can pick up a team in south London and dump it in a pasture in Milton Keynes?

In the coming years, if the game is recover and to flourish more equitably, the fans have responsibilities too. The responsibility to understand who is running their football club and how, and to ask questions of these people. And to act when they see something they do not like or that is so obviously against their interest. This can only be achieved by bothering to extend the interest on the pitch, off it and into the boardroom.

The millions of football fans who follow teams in the Nationwide Leagues are now all too aware of how vulnerable their clubs actually are. It would be unreasonable to have expected the fans to pick up the flaws in the ITV Digital contract, especially as to most reasonable people, at the time it was struck, it seemed like the deal of the century. But they are entitled to ask, and indeed they should, why it is that perfectly sustainable businesses with anywhere between 5,000 and 25,000 paying customers a fortnight should so often be such financial basket cases, when others in the same boat (admittedly not many) are viable businesses.

And if you think this is pie in the sky, consider the number of occasions when fans have made a difference; the umpteen times a season when it is the pressure from the fans that has put paid to many a manager; the Manchester United fans who repulsed BSkyB's attempt to by their club or the Chesterfield fans who picked up the pieces after their club went bust, and something of the same at Brighton, where fans have rescued a previously failing club. And who knows where the campaign by Wimbledon fans will lead?

Having doled out the brickbats we would also like to award some plaudits. We would like to extend our thanks and admiration to those fans and people working in football who have contacted us with stories and who, through dogged determination, keep tabs on events at the clubs they love and support. Particularly the Chelsea Action Group, a cyber organization, who have often been a lone voice of opposition to Ken Bates and his adventures at Chelsea, and also to Harvey Harris, a truly awkward customer at Spurs, whose complaints were the basis for 'Anyone for Prawns?', our investigation into corporate hospitality.

Our thanks too, to Cassiano Gobbett, *On The Line*'s Brazilian correspondent in Sao Paulo, who we came accross after he took a shine to our book and who has since proved himself useful to a whole host of programmes on TV and radio made by the BBC in Manchester. Thanks are also due to Derek Ivens of *Radio Five Live* in Cardiff for extensive help with the Welsh football programme and to Phil Robinson, Anthony Thomas and Leigh Dineen for help and hospitality in Port Talbot, where Afan Lido provided an inspirational example of a community football club.

Investigative journalism is expensive, time-consuming and fraught with legal pitfalls. And for having supported *On The Line* through eight years and 19 series we must thank: Jenny Abramsky, Roger Mosey, Bob Shennan, Mike Lewis and Moz Dee – who have all, at one time or another in the past, been responsible for commissioning the series on *Five Live*. In our office we couldn't do what we do without the support and help of Ian Bent our editor, who co-authored the first two books and worked alongside us for seven years and who still manages to keep a watchful and helpful eye on proceedings now that he has been elevated. And also to Amanda Queiroz and Alison Turner, who play important roles in getting the programme to air. And finally to the man at BBC Books, Ben Dunn, who ran with the eccentric idea that there might be some mileage in a book version of *On The Line*. This is the third one ... thanks, Ben.

CHAPTER ONE

Double Agents

Nepotism and Conflicts of Interest in the Wheeler-dealer World of
Football Managers and Agents

*Is it right that football managers own shares in football agents and that
they buy and sell players who are that agent's clients? Is it right that some
managers deal with agents who just happen to be their sons? Hundreds
of millions of pounds are spent on transfer fees and wages every season;
can fans be certain that the players at their club have been bought for the
best reasons?*

The first thing to meet you after you walk through reception into the
light, modern offices of the Proactive Sports Group PLC is a life-size,
waxwork figure of Peter Schmeichel, in full kit, poised to make a
save. Initially it is a strange and disconcerting sight but the Dane has
been an important figure in the rise of Proactive, one of the UK's
leading football agencies, which its current chief executive, Paul
Stretford, started in his basement in 1987. High-profile Schmeichel
is just one of the 260 clients the company now has worldwide.

The Proactive offices currently occupy several buildings in the
affluent Cheshire town of Wilmslow, in the heart of Manchester's
commuter belt. As well as Schmeichel, Stretford counts Andy Cole,
Colin Hendry and Jason Wilcox among his clients and they are just
one of the 170 FIFA-registered agents in England. This figure is more
than double the number of the next country, Spain, and each of
them is fighting for a piece of the lucrative football action.

In the season 2000–1, £423 million was spent on transfers and
£562 million on players' wages in the Premiership alone; like
modern-day prospectors, Stretford and his many fellow agents have
found gold in them there football hills.

After a tour of the offices, Stretford, casually dressed, eschew-
ing socks under his fashionable sandals, sits at the boardroom

table proudly beating the Proactive drum:

> We're a sports marketing group and football is one, and undoubtedly the sexiest, of the media interests that we hold. The sports marketing division is the fastest growing part of the company. As well as that there is our corporate hospitality division, and between those two sides of the business they account for 38 per cent of world revenue. That will give you the answer of what the football side is worth.

In May 2001 the company, which counts former Manchester United players Jesper Olsen and Kevin Moran as directors, floated on the stock exchange. City analysts proclaimed that companies like Proactive would soon be replacing football clubs as 'the new force in the sports investment sector' as their clients' wages continued to grow and grow. Stretford explained:

> It was a public offering ... a very public offering. It received a lot of publicity because the UK is leading the field in terms of floated sports marketing companies. It is the only country in the world where there are floated sports marketing companies and there are five currently floated in the sector, and I think we were number one or two. So obviously the publicity for ourselves floating was very high, and people were aware of it. We produced a prospectus which was available to over 45,000 people, and this was sent to virtually everyone in football, as well as those members of the public.

Among those who took up the offer to buy into Proactive were some of the most famous names in football management, some of whom, while shareholders, have bought and sold players who are clients of Proactive. Stretford protested:

> I don't know all of the shareholders. I don't constantly look at the share register. If you look at the volumes of

trade in our sector we would trade far more than anybody else in that sector. We have twice the amount of shareholders in the sector and we have a very high level of retail shareholders. It would probably mean I wasn't doing my job correctly if I sat there all day just looking who has sold and who hasn't sold.

If Mr Stretford had taken time out of his busy schedule to check the share register, though, he would have found that on the day he met *On The Line* the following were listed among the shareholders in his company:

Bobby Robson – 100,000
Graeme Souness – 400,000
Martin O'Neill – 172,000
John Gregory – 60,000
Peter Reid – 125,000
Craig Brown – 120,000
Steve Coppell – 40,000
Howard Wilkinson – 48,000
Kevin Keegan – 200,000
Sam Allardyce – 80,000

Also on that list were two members of Keegan's coaching staff, Arthur Cox and Derek Fazackerley, who hold 40,000 and 10,000 shares respectively, and Michael Dunford, chief executive of Everton FC, with 40,000 shares.

After contacting all the managers concerned, *On The Line* had only three responses. One was from Sunderland manager, Peter Reid, and in a faxed statement he said:

The 125,000 ordinary shares were purchased when Proactive Sports Group floated in May 2001 at a cost of £31,250. After the flotation there were over a million shares in the company and my shareholding equated to 0.01%. All shares in Proactive Sports Group Limited held in my share portfolio have been disposed of recently at a loss.

My financial advisors purchased the shares at the time of the public flotation. The acquisition was made in my own name so there can be no suggestion that this was concealed or of a lack of transparency as my holding was listed in the Companies House register which is in the public domain.

On 21 June Reid did sell his shareholding, as had, on 7 June, Bolton manager, Sam Allardyce. Everton Chief Executive, Michael Dunford, sold his in September, prior to Proactive adding teenage sensation Wayne Rooney to their client list. While Reid held the shares, though, he signed a Proactive client, the American Claudio Reyna, for £5 million. By doing this he contributed to the publicly listed company's profits and, by extension, he would have benefited personally as a shareholder – surely a blatant conflict of interest.

In a fax from Martin O'Neill's solicitors to *On The Line* dated 13 May 2002, they demanded his name be removed from the programme. Despite the record of his shareholding being in the public domain, they told *On The Line* that Mr O'Neill 'will be taking steps shortly to ensure that no potential conflict of interest will ever arise'. But by the time the first Old Firm game of the season took place in October 2002, the Celtic manager still had his 172,000 shares.

No one is accusing any of the managers, coaches and directors on the share list, or indeed the Proactive Sports Group PLC, of doing anything illegal, but by the end of October only Reid, Dunford and Allardyce had sold up, the others all retaining their shareholdings.

Dr Bill Gerrard of Leeds University Business School specializes in football finance, keeping a keen and critical eye on the game. As he says, the maximum wage in football was abolished in 1961 and television by then was already making stars of the players, and that was when the need for agents seemingly became greater:

It's been a gradual process. The sports agent began in the 1960s with Mark McCormack representing the golfers, and as sport has moved into the commercial age and the money has got bigger, and the individual players have got bigger, there is a need for the legal and financial services of agents. So there is a clear role for the agent, and it has grown over time, as the financial rewards have got bigger.

Dr Gerrard concedes that the public perception of sports agents places them somewhere between estate agents and traffic wardens:

> You have got to look at two sides. Yes, there is the public perception of them as Mr 10 per cent, who gets that for doing nothing. [People want to know] why do the players have them? What do they do? Well, when you get down to basics, the agents provide services, they provide the legal services, they provide the financial services, etc., which enable the players to maximize their income. Agents do not exist in a vacuum, agents are not around for nothing, they are there to provide necessary services.

Dr Gerrard advises the FA on transfers and he has devised a system to add some objectivity to player evaluation that has been used by a number of clubs in both the Premiership and Football League to assess the worth of their squad. He says that there is no reason to believe that the dealings undertaken are not above board but it is imperative to be 100 per cent sure: 'The only way we can see that everything is above board is that any conflict of interests is declared by those involved, so that fans know their motivation. And if there are clear conflicts of interest, then it should be a requirement for those [people] to remove themselves from the transaction.'

The biggest holder of shares on the managers' list was Blackburn manager Graeme Souness, who had 400,000 shares, which represents a small fraction of the total bought when the company floated at 25p a share. Just after Christmas 2001 Souness, sensing a relegation dog fight at the bottom of the Premiership, paid Manchester United £8m for Andy Cole, one of Proactive's highest profile clients. FIFA rules stipulate that agents should take roughly 5 per cent of any deal, meaning that Proactive and its shareholders, Mr Souness included, were nearly £400,000 better off. One wonders how many Blackburn fans knew that their manager had such a stake in the company when the deal was being done.

Naturally, Paul Stretford bullishly defends the transfer and says that if they did know, they wouldn't have cared:

> What I think was more important to the Blackburn fans was that Andy Cole came and scored 13 goals in 20 games and Blackburn are in Europe, and finished tenth, and they won the Worthington Cup, and he scored the winning goal in the final. Virtually all the Blackburn fans will tell you that that is the most important factor.

Again, one wonders if this would have been their reaction had they known. Again, Stretford feels this just isn't an issue:

> I don't understand why such a point would come up. Graeme Souness is on a public list of shareholders and you have chosen to name an individual ... the transfer, as I have said, was based on what Blackburn Rovers needed at the time. They needed a striker who could score goals, and Andy Cole has given them that. Every Blackburn supporter will tell you that, every Blackburn Rovers player and member of the coaching staff will tell you that, and that was the only reason he was bought, no other reason, and that is the only reason that is valid.

Stretford is absolutely correct, of course: no one has hidden anything. The list of shareholders with Souness's name and those of all the other shareholders on it is available to public scrutiny, deep in the expensive computer databases at one of the six branches of Companies House in the UK, though these are not, it might be suggested, the natural domain of the average football fan,

Dr Malcolm Clarke is chair of the Football Supporters' Association and he disagrees that fans don't care; as he explained from the office he has at his home in Sale near Manchester:

> Fans have a great interest in what goes on at their clubs. Most of them love their clubs, and have supported them for life, so they have a great interest in what goes on at

their club and a great desire to see things done only in the interest of the football club, not in the interest of people who might make any money out of it.

Blackburn started the 2002–3 season against Peter Reid's Sunderland, ironically, with Proactive shares standing at just 7.5p. As Stretford points out, this meant that Souness's initial investment of £100,000 was now worth just £30,000 and so he cannot have benefited. This is hardly a valid point, though, for Souness and his fellow managers would surely, like any investor, expect and hope to make a profit. Who really invests such a large amount of money with the intention of making a loss?

Souness refused to speak to *On The Line* but a spokesman from Blackburn Rovers did tell the *Observer* that, 'Graeme has a minor equity stake in this company, but we are satisfied that there was no conflict of interest in our signing of Andy Cole.'

Another Proactive client to be bought by a manager who held shares at the time of the transfer was the man immortalized in wax behind the reception door at their Wilmslow office. At the end of their Division One Championship winning season, Manchester City signed 38-year-old former international Peter Schmeichel. In time-honoured fashion the City manager, Kevin Keegan, posed for photographs with his latest acquisition – while he held 200,000 shares in Proactive.

Again Stretford vigorously defended the deal:

The only reason I would see unease was if the fans didn't see the talent was coming to their club was suitable to the requirement. I am glad you used Peter Schmeichel to be honest, he has a worldwide reputation, he has won everything in the game, he has personal honours and recognition from FIFA and UEFA.

Obviously angry now, he continued: 'And correction: neither manager has bought him – they didn't. He has appeared at both clubs on free transfer, so there would be no exchange of monies between clubs for Peter's services.'

Asked if his company and shareholders would benefit from the transfer, Stretford said:

> Peter is contracted to the company as are 262 other players and within that contract it shows that we would receive recompense for conducting their contractual affairs in the same manner as it would with anybody else in the company that works in the field. In my experience the sole reason for people taking players is what they do on the pitch, and unless that is backed up on the pitch, they will lose their jobs. At the end of the day, they can only produce their results on what they buy and put together and coach, etc.

Although the agents are licensed by FIFA, none of them wanted to be interviewed, saying they had ceded control to their national association. The FA also refused to be interviewed but they did issue a statement:

> In itself these shareholdings are not unlawful or against regulations. What is important is that any conflict of interest or any deal is disclosed and dealt with. The people who would most want to ensure this area is covered by the club, its Chairmen and Shareholders. Transparency is the key, provided people know about any conflict they can deal with it. Conflicts are not in themselves the issue. In relation to agents FIFA has ultimate world-wide jurisdiction, there is then jurisdiction delegated to National Associations there is no disagreement over this.

It was this second sentence that 'the club, its Chairmen and Shareholders' are the body that would most want to ensure any conflicts of interest are covered, that most interested Dr Clarke at the Football Supporters' Association. As he stared incredulously at the faxed FA statement he said:

> I am appalled and amazed that the Football Association

do not include supporters in that list of people who would be most concerned. I would suggest that supporters would be the single group of people who would be more concerned than anybody else. We often refer to supporters as the emotional shareholders; I think the FA there were only thinking of the financial shareholders.

Dr Gerrard at Leeds University agrees, and he thinks that football has to take more care than any other business because of the unique emotional bond between the companies and their customers or, to put it another way, the clubs and their fans:

It's a double-edged sword, the very intensity of the fans makes the conflict of interest in football as opposed to other industries more and more significant. There are financial misgivings in other industries, but they do not capture the imagination, they don't create the sense of outrage that they do in football, just because of the bond the fans have to the game, it's that intensity that creates the commercialism that creates the value, and hence creates the incentives to create those conflicts of interest. It's the fans who are most outraged by the conflict of interest if they affect the financial fortunes of their club.

In the late 1990s the FA responded to fears that the game might be susceptible to the effects of organized gambling and concerns over 'bungs' in the game by bringing in the former deputy commissioner of the Metropolitan Police, Sir John Smith, to investigate. Since then he has sat on the Football Trust as well as keeping a vigilant eye on the game from the sidelines.

'I would be absolutely appalled,' he says, 'if someone suggested to me that a manager had shares in an agent. It seems to me that it has all the hallmarks of something quite unsavoury and shouldn't happen.'

He agrees with Dr Gerrard that football has to become more transparent so that the shadow of suspicion doesn't linger over it:

If you are really interested in building up a business, first and foremost you have to establish the governance and regulation and transparency, it's the way that most businesses establish the confidence of their customers. If football is to continue to become more and more popular, as it has in the past, then the display of its obvious integrity is absolutely key. If people are doing things which appear as though they could be abused, acting to the disadvantage of clubs and individuals, then something has to give. Any football supporter wants to know that somebody, somewhere views it seriously enough and erase any doubts.

Surely, though, there must be doubt when there is such a conflict of interest, not helped, according to Sir John, by the way football operates itself:

The lack of transparency really seems to be protected by football. It doesn't seem to need to make its activities transparent to the general public. Of course, transparency is a precursor to good governance, it is something which it should strive to do although it has to be said, that any organization will always need a degree of secrecy to operate.

It is a view shared by Dr Gerrard, who recognizes that deals are thrashed out behind closed doors so those of us on the outside can only act on the perception from the little evidence we are allowed:

The problem arises in football because many of the transactions in football are not particularly transparent and information isn't disclosed into the public domain. We cannot reach objective valuations of how a deal has been done and when you have got that sort of environment it creates a suspicion. The reality may be that there is little or no conflict of interest, but the perception is that there could be significant conflict of interest.

Transfer negotiations are as mysterious and distant to a supporter as the last-minute team talk or the vagaries of the treatment room. It is the perception that is all important – football more than any business thrives on gossip and hearsay – and newspapers, avidly digested by fans every morning, eagerly latch on to that gossip and in many cases report it as near fact, which is why football must be so closely aware of its own perception.

'Football is the family game' is the modern-day mantra we are constantly fed, mostly by sharp-suited PR executives (of course, families have never gone to football matches ever before). We have family stands, family season tickets, family enclosures and even match day crèches. Families, though, play a far larger part in the game than is realized, especially when it comes to the transfer of players.

On the Line learned that within the game in England there are six agents or consultants who are the sons of managers or football club directors. Some, though not all of the clubs concerned have dealt with these agencies regarding the buying and selling of players.

> Mark Allardyce – son of Sam, Bolton Wanderers manager
> Matthew Francis – son of Trevor, Crystal Palace manager
> Jamie Hart – son of Paul, Nottingham Forest manager
> Kenny Shepherd – son of Freddie, Newcastle chairman
> Jason Ferguson – son of Sir Alex, Manchester United
>   manager
> And Darren Dein, – son of David, vice-chairman of
>   Arsenal, is a solicitor who acts as an adviser to at least
>   one well-known agent.

The image of the agent in football, as Dr Gerrard says, is that of a somewhat seedy, opportunistic Mr 10 per cent, exploiting the game's wealth and its vulnerable players, all the while earning themselves a great deal of money for doing very little; of course, in the majority of cases this is unfair. Rachel Anderson, who is the only female licensed agent operating in England, is one of those who actively encourages family involvement, and is accompanied by her son as she travels around Europe. In her opinion football is just like a little village:

There are certain parts to it that I don't object to. There is nothing wrong with one manager ringing another and saying, 'Have you a job? My nephew is looking for work.' I cannot see what's wrong with that at all. It's when there is a conflict of interest, that's when I find it a bit difficult, when there is a manager or director of a club whose relative is representing players you are bringing in and out ... that must be difficult.

There is a huge amount of money sloshing around the game, but it's not infinite, so an agent will use any extra advantage he can. And sometimes, according to Anderson, it can get a bit dirty: 'Oh yes ... I am giving my secrets away now ...' She laughs, mindful, perhaps, of some sort of fraternal club rule she is breaking, 'Oh well, never mind. There are well-documented agents who have no qualms about oiling the wheels financially. So if it's a club I haven't dealt with before, or if it's a new regime, if I want to find out just how reasonably honest they will be, then I would speak to the sort of backroom staff. If they come up with tales of what a great guy he has been, you know, "We all went to the races and we went here and we did so and so". Why would you take the third kit man out to the races? I am sure that he is a nice guy, but that just alerts me I have to be a bit more careful.'

Building a close relationship with a club is important, as Anderson knows, but how fortunate if all the years of groundwork, building that professional relationship and getting on the inside has already been done, – all thanks to who your dad is.

Again, nothing illegal is being done here, but questions have to be asked if managers or other club figures are recommending deals which benefit their sons' companies.

In readiness for Sir Alex Ferguson's planned departure from Old Trafford at the end of the 2002 season, journalist Michael Crick wrote the Manchester United manager's biography. Of course, Sir Alex changed his mind and stayed on, signing a three-year contract. In this book, *The Boss: The Many Sides of Alex Ferguson,* Crick devotes a chapter to one of Sir Alex's three sons, who has successfully reaped the benefits of his father's powerful position.

Jason Ferguson didn't quite make it as professional footballer and decided in his 20s to make his mark in a new field, journalism, joining Granada Televison in Manchester. He left Granada and, after a spell working with orphans in Romania, he came back to Britain and joined Sky TV. Crick, who first came to prominence detailing the life and lies of Jeffrey Archer, takes up the story.

> Clearly he was helped in his Sky career by Sir Alex, and there were occasions when he would get tip-offs about stories that other journalists did not have, but you are not going to become one of Sky's best football directors, without a real talent for the game and people say he was passionate for the game, or dispassionate in a funny way. If he saw that his father was going mad in the dugout he would shout, 'Switch the shot quick, Fergie's going mental!' He was highly admired by his Sky colleagues, but towards the end of the 1990s he felt he wasn't being paid enough and quit TV and decided to become an agent, where the money is better.

In 1999 Jason Ferguson linked up with a Manchester agency, L'Attitude. Crick told *On The Line* about the company:

> L'Attitude was formed by two people, Andy Dod, who was manager of Mick Hucknall, and Kieron Toale, who was in the United youth team – he never really made it and trained to become a barrister. They came together and formed L'Attitude knowing that they had Alex's backing. Alex knew Dod through Hucknall, who was a great friend, and Toale was also a friend of Ferguson's sons. They set up L'Attitude and initially Jason's wife Tania took shares in it.

Crick goes on to describe how a leaked fax on L'Attitude headed notepaper listed the names of several United youth team players whom the club were making available for transfer – this came as a shock to many of the players, especially those who had agents already. The father of one of the players on that long list who has since gone on to a successful league career told *On The Line* that he was forced to confront L'Attitude after his son's name appeared on the transfer menu.

In 1999 L'Attitude claimed their first big United deal, although it is probably one they would rather forget. After Peter Schemichel left to play in Portugal, the role of filling his gloves was given to Massimo Taibi, an Italian signed from Serie B side Venezia. It only took him a couple of weeks to become a laughing stock. Football fans around the country watched with barely disguised glee as a weak and speculative shot from Southampton's Matt Le Tissier trickled through the hapless keeper's hands and into the net in front of a packed and incredulous Old Trafford.

Taibi's Old Trafford career lasted four games, at roughly £1,125,000 per game. He was quietly moved out on loan, and then permanently to Italian side Reggina. Crick traced L'Attitude's role:

> Massimo Taibi was the only player they actually sold for United. He was one of the most notorious players in United history. He let in 11 goals in the course of 4 games – he was a big disaster. He was bought for 4.5 million and they wanted rid of him and they asked L'Attitude to do that for them. So they fixed a club for him in Italy and L'Attitude was paid 25,000 pounds – a very small commission that reflected some unease at the club.

Reggina confirmed to *On The Line* that L'Attitude did play a role in Taibi's move.

One agent with a number of Premiership and League players, who didn't want to be named, told us that he and his fellow agents resented that they have had to work for many years to build up contacts, and their business, while Jason Ferguson and his colleagues have seemingly leapt straight to the top table, helping themselves to large slice of the lucrative United cake, as the rest looked on, noses pressed against the window.

Rachel Anderson agrees and is obviously frustrated too:

Honestly, people are jealous of it, people are quite jealous of it. It must be quite easy if you can ring up your dad, or brother, or your uncle, and say, 'Can you look at so and so?' or 'Do you fancy him?' But I couldn't imagine having to negotiate on behalf of my player with my father, or brother, because it's families first, it would be extremely difficult for me to stand head to head with them and let them lose, it would be very hard.

Singling out Manchester United would be unfair as they are not alone. Only a couple of the 'sons of bosses' have distanced themselves from any transfers. For example, in the summer of 2001 Arsenal paid £8 million for teenage striker Francis Jeffers, whose agent is Jerome Anderson's company, Sports and Media Entertainment Group, who use as a consultant Darren Dein, son of Arsenal chairman David.

Anderson's solicitors told *On The Line*:

Mr Dein is a consultant to the group. We are instructed that he is a qualified solicitor and provides advice to it in relation to legal and commercial matters particularly in relation to image rights and commercial opportunities.

The statement goes on to say that Darren Dein is not and never has been involved in any transfer negotiations involving either party or any other football club.

Mark Curtis is another successful agent with a fantasy league team of clients on his books – he employs Mark Allardyce, son of Premiership manager Sam Allardyce. During Sam Allardyce's spell as manager at the Reebok, Curtis has represented several Bolton players, including Michael Ricketts and Kevin Nolan. Curtis showed *On The Line* part of Craig's contract, which states that he is prohibited from having any discussions with any club where his dad holds any position.

Former deputy commissioner Sir John Smith has probably dug deeper into the murky depths of the game than anyone else. Just like the issue of shareholdings in agents, he thinks transparency is paramount in order to ward off any doubt:

I think I would be concerned about the way things appeared to be. Of course, if a relative of a manager was becoming involved in a transfer I would want that to be declared publicly; you would want them to say that this would not impact the position of the club. The position of the club is something which is paramount, and has to be protected, over and above the relative. It can be protected and you can do that by building Chinese walls, so that over the breakfast table it doesn't slip out that a particular player is looking for a transfer or something that would be of material benefit for that agent.

Manchester sports lawyer Chris Farnell, who acts for a number of players, agrees. Looking out over the ever changing Manchester skyline from his office, he said:

What you have got to look at is this – if the agent is related to the manager, or indeed any member of the coaching staff, they will have access to a lot of information that is privileged. For example, they may know the name of a player that the manager wishes to sign. It is therefore open to the agent to liaise directly with the player, i.e., 'This club is interested in you; if you want to come here you have to use me.' And that gives them that side of the information.

There is another side to this, according to Farnell:

If a manager was unhappy with a player, and knew that a first team player was unhappy and wanted to leave, and that relation has that information, it gives them a lot of power in actually looking for clubs for that player, prior to the player himself knowing that he is no longer welcome.

In other words, inside information passed on with the tea and toast over the breakfast table – a scenario that Rachel Anderson again, is less than happy to consider. Pausing to choose her words carefully, she said:

> I am appalled! I am terribly appalled but there is nothing
> ... To do something like this and to try and wipe it out
> single-handedly is impossible. The only people who can
> do this are the authorities. FIFA and the FA are the only
> people who can stop the underhand things going on. As
> soon as they are made aware of it, they have the power to
> stop the transfers of that club for 12 months. That would
> cripple the club whether it would be non-league or right
> to the very top.

As part of his final report, Sir John Smith also called for the FA to set up an investigative unit prepared to act against anything untoward. However, more than ten years later he is still waiting:

> I never imagined that an effective compliance unit would
> effectively consist of one person. As good as that person
> is, he certainly couldn't manage this job alone, so per-
> haps there should be five or six people and even then
> they need to be augmented on occasions to deal with
> whatever inquiries it undertakes.

Dr Gerrard agrees that some form of transfer clearing office could be the answer:

> It doesn't necessarily have to be that all information on
> all deals is released for all consumption. There is clearly
> a role for the football compliance unit; it has a potential
> role to monitor all dealings and provide a report that is
> put into the public domain to show their belief in the
> good financial and ethical standards in the financial
> dealings of clubs.

As Sir John states, the FA has a compliance unit but it is not as big, as influential or indeed as well supported by the association as he envisaged or asked for in his final report. As the 2002–3 season kicked off, some newspapers hinted that a beefed-up investigative body would be set up, but Sir John and others have heard these same rumours before.

Maybe self-regulation is the key. *On The Line* asked the League Managers Association (LMA), the umbrella body for the game's bosses, their view on their members' deals. They refused to comment but they did post a statement on their website, which said: 'At this moment the LMA's position is very clear – we are working very closely with the FA and the PFA to introduce regulations which will cover all activities concerning agents in football.' And LMA chief executive John Barnwell was quoted: 'We have always recognised that there needed to be clearer guidelines, and we have stressed to managers that they must always act responsibly, transparently and with complete professionalism.'

Obviously, as the country's biggest club with the country's highest profile manager, the spotlight falls on Manchester United, Sir Alex Ferguson and how they go about their business. And in 2001 the spotlight exposed one of the club's most perplexing episodes in recent history.

Not long into the season, defender Jaap Stam was told a deal had been done and he was to join Rome club Lazio. The Dutchman, a major part of United's 1999 treble winning team, was, along with the rest of the football world, a little shocked by the move.

By this time Jason Ferguson had left L'Attitude and had become a director of another agency, the Elite Sports Group, along with another former United youth player, David Gardner, and a man called Francis Martin, who is the person who actually holds the FIFA agent licence. At the glitzy draw for that season's Champions League in Monaco the Stam deal was hatched – with Elite's full involvement, according to Michael Crick:

> It is known publicly that Jason's company, Elite, was involved in the transfer of Jaap Stam to Lazio. Francis Martin, one of the Elite partners, told my researcher that they billed Lazio for that transfer, and yet senior people at United do not seem to be aware of that fact, and don't

seem to want to ask Alex Ferguson. If Elite and Ferguson
and United came out and there was openness, if they said
'Elite were involved in this transfer, our role was to do
this and as a result we billed Lazio for x million or x thousands of pounds', this would help everybody.

Neither Manchester United nor Elite were willing to talk to *On The
Line* but Stam's Dutch agent did. He said that although he didn't
negotiate with Jason Ferguson he did talk to a Monaco-based FIFA-
registered agent, Mike Morris, who is an important player in the
business world, according to Crick:

They are very close through one of Jason's partners,
David Gardner. He used to act as a driver for Mike Morris,
so the links between Mike Morris's agency and Jason's
agency are very, very close. Mike Morris was one of the
other agents in this transfer.

This illustrates how all of a sudden, these transfers have become
extremely complicated. Michael Williams, Stam's British agent, was
also involved. He told the BBC:

He [Stam] was obviously totally bewildered, he couldn't
understand what was going on. One minute he was the
key player, the next minute the manager was telling him
he wasn't required. Jaap had said that he felt he was
treated like a piece of meat on his departure from United
but I think what he was really trying to say was that he was
treated with a lack of respect. Certainly Manchester United
in conjunction with Jason Ferguson seemed to have put
the whole deal in a box and put ribbon round it.

A telling last sentence from Williams, proving that knowledge is
undoubtedly power. As Crick says:

If you know that a player is available for transfer and
nobody else knows, that is very valuable knowledge. If I

know Alex Ferguson has decided to sell Paul Scholes, and nobody else knows that, people will pay me a huge amount of money to be tipped off – especially if I tip them off and I don't tip anybody else off. Now that may be at the heart of the Stam transfer. Jason and Alex Ferguson refuse to talk about it and until there is transparency we will never really know.

Sir Alex refused to contribute to Michael Crick's book and also to *On The Line*. This example is a summary, though, of one particular transfer, which highlights the potential for abuse.

An agent's job is simple: to get the most money and the best possible deal for the client and, by extension, himself. The clubs will also want the best deal but in their case this means keeping their monetary outgoings to a minimum. If a manager's son is involved in a transfer then the same family has a financial stake in both sides of the deal and the potential for a conflict of interest is inbuilt. As sports lawyer Chris Farnell recognizes:

> Unfortunately it's been said that perhaps that one or two agents have been acting not only on behalf of the player, but also the club. That leads to a genuine problem, as you cannot act for two parties in one transaction. That is clear under FIFA guidelines. The reason is that if you are receiving monies from the club for acting in their best interest, the club is open to allegations that you are not acting in the best interest of the player. You cannot negotiate for both parties in any one deal, it simply cannot happen.

Agent Rachel Anderson knows that all parents want the best for their children, but such is the nature of the transfers negotiated and the amounts of money involved, she acknowledges that she and her fellow agents should be more open to account:

> It has to be whiter than white, more so now than it has for years, and this is what people have been campaigning

for. To have someone in power who employs someone else in their family, I can see the absolute sense in that, because you trust them, but what worries me is when the member of the family is acting for somebody you are trying to buy. It is very hard to be impartial, some might argue you try harder and that blood wins – it has to, hasn't it?

A manager of a football club is without doubt the dominant figure; he deals with players on a day-to-day basis and influences their careers more than any other person. And an effective manager will be responsible for all football decisions (including the bad ones) that affect a club, especially when it comes to transfers.

In the view of Proactive's chief executive, Paul Stretford, nepotism is not a crime and, of course, he is right, it isn't. And he should know. His company employs Jamie Hart, son of Paul, the Nottingham Forest manager, and also Kenny Shepherd, the son of Newcastle director Freddie. In fact, Newcastle United PLC is itself a former shareholder in Proactive and Mr Stretford has travelled extensively with officials of the club, Bobby Robson and Kenny Shepherd included, to help build links for it in Australia and China. As Stretford says:

All companies are run on knowledge and contact and I think that's the same of any business, whether that's the media or anything. It is not indicative of football but because it is football it is taken out of context – because of the emotion. I think you will find in all these cases football has been a family agency from before they were born or growing up, and that people work in the business of their fathers in some way or other.

In February 2002 Newcastle's shareholding manager, Bobby Robson, bought teenage starlet and Proactive client Jermaine Jenas from Nottingham Forest for £5 million.

Whenever there is a danger of a conflict of interest it is surely in everyone's best interest that it is declared, and that all parties affected remove themselves. It is an imaginary scenario, which could happen with any transfer, with any club and involving any agent. As a tense day of negotiations comes to an end, both sides are satisfied they have come out on top. The wily old manager crosses the room to the group of agents huddled around their player. 'Well done, you drive a hard bargain,' he whispers in the young man's ear. A smile of recognition greets the unlikely praise. 'Oh, by the way,' the manager whispers again, 'your mum said to ask you to whether you'll be home for dinner, she's cooking your favourite.'

CHAPTER TWO

Swansong

Ken Bates has steered Chelsea through the most glorious epoch in their history, but at what cost? The club are heavily in debt and even contin-ued success may not stave off a reckoning. This chapter explores Ken Bates business past and how it has played a part in the curious ownership arrangements at Stamford Bridge which have enabled Bates to push his controversial vision for the club.

Not too many weeks go by in a football season without Ken Bates, the ultimate supremo at Chelsea Football Club, pronouncing on one matter or another. The government, the Football Association, the morality of vivisection (he is in favour), the European Union, Chelsea Football Club's chances of world domination – they're all subjects that have provoked public outpourings from one of the most recognizable faces in British football.

Most newspapers have ample stock photos of the great man, seemingly in the act of a bellow, which is surprising for someone who tends to speak without moving his lips much. Yes, given the opportunity, Ken Bates will put you right on most subjects. Most, but not all. Take his own business history, for example, or the ownership arrangements at Chelsea Village PLC (the company that includes the football club), or his relationship with a man wanted in the USA to answer for an alleged multi-million dollar bank fraud.

Push Bates on his past and you will, as likely as not, get more edits than a pop video. Ask him who actually owns Chelsea Village PLC and he won't tell you. Not even if you are a director of the com-pany. Ask him why he invited a man on the run from massive bank fraud allegations to be his guest at the 2002 FA Cup Final and he won't play ball. Even though the same man apparently used Bates's name on a share certificate to help him perpetrate the aforementioned bank fraud in the United States.

Not that this, on the surface, bothers most Chelsea fans. By and large, they are a happy bunch. The club's official web chat page buzzes with the kind of chatter you would expect from a team camped at the upper end of the Premier League. On the pitch, they still – just about – ooze promise. Its team sheet since 1997 has featured World Cup winners and performers poached from the finest leagues and teams in the world. No longer can Chelsea's London rivals scoff.

Look around the 'Bridge' and it is unrecognisable from the dump of a ground of yesteryear, its most famous stand, the 'Shed', being an apt description of what the fans were housed in before Bates. Most importantly, serious silverware now jostles for space in the trophy cabinet, including two FA Cups and one European Cup Winners Cup, which makes the years 1997–2000 the most successful in the club's history. When you are winning, fans tend not to ask questions. But perhaps more of them should, because there are financial storm clouds gathering over Chelsea Village PLC that even the silver lining of these recently acquired trophies won't dissipate for much longer.

It may be that Claudio Ranieri, a man with a face from another century, will be able to mould a championship-winning team from the mixture of highly-paid stars and youth team graduates currently on the club books. He will have little choice because there is no money to spend on squad strengthening at Chelsea. Chelsea Village PLC, the personal vision of its chairman, Ken Bates, is struggling with debt. The majority shareholder since the Village was born, Swan Management, has recently dumped its holding and the immediate future of the company now seems to rest on the goodwill of the several banks and bondholders who between them are owed over £100 million by the club, making Chelsea one of the most indebted clubs in Europe.

If it all unravels, there will be only one person to blame. Chelsea Village and all its works are the vision of one man and one man only. Ken Bates. Its structure, proposition and execution of dozens of vaguely related businesses under one roof come straight out of the great man's business past. For a time, he was handed control of the Wembley Stadium project and could not help himself, driving hard to create our new National Stadium in the Chelsea Village image. The idea that football couldn't survive without a cluster of hotels, conferencing facilities, posh boxes, nightclubs and expensive dinners actually gained currency for a time but thankfully, under wider scrutiny, his ambition was exposed as preposterous and he walked. But at Chelsea, because he owns it or at least has the confidence of a clear majority of shares, he is unassailable. There is no one with the clout to stand up to him.

Increasingly, the businesses that make up Chelsea Village PLC are struggling to make ends meet. Except one – the football club – which has made a profit more often than not and has strong revenues. Although the Village was sold to the shareholders as a cunning safety net where each company would contribute to the others' financial security, such is the debt, and the less than wonderful performance of the group, that the Village has become a millstone around the football club's neck.

Dig beneath the surface of Bates's past business career and it's easy to see the Chelsea Village project coming. Its character and structure are an all-singing-all-dancing manifestation of the bold and the Byzantine but ultimately flawed essence of the man. He has pursued many enterprises in his time. All over the world. What unites most of them is controversy, complication and collapse. But it seems that whenever a business has failed, or in some cases never materialized, Bates is already off somewhere else, looking none the worse. Ominously for Chelsea fans, the current creaking corporate structure at Chelsea Village bears a remarkable similarity to his first public venture.

At heart, Bates is a property developer. That was what attracted him to Stamford Bridge in the first place. Chelsea Football Club has had the fortune to occupy the most expensive real estate in British football and its value continues to soar by the day. When Bates first set eyes on Chelsea he could see the fulfilment of a life ambition. The fact that it included a football club was icing on the cake. Bates had had a taste of football back in the 1960s when he became chairman of Oldham Athletic and in between times he was on the board of Wigan and also involved in a Scottish club. The Chelsea project represented an opportunity, a synergy – nay, a destiny!

Bates turned over his first significant bob or two in early 1960s Lancashire in the days when it really was grim up north. An impression he no doubt played his part in perpetuating, in that his firm, Northmix, was churning out some of the concrete with which builders were busily covering our city centres.

In those days he came across a man called Eric Cookson, who ran a firm that specialized in repairing and refurbishing schools. Cookson was friends with a local family of builders, Howarth's of Burnley. After Mr Howarth passed away in the late 1950s and much of the day-to-day running of the firm fell to his widow, Cookson bought her shares. Bates bought Howarth's from Cookson in late 1961.

Good timing! Howarth's had just tendered for the contract to rebuild Burnley town centre. The formidable alliance of a man who knew about concrete, Bates, with one who headed a firm of well-respected local builders, Cookson, put the Howarth tender in the 'box seats' and they were duly awarded the business.

In all it was worth £5 million. A considerable sum in those days. The House of Commons library has published a calculator to convert sums of money into modern purchasing power. £5 million in 1961 comes out at close on £60 million in 2001.

What should have been a straightforward affair, however, in a style that was to typify Bates's business dealings in future, soon became a complicated one. In a bold move he persuaded his partners to float the company on the Manchester stock exchange. In January 1965 Howarth's went to market with a paper value price of two shillings a share. Its price doubled on opening and just four months later it had doubled again.

A firm capitalized at £40,000 in January 1965 was worth £250,000 by April. In the same period the fistfuls of shares Bates held in the company had quadrupled in value. As principal stockholder, he was sitting on a fortune.

Not that everyone who helped create the business at Howarth's shared in the instant wealth created by the flotation of the Burnley construction group. Take Charlie Bradley, a plasterer whose firm had plastered the shopping centre and the Kierby, a spectacular hotel, for its time, in the centre of Burnley and also built by Howarth's. Charlie was used to fighting battles. He had been in one of the worst in the Second World War, Monte Cassino, where he had taken a shrapnel wound. But getting his dues out of Howarth's ultimately proved beyond him. Now retired and living a comfortable life on a steep yellow brick terrace in the Rossendale Valley, Charlie positively boils at the memory of events over 40 years ago. As does his wife. 'It wasn't Cookson but Crookson should have been his name,' she says, referring to Bates's now deceased former partner at Howarth's.

'It were terrible,' says Charlie in a booming central Lancashire accent. 'You would send in a bill for a couple of thousand for doing a house or whatever and you would be paid hundreds. I have still got all the jobs listed in a book in the attic.'

One of the reasons that squeezing money out of Howarth's was a bit of a trial at the time could be that the company was busy spending its reserves acquiring subsidiary companies all over the north west of England. House builders, plumbers, plant hire, aggregates merchants – it was a dash for growth to turn Howarth's of Burnley into a mighty force to be reckoned with on a national scale in the building trade, no doubt. The stated logic underpinning these purchases was that each would develop into a profit centre and help sustain the group through any recession – sound familiar?

It did not work out like that. By 1967 a number of acquisitions were in trouble. Far from protecting Howarth's, they ultimately brought it down. The group's debts and liabilities mounted and by 1968 the parent Howarth company was on the slide. Angry shareholders packed a meeting at the Kierby Hotel to hear what the chairman had to say.

Anyone used to reading Bates's chairman statements at Chelsea Village PLC after yet another loss account will recognize the tone of bluff optimism. The *Burnley Star* newspaper reported the 1967 meeting thus:

Bearded Ken Bates, Chairman of Howarth of Burnley Limited, told the shareholders of the company: 'I am not getting out. I am fully involved in the group.' Mr Bates

revealed that he and managing director Eric Cookson
had injected £100,000 into the group [he said] as tangible evidence of faith in the group's future.

By this time Charlie Bradley and other creditors were becoming
nervous about their unpaid bills. He went to visit Bates one day at his
offices:

I went in and asked about my money. But he was evasive
and did not answer my questions. In the end, he was a bit
cheeky and I had him by the throat and offered him to
come outside, but he wouldn't come. I was not the only
one. He was terrible to get hold of, always dodging out of
your way. I can see him now, in the precinct centre that
we had all built, promising to reckon up but you could
never get nowhere with him.

In May 1969 Howarth's shares, which four years before had soared
to eight shillings and four pence [41.6p], were suspended at ten
pence [4.16p]. A year later the company was wound up in the
chancery court in Liverpool with debts of £1 million. Charlie
Bradley says he was owed £39,700, the equivalent today of a shade
over £400,000. Bates had actually left the firm in late 1968 or early
1969 but, as the directors' report for the financial year 1967–8 makes
clear, the struggling affairs of a building firm in rainy central
Lancashire were not his sole concern at the time.

The directors confirmed to the shareholders that year that
Bates had paid the firm £41,000 to purchase all rights to future profits from a subsidiary of the group called Howarth Securities (Pty) in
South Africa. It seemed to be the kind of place he felt he could do
business. In defiance of the government of the time, he had taken
Oldham Athletic on tour to Southern Rhodesia (today's Zimbabwe)
in 1965. There is even a photo of the great moment when he met Ian
Smith, the man who had led the country out of colonialism and into
minority rule, fearing Britain was preparing to hand the country
over to its majority African population.

Sometime around then, Bates met the man who to all intents

and purposes has become the most important business associate of his life. Stanley Tollman. People who know them have described them as peas in a pod. Bates speaks warmly of Tollman in his book *Chelsea: My Year,* published in 1984. He even called one of his dogs 'Tolly'.

South Africa in the late 1960s was gearing up for an orgy of property speculation and Bates, with Howarth Securities and Tollman, with a number of firms, were there to take advantage. Tollman was into hotels and had several named after himself, including the Johannesburg Tollman Towers, the Tollman Airport Hotel and so on.

Ian Fife is a property journalist with the *Financial Mail*, a Johannesburg-based publication, who recalls Tollman in that era:

> The business environment at the time is key. It was cowboy country in the property market. A lot of asset strippers from the UK had arrived smelling the opportunity and were teaching the South Africans the advantages of buying well-established listed companies, breaking them up and selling off the assets.

Whether by accident or design, none of the companies that Bates and Tollman operated through during those heady days are around in the here and now to tell the tale.

With Howarth in its death throes and the South African operation in its early days, Bates had taken to the role of global entrepreneur with relish. He had simultaneously spotted an opportunity on the other side of the globe, in the British Virgin Isles, in the Caribbean. The Howarth creditors may have struggled to wring a penny or two out of the company but, in 1967, Bates laid out $200,000, plus rent of $30,000, to secure a lease on two thirds of the second biggest island in the British Virgin group. It was called Anegada.

The Virgin Isles are the quintessence of a tropical island paradise. Guaranteed to entrance Europeans weary of their home climate. It certainly tickled Bates's fancy. He is still an occasional visitor. His own personal trust, Mayflower Securities, is registered in the capital Road Town, which back in 1967 consisted of just that: one main road. Across the water is Anegada, hugely underdeveloped – virgin territory, you might say.

Bates's acquisition of the lease was a curious business and ultimately proved the undoing of his plans for the island. He had acquired it from the colonial administration just weeks before the Commonwealth Office in London handed the British Virgin Islands over to a measure of direct rule, called the ministerial system. What was odd about the lease was the length of it: no less than 199 years, which is more than twice the term of any other commercial lease in the territory.

Ralph O'Neal, First Minister of the British Virgin Isles, recalls the rumblings of discontent:

> He had about two thirds of the island, which he acquired for less than $200,000. It was considered too little and the lease too long a time period. Because up until the time of his coming, leases here had been granted only for 99 years. I think he got these concessions because the government recognized the need to develop the island and he was the man on the spot.

Bates wanted to build a marina and commercial development. Part of the deal was that he would bring basic social infrastructure to the island. In return, the inhabitants, who had never paid to live or work the land that had been theirs for generations, would pay some rent, as O'Neal explained:

> In Anegada, the people were accustomed to using the land without paying any taxes at all. All this privilege was taken from them because the land was now leased to Mr Bates, so it disturbed their way of life and his manner in dealing with the people was what you might call crisp or perhaps hard.

Worse, from the British government point of view, there had been a political uprising in the nearby island of Anguilla. The British were anxious that social and political discontent should not spread through the region and wanted to gain control of any event that might lead to more insurrection. They decided to empower a committee of inquiry to look at the circumstances surrounding the granting of the lease to Bates. Led by an eminent QC, the committee concluded that the lease had been secured on excessively favourable terms.

However because it had been signed by the Queen's representative at the time, Bates and his associates were due compensation. The UK government lent the British Virgin Isles the $5.8 million needed to pay Bates off in 1971. He took his money, possibly the biggest payday of his life, and sailed off.

His next port of call in 1971 or thereabouts, and indeed for most of the following decade, was Ireland. With capital in his back pocket, he set up two companies. One, a trust in the tax-lenient Isle of Man, the other, a bank in the Republic of Ireland. Once more, the focus of the business was property, once more he constructed a convoluted business entity and once more it ended in tears.

Like South Africa, Ireland represented a major opportunity to develop land from scratch and it was not a bad call from a business point of view. But the Irish government, wary of the number of property developers and banking institutions pouring in to take advantage of the development opportunities, had no wish to see the country turn into some kind of offshore haven for 'here today gone tomorrow' speculators.

The government decided to overhaul their banking system and to introduce tighter regulation. The Bank of Ireland's interest in Bates's new company, the Irish Trust Bank, was kicked off by an enquiry from a credit agency that wished to know if the K W Bates of the Irish Trust Bank was one and the same as the K W Bates, late of Howarth's of Burnley.

Of course, it was. And the Irish were angry. Bates had initially left off any mention of Howarth's in his application for a banking licence in Ireland (although he later rectified this). The Irish Central Bank was not happy and tried to impose a condition that: 'Mr K W Bates will cease to be a director of the Irish Trust Bank limited, on or before April 2nd, 1972 and from that date shareholders of the Irish

Trust Bank shall not include Mr K W Bates or any nominee of K W Bates.'

They were trying to ban him from his own banking business. He sued. The Irish Central Bank came out all guns blazing. The deputy secretary, Mr O'Grady Walsh, admitted in cross-examination that there was nothing unusual about businessmen having been involved in a previous collapse of an enterprise but he found that Bates's omission of Howarth's from his original submission to be 'extraordinary and evidence of his lack of forthrightness'.

Bates's lawyers accused the Irish Central Bank of spreading unreasonable suspicion. In the end the judge, Mr Justice O'Keefe, decided that the Irish Central Bank had acted with undue haste and had not given either Bates or his fellow directors on the Irish Trust Bank board enough time to reorganize their affairs by the deadline they had set for Bates to disentangle himself from the company's affairs and so he threw out the Irish Central Bank's claims.

However, in his summing up in November 1973, Mr Justice O'Keefe added: 'Let me say any decision I arrive at is not arrived on the basis that Mr Bates is necessarily a suitable person to be a director of a banking company.'

The circumstances surrounding Howarth's collapse were not fully available to the court because the official receivers' report into it was not completed until a year later. It had taken four years and two insolvency practitioners to unravel the collapse. Bates's part in its downfall was additionally clouded by the fact that he had left the company a year before it actually went out of business. But when the receivers' report did finally emerge it came to the following conclusions over the cause of Howarth's dramatic demise from profitable company to heavily indebted busted flush:

> In the absence of any information from Ken Bates, who is believed to have left the country, the failure appeared to be due to the building up of the company as an apparently prosperous holding company with a public quotation for its shares, without proper regard to the continued profitability or otherwise of the businesses acquired.

The clear message being that the many acquisitions of Howarth's had in the end benefited only the share price of the holding company of which Bates and his then wife, Teresa, were major stockholders, and had proved detrimental to the business itself.

(Chelsea fans might like to reflect that other than the pound he paid to acquire the club and some money he paid in to cover the players' wages, it is difficult to see how much more money Bates has personally committed to the club. Yet when Chelsea Village floated he held 17 per cent of a company that was worth at one stage over three times its float value, in other words, millions of pounds. A hell of a return on a pound!)

It was at this point, in the mid to late 1970s, that world events had the effect of pushing both Bates and his South African friend and associate, Stanley Tollman, into the affairs of a struggling west London football club. It began in Vienna, where the member countries of the oil-producing nations, or OPEC, decided that the world had had their oil on the cheap for far too long. They doubled the price.

The impact was widespread. Inflation rose worldwide and most businesses suffered but property, whose profitability is closely related to low and stable interest rates, was savaged. In Ireland Bates's principal vehicle, the Irish Trust Bank, got into difficulty. It had bought property but had yet to realize the full income streams from its investments. Liabilities exceeded assets. It has to be said, Bates's reasonable protestations, that if creditors would keep their nerve, property prices would recover, had some merit. The Irish Central Bank was having none of it and closed his bank down. There was further excitement during the winding-up process when a warrant was issued for Bates's arrest in the Dublin High Court for allegedly removing papers from the bank's boardroom. Bates turned up in court claiming they were personal papers. The warrant was quashed.

In South Africa, Tollman, who had built up an empire in eponymous hotels, could not sustain his borrowings either. Both businesses collapsed and both men wound up sharing an address in Monte Carlo, indicating that, once again, they had gleaned enough money from their various doomed enterprises over the years to still live the lifestyle of the rich and famous.

At a loose end, Bates happened to renew his acquaintance with Brian Mears, a regular visitor to the Principality. The Mears family had owned Chelsea Football Club since its inception in 1905. The club was on its uppers but obviously, given its location, was sitting on considerable assets. The Mears family had split the enterprise into two companies: the club itself and another company that owned the land upon which it sat, plus the 12 acres that surrounded it.

Bates agreed to buy the club for £1. There is some dispute between Mears and Bates about the second deal on the table. Mears said he offered the land, wrapped up in a company called SB Holdings, to Bates for £600,000. Bates claimed the price was £800,000 and out of his reach. In any event, Bates could not or did not buy SB Holdings. It was sold to a property developer called Marlar Homes in 1982 for £1.2 million. They in turn sold it on to a listed property developer called Cabra in 1986. So, over a six-year period the price for the whole caboodle rose from a few hundred thousand to a couple of million.

It is firmly fixed in Chelsea folklore that Cabra were, to use Bates's own words, taken from a programme note: 'Spiv developers intent on pulling down the Bridge and replacing it with expensive housing.'

The heroic version is that it was Bates who dug in to repulse and drive these 'home builders' from the site. Not entirely true. Cabra did have a plan to develop the site minus the football club but less well known is that they also had one to develop one with the club. John Duggan, still in the property business, ran Cabra:

> We offered to go fifty-fifty with Bates. He would put in the club and five million and we would put in the land and five million and develop the site and the club together. The problem was Bates did not have the money.

Cabra went bust in 1992, suffering from much same malady as Bates had in Ireland, after the local authority, Hammersmith and Fulham, rejected a planning application and Cabra, although they owned the site, did not have any income coming in from it and could sustain the delay no longer. The Royal Bank of Scotland was the main creditor when Cabra was liquidated and they held the lease to the whole site. They agreed to sell their lease on the property to Chelsea Football Club for 20 years at a fixed price of £1.5 million per year and further allowed the club the right to buy the lease outright at any time during that period.

During this fraught period in the club's history, Tollman was a regular visitor to the club, and why not? He was on its board. Bates had appointed his great friend to the position in 1982. There are numerous references in Bates's book *Chelsea: My Year* to Stanley, of football matches and the good times enjoyed by the pair in a chain of hotels that Stanley and his wife, Bea, had acquired (and Bea still owns) in London.

But the main focus for Tollman was in the United States. He was back into hotels and this time in the biggest market in the world.

Like Bates, Tollman had a preference for using other people's money when it came to building up and acquiring enterprises. He and another associate of his, Monty Hundley, set about building up a dynasty of hotels, leisure resorts and, later, casinos, throughout the south and eastern seaboard of the United States, which they achieved largely by heavy borrowing from a series of banks.

Money was clearly tight for the pair of them but Tollman, who had, it seems, an almost messianic belief in the commercial potential for hotels, was prepared to take an enormous risk with debt to achieve his ends. All this was possibly an influence in the scheme that had been taking shape in Bates's mind, a scheme that involved grafting hotels, luxury penthouses and leisure facilities onto the football club. But Bates had a problem. Matthew Harding.

Harding was an insurance whizz-kid who had cleaned up in the London re-insurance market through his company Benfield. At first the two got on like a house on fire. Harding put up the cash, around £5 million, to start the desperately-needed rebuilding of the Stamford Bridge ground. Additional money was granted from the Football Trust, a government-funded quango, whose purpose was to raise the standard of accommodation at football grounds so that fans would never again be crushed to death or burnt alive, as had happened at Hillsborough and Bradford in the late 1980s.

Harding, a dyed-in-the-wool fan of the club, was convinced

that Bates had little cash of his own and was curious to find out who it was that backed him. Chelsea FC had been collapsed in 1992 and re-emerged as Chelsea Village Limited. The majority of stock in the new company, 80 per cent of it, was administered in Hong Kong by a firm of accountants called Saffrey Champness, in an account named Rysaffe (an anagram of Saffrey). The 80 per cent was divided into four chunks, all administered by Rysaffe. Harding made several attempts to get to the bottom of who was benefiting from these shares. All were unsuccessful.

Curiously, when the new company emerged, it seemed there was no sign of Tollman. Ostensibly, he had disappeared from the club's affairs when Chelsea FC, of which he had been a director, went out of business to be replaced by Chelsea Village Limited.

So who were the 'new' club's owners? David Cooper was Harding's lawyer and, after his death, legal adviser to his estate. 'We did ask the question, both when Matthew was alive and after, but we never got to the bottom of it,' says Cooper. 'We would have preferred to have known who they were and the executives be invited on to the board but they never were.'

All Harding knew was that Bates spoke for the trust when it came to a vote. Basically, in any power struggle, Bates was unassailable. But it was clear that, whoever they were, Rysaffe at this stage could not or would not cough up the cash to buy the land outright from the Royal Bank of Scotland. The relationship between Bates and Harding soured in 1994, when they were on holiday in, ironically, the Virgin Islands. Matthew Harding had bought the lease behind Bates's back. Harding now owned Stamford Bridge

Harding had been alarmed at Bates's insistence that the future of the club would be best served by creating a holding company to develop the land around Stamford Bridge into a property, hotel and leisure group, with the football club at its heart, driving the whole enterprise with its brand.

Harding believed the best interests of the club would be served by building a bigger stadium and sticking to the football business. Later that year Bates returned the favour. When Harding went to the United States on business he returned to find that Chelsea Village had been floated on the Alternative Investments Market, or AIM.

Harding's loan for the new stand had, as per agreement in the event of a flotation, been converted into stock.

In the new company, Chelsea Village PLC, 60.1 per cent of the shares were owned by something called Swan Management, which, like Rysaffe, had transferred its voting rights to Bates. Harding owned the land, Bates controlled the company. There was a fierce falling out between the two. It proved impossible to accommodate both men in the same boardroom.

Harding was convinced the Village project was a giant mistake and was worried by the extent to which it might, in time, harm the club in which he had invested £5 million of his own money. There was a stand-off in the summer of 1996, which was ended when a compromise was worked out. A friend and associate of Harding's, Peter Middleton, who had a track record in the City and banking, would serve on the Village board while Harding would serve on the football club board.

Middleton too enquired as to the identity of Swan Management: 'There was some mist covering the ultimate beneficiary of these chunks of shares in Guernsey. I was always surprised by it. Ken is a secretive person by nature but I did not feel he had anything to hide.'

Like everyone else, his enquiries were rebuffed. And although he has worked in a wide variety of PLCs and other companies he says he had never come across, before or since, the phenomenon of a majority shareholder being a mystery to the board of any company – never mind one with a public listing.

In October, 1996, while returning from a Worthington Cup game at Bolton, Matthew Harding's helicopter crashed in Cheshire and he was killed. Shortly afterwards, Middleton resigned. With no opposition to speak of, Bates pushed ahead and began his hotel and other diverse developments around Stamford Bridge. The capacity of the stadium was capped around the 45,000 mark, with two hotels taking up much of the space where the historic Shed had once stood. A seething mass of 16,000 hard core club supporters was to be replaced with a seated stand of 6,000.

Bates borrowed £75 million raised in a Eurobond arranged by the City bank Warburgs. He used this to buy the land off the

Harding estate and to fund the construction of the two hotels, restaurants, penthouse apartments, restaurants and other elements of the Village.

With the kind of classic miscalculation that has marked his career, Bates remarked of the size of the loan and its £7 million a year interest payment: 'In 2007 [the due date for repayment] £75 million will be no more than the price of a decent left back.'

Bates, an avid Tory, was assuming that the new Labour government would usher in an era of high inflation. In fact, inflation has remained consistently below the government's proclaimed target of 2.5 per cent.

Try as you might, you will find nowhere in the Chelsea Village accounts any mention of the repayment of this huge sum by 2007. It is effectively a kind of endowment mortgage – but without anything resembling a life policy to generate the lump sum needed to pay off the initial loan at the end of the term.

During this period, the City had not quite cottoned on to what a bad investment football would prove to be. With the Village still a hole in the ground, riding the logic of speculators thinking with their wallets and not their heads, the share price rose up and up, peaking in 1998 at 173p.

Meanwhile, the mysterious Swan Management cashed in, selling off around 20 per cent of their shares at between 60p and £1. Remember, they had received this paper for nothing, or at least very little. On flotation, the market valued the shares at 56p and Swan held more than 50 million of them. All in all, Swan were sitting on a tidy sum. One that dramatically increased when they sold a further 10 per cent of their holding (about twelve million shares) to BSkyB at a price of 163p.

Swan, whoever they are, have taken out millions from Chelsea Football Club with little obvious cause. After all, Harding and the Football Trust paid for the stadium, and the Village development was funded by massive loans. It seems that, ultimately, the football club (i.e. the supporters) will pay for these while strong revenues from the club have been bankrolling the glamour signings of the last decade.

The role of Swan is important because, although they have

contributed little in a material sense to the business, they have given Bates the power to push through his vision for the club – a vision that was laughed out of Wembley in the end but is apparently good enough for Chelsea. The only power football fans have is the one of protest. But if they don't know what is going on, what is there to protest against?

The Football Association claim to have rules relating to ownership. A compliance unit is supposed to ensure that the affairs of member clubs are above board and present no threat to the crucial entity of which they are all a part – the Premier League in Chelsea's case. But despite the biggest chunk of one of our biggest clubs being a mystery, the FA has apparently never enquired into the matter.

Some fans, however, are not so supine. A small collection of financially savvy individuals has been poring over the accounts, analysing the claims being made for the Village and they are appalled by what they have discovered. They set up a cyber protest movement, the Chelsea Action Group, and began to publish their research on their website, Chelseaactiongroup.com

They were particularly interested in the role and influence being exerted by Swan. One thing was clear to them – whatever Bates said, he and Swan were closely associated. A spokesman for the Chelsea Action Group said:

> One characteristic that always comes through is that Ken Bates likes to deal with people that are close to him, an inner circle of people that go back a long time. The Village development he has described as his vision. The notion that such a huge chunk of the company could be owned by someone he did not know just seems to us completely implausible.

Tollman is the obvious candidate for the man on the receiving end of the Swan investment. He had been on the board of the old Chelsea FC and he and Bates had enjoyed business connections going way back to South Africa. They had once shared the same address, both used an obscure company of auditors, Hargreaves, Brown & Benson, from the tiny Lancashire town of Colne, to audit the books of their companies and, as the FBI revealed in April 2002, Tollman's businesses were operated from the same Guernsey address as Swan Management. Most telling of all is the lack of a plausible alternative.

Bates's only public statement on the issue was in the programme notes to the Champions League match against Marseilles in March 2000, when he wrote: 'They are the same people who backed me when I took over the club in 1982 and if they are sitting on a nice fat profit as a result of their investment then good luck to them.'

Then there is the timing of Swan's disposal of their entire stake in Chelsea: 26.3 per cent of the total stock, or 44 million shares, on 28 June, which coincided with some difficulties Tollman was experiencing with the FBI and other authorities in the United States. There was a lack of a compelling economic argument for disposal: the shares were at their lowest point ever – just 18p – at the time of disposal.

When Tollman left the Chelsea board at its dissolution in 1992, he was, claim the American authorities, in the middle of cooking up a most audacious scam on a collection of banks in New York.

Tollman and his partner, Monty Hundley (another guest of Bates at Stamford Bridge down the years), had been in hotels for over a decade. They bought the Days Inn of America holding company in the late 1980s, just as recession bit. Between them their various companies had borrowed over $100 million to build their empire. In 1991 they told the banks they were broke and couldn't pay the money back.

According to the indictment put before a grand jury in the US court sitting in New York in April 2002, this turned out to be a lie. They had sold the Days Inn back to its original owner and had received, as part of the deal, stock options that by 1995 were worth over $100 million.

This was siphoned off, say the FBI, into various accounts based in Guernsey. Tollman and Hundley had made some agreements with creditors but in 1994 they still owed $50 million. They knew the banks were not hopeful of getting their money back and so they set up two companies to approach the banks with a story that they were both planning to do business with Tollman and Hundley. And to give them extra leverage in the deal, they said they would like to buy the debt from the banks.

This is a fairly common device in such circumstances. The banks, believing there is a good chance they will end up with nothing, sell the debt to an independent third party at a considerable discount. In the biggest single alleged fraud, a company calling itself Chelsea Acquisitions approached the Chemical Bank of New York (now JPM Chase Manhattan) and offered to buy a debt of $21,170,000 for $2.1 million.

The bank agreed to this 90 per cent discount as long as they received assurances that neither Tollman nor Hundley were in any way connected to Chelsea Acquisitions. They received such a letter from the president of Chelsea Acquisitions, who is described in the indictment as 'a foreign business associate of Stanley Tollman'. The indictment also describes how '*another* foreign business associate of Stanley S Tollman was caused to serve as an additional shareholder of Chelsea Acquisitions.'

This 'additional shareholder' is almost certainly Bates because, in the summer of 2002, his lawyers issued a statement to the press, declaring: 'Kenneth Bates understands that there is a share certificate issued in his name but he has no idea why.'

In fact, says the indictment, Chelsea Acquisitions had no intention of collecting on the debt they had purchased from Chemical because the purpose was, effectively, to defraud the banks of the sum. To support this claim, the investigators say they tracked a transfer of funds from an account controlled by Tollman in Guernsey to Chelsea Acquisitions – money that was then used to pay Chemical for the debt.

On 24 April 2002 Tollman failed to appear to answer the summons in New York and was declared a fugitive from justice. Six months later he was believed to be living in London, holed up in a flat opposite Buckingham Palace.

Even though Tollman had apparently used his friend's name to help perpetrate the fraud, it seems there were no hard feelings. A week before the indictment was published, Tollman was a guest on the top table at Chelsea Village at a party thrown to celebrate Bates's 20th anniversary at Stamford Bridge. Even if Tollman had let Bates in on his little difficulty and the role he had assigned to him, there was no obvious sign of animosity between the two when Tollman was Bates's guest at the Millennium Stadium for the FA Cup Final between Arsenal and Chelsea shortly afterwards.

Where before there was one major mystery behind Chelsea and the ownership arrangements behind the Village, there are now many. Bates has taken up half of the Swan disposal and he now holds 29.5 per cent of the company. The figure is significant because if he owned 30 per cent of the company he would be obliged to make an offer for the whole company – not something he would want to do, given the current financial status of the Village

But where the other half of Tollman's shares have gone – 15 per cent of the company – is anyone's guess. Chelsea already have a huge number of offshore nominee companies that own tiny bites of shares. These companies never have enough to be declared major stockholders but *en masse* they add up to a significant proportion of the club's stockholding. It is odds on that the 20 million-plus shares have been distributed throughout similar offshore trusts – not that these trusts will see any benefit from them anytime soon. As a spokesman for the Chelsea Action Group points out:

> You have to remember, for anyone buying shares, the reason the share price is so low is because anyone who wants to invest in the company will look at the level of debt. Now, at Chelsea Village, that translates as a significant debt per share. So to buy a share in Chelsea Village today you are not so much buying a share of the business as a share of its debt.

There is an additional worry for fans if it turns out that Tollman was behind Swan. The US government have made it clear that they will pursue Tollman's assets, even if they have been sold, diluted or put beyond the jurisdiction of the courts. Under an agreement between HM Customs and Excise and the FBI, the American authorities are known to have cleared an enormous amount of paper relating to Tollman and his business activities from the same Guernsey address where Swan Management was registered. The FBI have promised to put more information on public record, so soon we will all know, one way or another.

There is, from Bates's point of view, one advantage he enjoys now at Chelsea Village that he has never had before and it is this: the club is unlikely ever to go bust. For despite the appalling financial squeeze in the Nationwide League, the odds are that something will be worked out because in Britain a football club is more than a business – it is both part of a larger entity, a League, and, crucially, an unassailable cultural phenomenon.

No club that is firmly part of a league that turns over more than £1 billion a season is going to find closed signs up at its entrance. Football's financial problems are mostly about its inability to deal with the huge increase in its business rather than a scarcity of resources. Like other established Premier League clubs, Chelsea's revenue stream is strong and will remain so for the foreseeable future. It may be that the worst the Village will do is rob the club of the kind of resources it might have had as a stand alone football business, trying to compete with Manchester United or Arsenal.

Chelsea would not be the first club to blow a fortune on building a vision that turned out to be an illusion. One thing is certain, the continued veneration many fans feel for the man who 'saved the Bridge' is neither healthy for them nor for the club they support so passionately.

Meanwhile, the FA say they will soon establish a set of criteria to ensure that those who run football clubs are 'fit for the purpose'. Their report, if it is ever applied to Chelsea Village, will make interesting reading.

CHAPTER THREE

Take Your Seats

The Well-connected Stadium Seating Firm that Cashed in on Hillsborough

In February 2000 On The Line *charted the remarkable rise of a stadium-seating company that had been formed in the wake of the Hillsborough disaster and had dominated the post-Taylor Report demand for plastic seats. The company's prime movers were key figures in the game – former senior administrators and club chairmen. They had made millions of pounds.*

In the middle of a dour industrial area of Oldbury in the West Midlands lies Rood End Road. Most of the firms in this quarter of the Black Country are solid, time-honoured metal-bashing firms but halfway along the road lies a business called Pel, which, with its modern minimalist frontage and company logo beamed onto the reception area, sticks out like a sore thumb.

Interior design and project management are not the kind the businesses you'd expect to find in Oldbury. But then Pel PLC is no ordinary company. It is a group of companies specializing in furnishing and shopfitting and its key customers include major High Street names such as House of Fraser and Marks & Spencer. Yet it is doubtful whether the remarkable turnaround of this company in the 1990s, from a firm that was going bust in 1989, would have taken place at all if had not been for a sudden increase in the demand for plastic seats at football grounds. The men behind it are some of the biggest names in the game's administration.

In 1989 Pel (formerly known as Accles and Pollocks, a company that dates back to the 1930s) was losing money. It was a failing furniture manufacturer that specialized in educational seating – the sort of plastic chairs found in schools all over the country. In the summer of 1989 Pel was bought by Mike McGinnity, a retired Black Country businessman, who was a director of nearby West Bromwich Albion.

McGinnity had built up his own shopfitting business but, at the age of 49, had sold up and retired. Fed up with kicking around the house, he decided to come out of retirement after just five weeks. He told *On The Line* he was, 'talked into buying Pel' with the aim of setting up a specific stadium seating division. The company had flirtations with this particular market in the past – they had the tools to make the seats but the opportunities to supply them to the British sports industry had been few and far between.

Things were about to change. Pel would supply and fit millions of seats at football grounds. McGinnity, who would later become chairman of Coventry City, employed former FA secretary Ted Croker as Pel Stadium Seating's first chairman. Croker's son-in-law, Nick Harrison, was soon on board as sales director while McGinnity's former West Brom boardroom colleague, president of the Hawthorns club, and former FA chairman, Sir Bert Millichip (who sadly died in December 2002), would be employed as an adviser. Pel's connections would leave them sitting pretty as the UK's leading sports seating supplier. It would prove to be a very lucrative business.

The opportunity for Pel Stadium Seating to clean up arose from English football's darkest day. 15 April 1989 is a day remembered simply as Hillsborough – the day when 96 Liverpool fans lost their lives and hundreds more were injured in a terrace crush at an FA Cup semi-final between Liverpool and Nottingham Forest at Sheffield Wednesday's Hillsborough ground. The disaster symbolized the state of the national game. Although there were unique circumstances that led to the disaster, it could have happened anywhere. Decaying grounds, repressive regimes to combat hooliganism, scant regard for spectator safety. Hillsborough was a watershed. It was time for a change.

In the subsequent public inquiry – the infamous Taylor Report, published in January 1990 – Lord Justice Taylor called for 'the fullest reassessment of policy for the game'. He unleashed a searing attack on what he called 'poor leadership of the past'. The Football League and the FA, the game's governing body, he said 'had failed to give a lead on safety'.

'One would have hoped that the upper echelons would take a lead in securing reasonable safety and comfort for the spectator and in enforcing good behaviour by precept and example ...' said Taylor. 'Unfortunately these hopes have not generally been realized.'

On the subject of football club directors, Taylor delivered this damning indictment:

> In some instances it is legitimate to wonder whether the directors are genuinely interested in the welfare of their grassroots supporters. Boardroom struggles, the wheeler dealing in the buying and selling of shares sometimes suggest that those involved are more interested in the personal financial benefits or social status of being a director.

Taylor's interim report made no mention of all-seater stadia but after recommendations from the FA it formed a controversial part of his final report. In February 2000 *On The Line* revealed that some of those involved in football administration – those people so roundly criticized by Taylor – saw the massive stadium rebuilding programme as a commercial opportunity and a means of getting rich. The football directors and administrators of Pel Stadium Seating would make money from the changes implemented after Hillsborough

Graham Kelly, chief executive of the FA at the time of Hillsborough, recalled that he had rallied for the introduction of all-seater grounds as early as the evening of the disaster:

> I said we had to move the fans' preferences away from standing on the terraces and the view, generally, at the FA was that we should move to all-seater in the top divisions as quickly as possible. We took a view that radical change to the game was necessary because of the scale of the disaster at Hillsborough. It was so awful that we felt that in order to restore confidence in the game we had to make the bold move towards all-seater.

Although the all-seater recommendation was never made FA policy (they submitted joint evidence to the Taylor inquiry with the Football League, whose lower league members understandably did not support the FA's initial call for compulsory all-seater grounds), the FA's hierarchy did give evidence to the inquiry, recommending massive public investment in rebuilding the nation's football grounds. 'Six hundred million pounds was spent upgrading grounds in the next ten years,' said Kelly. 'It provided the opportunity for English football to launch a World Cup bid for 2006.'

The subsequent redevelopments after the final Taylor Report would provide a boom time for all kinds of stadium contractors, who were competing for their share of the market. Builders, architects, caterers – and the makers of plastic seats. Millions would be installed in soccer grounds over the next decade. Pel would supply and fit 60 per cent of them in the UK.

The timing of Mike McGinnity's purchase of Pel in the summer of 1989 came after Hillsborough but before the Taylor Report was published in January 1990. It could, of course, have been excellent commercial anticipation. But, equally, he was well connected. The FA's chairman at the time, Sir Bert Millichip, was a boardroom colleague at West Brom. Ted Croker, Pel Stadium Seating's first chairman, had recently retired as FA chief executive. This gave the company status and prestige. They would have access to the type of people who could give them work. In an interview for *On The Line* Mike McGinnity said: 'The seating market presented itself following on from Lord Justice Taylor's report. The capacity and the ability to make stadium seating was already there when I bought the company but the size of the market followed on from the report.'

Supplying and fitting stadium seats is not rocket science. An employee of one of Pel's rival companies, Metaliform, showed me how easy they are to fit. It takes seconds to drill holes into concrete and install the seat leg fixing. Then a seat ring slides on and you fit the back.

Pel were tooled up for manufacture before Mike McGinnity bought them. Making plastic seats wasn't the problem, selling them was. There was little demand for stadium seats prior to Hillsborough.

Pel had dipped their toe in the limited market there had been – they supplied the seats for the main stand at local club, West Bromwich Albion, in the early 1980s for instance, but with clubs reluctant to upgrade their grounds until they were compelled to, Pel had installed just 4,000 stadium seats the year before Hillsborough. The year after, they fitted 40,000 – and it increased throughout the 1990s.

Back in 1990, for the handful of seating manufacturers, the Taylor Report seemed like an unfortunate blessing in disguise. Tony Sharrett, who was the managing director of seat manufacturers Hille, explained:

> Those of us in the industry thought that this might be an excellent opportunity. We'd spent many years in the wilderness with expensive tooling and facilities getting little business. There were a couple of bit players like Grandstand Tribune, who did some seating at West Ham, and SIS, who'd done some work in the north of England, but the major suppliers were Restall and Hille.

But it was McGinnity's new company, Pel Stadium Seating, who were to become market leaders. Sales director Nick Harrison told *On The Line* that by 1999 Pel had installed 1.6 million stadium seats in the UK and that their market share 'had fluctuated anywhere between 40 and 60 per cent of the marketplace over the last ten years'. Their millionth seat was put in at Aston Villa (a ground where Pel have supplied every single seat). Harrison, who joined Pel in January 1990, added: 'We tend to put in 150,000 to 200,000 seats a year. I think the timing with any business is the key thing and obviously the time for us in the expansion was right in the UK market.' He admits that Pel's senior figures helped enormously:

> There is no doubt that the connections we have with the game, with the fact the chairman of the company, Mike McGinnity, is the vice-chairman (now chairman) of Coventry City. I think that has helped within the game. It gives people the confidence that we are going to do the

job on time and on budget because the chairmen of other clubs up and down the country know they can speak to the chairman of our company very easily.

Harrison is Ted Croker's son-in-law. He told *On The Line*:

When Ted joined the company back in the late 80s obviously he'd just left as chief executive of the Football Association and so he was extremely well known, not only to football clubs but also to FIFA, UEFA and everything else. It certainly helped. Because he had never had any allegiance to any particular club he was seen as a fairminded person so it was certainly very handy to have him as figurehead of the company.

McGinnity confirmed that connections were key to getting business:

We were very successful in Ted introducing us to the various clubs. What we set out was for Ted to endorse it. With his credibility it immediately got the confidence of the chairman or stadium manager. Although they had to put out the jobs for tender to three separate companies to satisfy the demands of the Football Trust who were financing so much of the rebuilding, it helped us enormously. Ted totally believed in the quality of the product.

In fact, Croker was wearing two hats. He was also a vice-president of the FA and it was in this capacity, rather than as a chairman of a seating supplier, that he was invited to address a sports stadium design conference in 1990. It was organized by Owen Luder, who was then president of the Royal Institute of British Architects:

Ted Croker was one the top speakers that I managed to recruit for this seminar on stadia after Hillsborough, because clearly things were going to change. He started off with the words: 'The scene is set, the sun is out, the moment admired all over the world. The pageantry, the

passion and the glamour of the English Cup Final' – and
the background music was 'Abide With Me', which really
was quite an emotional start to a seminar which, after all,
stemmed from the fact that Hillsborough was a very
emotional, heart-rending event.

For the chairman of a seating manufacturer this was an ideal opportunity to press the flesh and make a personal pitch to the people
who could give you work. It raises just one of several important
questions surrounding senior football figures who used their
reputations and contacts for the benefit of Pel – in Croker's case
representing the FA while serving as chairman of a stadium subcontractor at the same time. Luder remembers talking to Croker about
this: 'He started off talking about the impact of Hillsborough and
then, very nostalgically, ran through the way football developed and
the way stadia had developed. He finished on this heartfelt plea that
now was the time when we really had to get it right.'

McGinnity explained how Pel made best use of Croker as their
chairman: 'Ted would be at a game involving a club who were going
for a grant from the Football Trust to develop their ground. He
would say he would be involved on some occasions. Would we be
allowed to tender along with other manufacturers? It was word of
mouth recommendations.'

Sheila Spiers of the Football Supporters' Association questions
the ethics of Croker's dual role:

You've got people who are directors of clubs and with
links to the FA, and at the same time the FA making recommendations to Taylor about what should be in his
report. Was there a conflict of interests with some people
who suggested it in the FA report to Lord Justice Taylor?

According to Tony Sharrett, of rival seating company Hille, Pel
made an immediate splash in the stadium seating market in another
way. In order to compete they had to come in at a lower price than
their competitors. 'They drove the price down and there's a limit to
how far down you can go,' said Sharrett. ' Pel introduced themselves

into the stadium market by advertising a stadium seat at £8–9. The average in those days had been £13–15, depending on the quality of the product.'

The first seating job that Pel undertook was the most significant and symbolic stretch of terracing in the Taylor Report – the Leppings Lane End at Hillsborough. *On The Line* discovered that after the seats had been fitted by Pel, the consultant engineers, Eastwood & Partners, had to call them back to make structural corrections to more than 2,000 seats.

Despite such a stuttering start to their new line of business, Pel rose inexorably. They would install more than 1.6 million seats in British football stadia – including 70 per cent of the seats in the Premiership. They became the most successful stadium seating company in Britain and their portfolio reads like a who's who of major football grounds: Old Trafford, Highbury, Anfield, Stamford Bridge, Villa Park, the Stadium of Light, the Hawthorns, St Andrews, Upton Park, Molineux and Highfield Road, the home of Coventry City, where Mike McGinnity is now chairman.

Pel have also installed seats at national stadia like Wembley, Hampden Park, the Millennium Stadium, No 1 Court at the All England Tennis Club at Wimbledon, Twickenham, Aintree and Silverstone. As Nick Harrison explained:

It expanded by word of mouth. These football clubs all talk to each other. One of the things chairmen will ask each other when they need a new development is, 'Do you know who does this, who does that, and who did your seating?' Someone would recommend Pel and say, 'Oh, you won't have any problems with them, they're market leaders and good guys, I'd recommend them.'

McGinnity said that carrying out work at some of the major football grounds in the country helped Pel's progress. 'When people ask you which grounds you've done and you start talking about Man Utd, Arsenal, Aston Villa, Chelsea, Wimbledon Tennis Club and the Millennium Stadium,' he said, 'it's not a bad recommendation to have on your visiting card.'

It is difficult to estimate how much Pel Stadium Seating have made because they don't file separate accounts from the rest of the Pel Group. But McGinnity's boardroom connections have undoubtedly helped.

In 1992 McGinnity suffered the ignominy of being the first West Brom director in the club's history to be voted off the board. He boasted to *On The Line* that Doug Ellis courted him for over a year and tried to lure him to Aston Villa. Ultimately, he ended up at Coventry City as deputy chairman in 1995, later taking over as chairman in 2002. All three clubs have their stadia totally fitted with Pel seats. There's nothing improper or illegal in that but McGinnity's association with them has given him the chance to talk business in boardrooms around the country. The sort of access Pel's rivals could only dream of.

On The Line asked McGinnity about his boardroom connections. Was he wary that some people might say there was a conflict of interest? Here he was, representing a football club at the same time as a stadium seating company. There are all kinds of negotiations going on between clubs, not least the transfer of players. Pel were supplying a key ancillary service. Was there a danger that to oil the wheels things might be confused? McGinnity replied:

> Not at all. We had the foresight to liase and connect with Ted Croker, followed by Sir Bert. The majority of football club chairmen and directors have been accused many times of the heart ruling the head but I can assure you that when it comes down to something tangible other than players there are many, many shrewd chairmen and football directors and managers and the only thing that would seal the deal would be the product itself: the delivery time and the price.

McGinnity insisted it was the first time he had heard any suggestion of a potential conflict of interests involving any of the people associated with Pel, whether it was himself, the late Ted Croker (who died in 1992) or Sir Bert Millichip: 'If there was any possibility of any of the inferences down the line that you are putting to me, Sir Bert certainly would not want to be involved with Pel and certainly we would not want to be involved with Sir Bert.'

Of the estimated £600 million spent upgrading British football grounds since Taylor, £160 million came from public funding – in cash grants issued to clubs by the Football Trust. Awards were made by a panel of trustees from different sectors of the game, including FA chairman Sir Bert Millichip, who knew his former colleague, Ted Croker, was also with Pel. 'I knew Ted Croker was there, obviously,' said Sir Bert. 'I was a personal friend of Mr McGinnity. I remained a friend of Mr Croker during his lifetime and still remain a friend of his wife.' He also knew how successful Pel had been: 'I was aware they'd put in the seats at Aston Villa in particular. I don't think I was aware at that time how extensive their activities had been but yes, I knew they were there and they were there in a big way.'

As a trustee of the Football Trust, Sir Bert helped to decide which projects would receive public funds, and Pel were a sub-contractor in dozens of successful stadium improvement applications. Although he was not employed by Pel at the same time as being a trustee, Millichip, like all trustees, was supposed to declare any interests in bids involving companies owned by what are called 'known associates', a term that would include old friends or former colleagues. It is a system designed to ensure the integrity of this allocation of public money. Phillip French was a spokesman for the Football Trust (which has now been renamed the Football Foundation and has been given a fresh task, since September 2000, to revive the game's grass roots). At the time of *On The Line*'s report in 2000, he explained:

> Trustees would be expected to declare any interests they have in a football club, in which case they would be excluded from the discussions involving that particular club. They're very strict rules and they are adhered to. We have a list of declarations of interests and if there are doubts then trustees are expected to declare them. For example, Sir Tom Finney played an active part in the workings of the Football Trust, and if there were any bids

involving Preston North End then Sir Tom would get up
and leave the room or be asked to leave.

 So the same would apply to Sir Bert and West Bromwich Albion,
where he had been chairman and was a president. But should a
trustee who had a long-standing friendship or association have
declared an interest if he had been on the same football club board
or served as chairman of the same firm of contractors? 'Certainly if
a trustee was involved with a major contractor that was bidding for
work at the Football Trust then he would be expected to declare that
interest,' explained French.

'What about a subcontractor?' we asked. 'If the trustee knows
that a subcontractor is bidding for that work or indeed that a major
contractor has a special relationship with a subcontractor and is
likely to be involved, then we would expect them to declare that
interest,' said French.

In his time as FA chairman Sir Bert did not inform the Football
Trust of his connections or friendships with people associated with
Pel Stadium Seating. 'I can't see there was a conflict of interests anywhere along the line either with Mr Croker, Mr McGinnity or
myself,' Millichip replied, when *On The Line* quizzed him on this
matter.

After his retirement from the FA, Sir Bert joined Pel as a consultant
in 1997. By this time Pel had exploited most of the seating opportunities available in Britain and were looking further afield. Nick
Harrison told *On The Line*:

> We are now looking for expansion into the European
> market. They are, effectively, behind the UK market. The
> business that has been generated in the UK over the last
> ten years will move on to the European sector where they
> are far behind us. We've got to get our timing right in the
> European market and the new emerging markets in
> the former Iron Curtain countries. There are enormous
> markets there.

Pel thought a formal arrangement with Sir Bert, who was still an executive member of UEFA, would help, as Harrison confirmed:

> Sir Bert very kindly agreed to give us his assistance particularly in Europe – especially through his contacts at UEFA. He was a European consultant for about 12 to 18 months. He was a personal friend of Mike McGinnity's and was known to me from my previous contacts and he was very helpful to us, but he is no longer associated with Pel.

Sir Bert insists he wasn't much of a salesman:

> What they wanted from me were introductions, mainly from clubs abroad, because they thought they were reaching saturation point within this country. I had colleagues out there who I tapped up to find out who was interested and who was not interested. I got some leads in the Czech Republic but as far as I'm aware nothing came of it.

Millichip confirmed that Pel paid him an annual sum, although he would not exactly reveal how much. 'Enough to keep me in Eccles cakes and gin and tonics,' was how he quaintly put it.

Although there was nothing illegal in Sir Bert's association with Pel, was he wise to work for them? During the making of *On The Line*'s investigation into Pel Stadium Seating, the english FA were preparing a bid to stage the 2006 World Cup. A sticking point had been Sir Bert's so-called 'gentleman's agreement', allegedly made with the German FA, that England would not launch a counter World Cup bid in exchange for Germany's prior support for England's bid to stage the 1996 European Championships. This was voted upon at successive UEFA meetings that Sir Bert attended. With Pel so keen to expand across Europe – and into Germany in particular, where the majority of grounds would require modernization for the World Cup – and Sir Bert's refusal to talk about his so-called 'gentleman's agreement' or his apparent acquiescence with

Germany being the sole European bidder for 2006, his actions have coincided with the business interests of Pel Stadium Seating and could easily have been linked to his association with Mike McGinnity.

Pel sales director, Nick Harrison, readily admitted that the company wanted the 2006 World Cup to go to Germany: 'Obviously from a patriotic point of view we would like to see England get the 2006 World Cup, but from a business point of view we'd prefer Germany or some other European country to get it because they still have a huge amount of work to do.'

In November 1999 the British Council launched Football Nation – an exhibition touring the world to promote the best of British stadium design. It was aimed at building international support and confidence in England's ability to stage the 2006 World Cup. Geoff Hurst, Gary Lineker and Sir Bobby Charlton were among the many roving ambassadors who joined Football Nation's global trek. Despite their business preference for the 2006 Finals to go to Germany, Pel provided the seats for the auditorium and were the only seating company approached to advertise in the accompanying brochure. Alex Latimer, the sales director at seat manufacturers Metaliform, said:

> I wasn't asked and I can't honestly say why I wasn't asked. It was a British thing so all sorts of British manu-facturers should have been asked to advertise. Obviously something which appears to carry unbiased recommen-dation is always useful. There was more than one con-tractor in the magazine and I would have thought they should have shown there is more than one seating sup-plier. It's a bit off frankly, particularly when you consider there are only three or four companies really making this product. I think all four should have been given the chance so from that point of view it's a bit galling.

In 1999 the Pel Group was a £75 million a year turnover company majoring in shopfitting. Stadium seating represented a small, though significant (in terms of profile), percentage of their overall business. The post-Taylor boom sustained them through early 1990s recession and their dominance in the market owed an enormous amount to their connections. Legally, Pel and the people concerned have not broken any rules but their links with former FA figures raise a number of ethical questions – not least the morality of the very people so roundly criticized in the Taylor Report for having overseen the neglect of grounds that led to the disaster, then making money out of the stadium rebuilding programme it instigated.

I put these concerns to former FA chief executive Graham Kelly. How did he feel about his predecessor (Ted Croker) and the director of a (then) Premiership football club making money out of a disaster and, some might say – and Lord Justice Taylor certainly implied it – making money from the consequences of the misman-agement of the game? 'I don't have any comment to make about that,' said Kelly. 'I don't comment on people's personal matters.' Surely he must have a view? 'No,' was his blunt reply.

Sheila Spiers of the Football Supporters' Association wasn't so reticent. A Liverpudlian who was at Hillsborough on the day of the disaster, she thought those who remember the tragic events of 15 April 1989 would be disgusted:

> The whole problem with Hillsborough seems to be it was the fans who suffered and died and they haven't got any benefits out of Hillsborough at all, and so many other people have. And this as an example of the people in the heart of the football organization and ruling bodies using Lord Justice Taylor's edict on all-seater to make large amounts of money is quite sickening.

Since our investigation the Pel Group has been completely restruc-tured. It was taken into private ownership by Mike McGinnity's son, Nigel, in May 2001. Mike McGinnity, who is no longer a director of Pel, became chairman of financially troubled Coventry City in 2002, ousting his predecessor, Bryan Richardson, in acrimonious circum-stances, which Richardson described as a 'boardroom coup'.

In the two years to the end of 2001 Pel's annual turnover dropped from £75 million to just £19 million. Its stadium seating market has decreased although it supplied the seats for Southampton's St Mary's stadium. Nick Harrison told *On The Line* that he was sure the company would offer a 'very competitive tender' to supply the seats for Coventry City's new stadium, which, when he took over as chairman, Mike McGinnity promised Sky Blue's fans would be ready by 2004. But with football's ever-tightening finances and Coventry being millions of pounds in debt, Pel may have to wait some time to tender for work at their former chairman's new ground.

CHAPTER FOUR

The Juggler
From Machester United to Carlisle:
The Weird World of Michael Knighton

Michael Knighton is the man who clinched the deal to buy Manchester United, then promised to take Carlisle United to the Premier League. He and Carlisle didn't quite make it – but they had some interesting times battling for Football League survival.

Michael Knighton first strode into football's consciousness at a packed Old Trafford on a sunny August afternoon before the first game of the 1989–90 season. Kitted out in a Manchester United sweatshirt and, for a near-40-something, somewhat minimalist white shorts, he juggled a ball on the pitch, dribbled it towards the Stretford end, then walloped a hat-trick into an empty goal. United fans, it should be remembered, roared back and he saluted them, arms aloft, beaming beneath his moustache. This was the man, the crowd was told, who had agreed to buy the club from the deeply unpopular Martin Edwards, and was promising to return the 'glory, glory' to Man United, who had not won the Football League Championship for 22 years.

Knighton unveiled his plans for United, arguably England's biggest club even then. He had agreed to buy the 50.6 per cent stake in United held by Edwards, whose father Louis, the previous chairman, had bought into the club steadily since the 1950s. Knighton, about whom the general public knew nothing, was paying £10 million for the stake and had agreed to invest a further £10 million to complete the all-round cantilevering of Old Trafford promised by Louis Edwards' blueprint drafted in the mid-1960s. 'It was that which swung it,' Knighton said. 'Martin wanted to see his father's vision fulfilled and I promised to do so.'

Before unravelling Michael Knighton's bizarre, unique sojourn in professional football, which was to last until he finally sold his 93 per cent of Carlisle United 13 years later, it is worth pausing to contemplate the deal he had with Edwards. Nine years later, in 1998, Edwards was negotiating the sale of United to BSkyB for £625 million – 30 times more than he agreed to accept from Knighton. Edwards himself made over £100 million eventually, by selling in slices the United stake the family had bought for around £1 million. Knighton's near-purchase, complete with surreal ball-juggling display, still sticks in the memory, bathed in sunshine, as a measure of how much football changed, so quickly, after the 1992 Premier League breakaway by First Division clubs and their subsequent multi-million pound TV deals with BSkyB.

Knighton has since successfully sued the media who repeated the story that he didn't have the finance to go through with buying United. He had, he said, 'secured, with the assistance of others, a £24 million overdraft with the Bank of Scotland to buy Manchester United'. It was the deal of the century.

Knighton told the press that he was a football fanatic, who had seen through the stigma and shame which then surrounded football – only three months after 95 people had died at Hillsborough – and could foresee the commercial revolution ahead. He produced his own blueprint, which talked about a stock market flotation and United as a 'brand' that could be grown and turned into a licence to print money. As a major shareholder, he would make a fortune too. This is now basic stuff but at the time the press ridiculed him: Football a business? United a brand?

The press delved into Knighton's background and the details of the deal, a spotlight that Knighton later described as 'tearing at his soul'. His backers, two wealthy businessmen, Robert Thornton, formerly of Debenhams, and Stanley Cohen of Parker Pens, withdrew. Knighton, although he had a signed contract from Edwards, bowed to the tremendous pressure and pulled out. In return, he was made a United director and served a decent portion of shares. When the club floated two years later he was a director of Manchester United PLC. He has always claimed that his ideas kick-started the commercial growth that United has pursued successfully and remorselessly, ever since.

In 1992 he decided to have another try. He and his partner, Barry Chaytow, a Manchester businessman, scouted the country for a club to buy. Knighton, the football speculator, drew up five qualifying criteria, his 'fundamental absolutes': The club had to be in a football town, have a large potential fan base, have 'brand monopoly' (no rival clubs too close), have 'brand potential' and have property around the football ground that could be developed. They looked at several but eventually Knighton decided that the lucky club was going to be Carlisle United.

Fans of Carlisle, England's northernmost professional club, do like to think they have potential. Perched north of the Lake District, with no other clubs for miles around to compete for the fans' affections, the whole of Cumbria (at least) watches for the Blues' results. The club is most famous for their single season in the old First Division in 1974–5, which they briefly, exhilaratingly, topped before being immediately relegated. Around the Brunton Park ground were 130 acres, which could be commercially developed. But when Knighton arrived there the club was bumping glumly along at the bottom of the Fourth Division and, under the board of local businessmen, broke.

'In ten years' time,' Knighton promised, 'this club will be in the Premier League.' As at the other United, the club's future success and Knighton's were to be intertwined, as he explained with his natural gift for the soundbite: 'I said I would be a full-time tracksuit chief executive chairman. I would be fully hands on. The club couldn't afford to pay me in the short term, but I did say one day it will pay me a gargantuan salary.'

He told *On The Line* that he paid £75,000 for his shares, and he borrowed the money that would help transform the ground and power the club up the divisions. Colin Seel, a former Football League referee and lifelong Carlisle fan, remembers how seductive Knighton's vision was:

> He said, 'This is Brunton Park as it stands but wait till it is a stadium, 1999–2000 season, when we're playing in the home leg of the European Cup semi-final. Picture it: 40,000 people in an all-seater stadium.'

> I said, 'That's a wonderful, wonderful dream.' He said,
> 'It's not a dream, that will happen, you have Michael
> Knighton's personal assurance that that will happen.'
> I thought I was in the presence of a saviour.

Yet, still very little was known about this strange, articulate, booming football man who was embodying the new age of football as a business. Although he was usually described as a businessman or property developer, Knighton's background was in fact in education. In 1977 he had begun teaching PE and geography at St David's, a private school in Huddersfield for the children of the middle-ranking rich.

Knighton's energy – he describes himself as 'a total workaholic' – impressed the old lady who ran the school, Mrs Katy Wilson, and she promoted him to be headmaster in 1982, when he was only 31. He says he made money in the 1980s from property, buying and selling houses in the environment of low interest rates and steepling prices that characterized the mid-Thatcher years. When Mrs Wilson wanted to retire she handed the school to Knighton and his wife, Rosemary, on what he himself described as 'very generous terms'. By the time the property market crashed, Knighton says he had made enough money to move to the Isle of Man, become a tax exile and retire from teaching – although he held on to St David's.

The application of the Knighton principles to the underperforming Cumbrian football club began happily enough. In 1993 he appointed Mick Wadsworth as manager, a highly respected coach who nurtured an exceptional youth team crop, which included Rory Delap and Matt Jansen. In 1995 Carlisle were promoted as Third Division champions and also went to Wembley, where they lost in the final of the Auto-Windscreens Shield. Wadsworth left, to be replaced by Mervyn Day. Carlisle were relegated the following season but were consoled with another trip to Wembley, this time to win the Auto-Windscreens. The following year they yo-yoed back up. It was then, in 1997, that the Knighton blueprint, the rapid, inexorable march to become champions of Europe, began to falter.

Knighton had rolled his sleeves up and become a totemic figure to the fans, who had believed, had wanted to believe, in his vision. Still a workaholic, he was constantly at the club, having to be woken up some mornings by the cleaners, who found him asleep in the physio's room, as he remembers: 'For the first two years I slept many nights at that football club on rock hard tables in the medical room. I would turn in about 2 o'clock in the morning and get up at 7. When I look back now you could ask: was it all worth it?'

The project to transform the ground itself began with the construction of a new east stand, opposite the old main stand. While other lower division clubs were refurbishing or installing cheap, functional all-seater stands, there was to be no such modesty of ambition for Carlisle. The stand Knighton built, opened in early 1996, was huge, with 6,000 seats, incorporating 18 boxes, function rooms, and a space underneath, which he hoped would house the national football museum – a lottery-funded project that ultimately went to Preston North End's Deepdale stadium. The eventual intention was to create an all-seater stadium with similar new stands replacing the main stand and the two terraces, one of them open, behind each goal.

The new stand overran the pitch and Knighton's plan was to move the pitch and rebuild the stadium as part of the major redevelopment of the club's land. This, the 'Carlisle Gateway Millennium Project', including a hotel, golf course and lake for water sports and wildlife, received outline planning permission in 1996. The Department for the Environment, however, asked for a detailed environmental assessment, which was never produced, and in October 1998 Knighton withdrew the application. The east stand still runs 16–20 metres too long; fans sitting in the far end overlook not the pitch but the waterworks end terrace, which is now closed. The Football Trust provided a £1 million grant for the east stand but the borrowing by the club, guaranteed by Knighton himself, was to become the unshakeable reminder to Carlisle of their true place in football reality.

Albert Doweck, a Manchester businessman and football enthusiast who had lent £100,000 to Carlisle and become a director, believed the project was too grandiose: 'It was a very heavy commitment, in the region of nearly £2.75 million. I didn't think we needed such a big stand at that stage, we could have built it in two stages.

It was a risk, really, which Michael decided he would underwrite personally.'

Some of the players signed at first to augment the Carlisle youngsters were also expensive, being paid fortunes for the lower divisions. The scale of borrowing on the new stand meant that by 1997 the spending began to slow down. Carlisle fans found that the European dream had reached its limits with a couple of brief stints in the Second Division and the Auto-Windscreens Shield. Mervyn Day left in 1997. It was said then that Knighton, always the frustrated footballer, became team manager himself but he has always denied it. 'I did some stretches on the training ground, but I never took a session and didn't pick the team,' he said. 'David Wilkes and John Halpin were directors of coaching. They were using me as a front man.'

Rothman's Football Yearbook, the most favoured directory, appears to compromise on this, naming Knighton as manager, along with Wilkes and Halpin as directors of coaching, from 1997–9. During this time, instead of the youngsters forming the core of an exciting new team, they were sold. In February 1998 Matt Jansen went to Crystal Palace for £1.5 million, Rory Delap went to Derby for £500,000, swelling a gloomy exodus, and in May Carlisle were relegated again.

Meanwhile, Knighton had made the national media again, this time for musing at a press conference about the time he had stopped on the M62 between Manchester and Huddersfield to watch an alien object flying overhead. Later, he made a cogent case for the rational possibility of the existence of UFOs but after his Old Trafford display, the sporting media were not generally interested in anything other than the idea that Knighton himself was on another planet. He fell out with the local newspaper, the *Carlisle News and Star* over this, and blamed their reporter for using the remarks – he said they were made off the record, which the paper denied. Relations descended into warfare when Knighton formed his own short-lived Sunday newspaper to compete with theirs, and peace would never reign again.

Relations with the majority of Carlisle supporters were fundamentally ruptured with the news that at least one of the promises

Knighton made when he took over was coming to fruition. But it was the wrong one – the one about the club one day paying him 'a gargantuan salary'. The club's accounts revealed Knighton as a chief executive on between £100,000 and £120,000 a year every year from 1995. He also had his wife Rosemary, daughter Chevonne, and son Mark on the club payroll, doing various jobs. Knighton justified his own pay packet – 'It's what you pay, the going rate for a quality chief executive' – and said the other family members were putting in long hours at low pay for the club. But seeing Knighton make so much at a club which was by now shipping players and money was too much for many fans.

They also began to question where the money from selling players was going; it was the beginning of virulent rumour-mongering, which would from then on engulf Knighton's Carlisle. He acknowledged what was being said but has always denied the stories: 'Well of course people tell you I trousered the money. The money went on servicing the debt we had on building the east stand and other improvements at Brunton Park. It also went on land acquisitions which we thought were right at the time.'

In May 1999 Carlisle hosted one of the most extraordinary matches in football history. Needing to win to stay in the Football League, they were drawing 1–1 with Plymouth, when on-loan goalkeeper Jimmy Glass – signed after Knighton sold Tony Caig, the club's only keeper – went up for a corner and scored four minutes into injury time to keep Carlisle up. The story has a crazy romance, part Roy of the Rovers, part Billy the Fish – so fittingly Knightonesque. Jimmy Glass is still Carlisle's ultimate cult hero but what most newspapers did not print was the blackness of the atmosphere at Brunton Park that day and the fury that would have been vented on Knighton by many fans had Carlisle been dumped out of the League.

Reality had bitten. There was no prospect of change under the Knighton regime, which had run out of money, backers and decent players. Knighton by now could give an incisive lecture on the self-destructive economics and excessive player wages of lower division football, but being the practical experiment for such a lesson was no comfort to fans who had been promised a bit of Manchester United in Cumbria. The following seasons, in 1999 and 2000, Carlisle again finished 91st out of the 92 Football League clubs, avoiding the drop to the Conference in 2000 only by finishing with a minutely less awful goal difference than Chester City.

Then, in September 2000, with Carlisle fans now bitterly opposed to the chairman, owner and director whom they saw taking money out of a beat-up club, came dramatic news from Knighton's former life. At a court in Leeds, Knighton and his wife were disqualified from being directors of any company for five and a half and two years respectively, a serious sanction to impose, after one of their companies went bust. They had paid over £200,000 from it to their own holding company, Knighton Holdings, even though it owed the Inland Revenue nearly £300,000 in unpaid tax. The company in question was not Carlisle, but St David's, the private school in Huddersfield.

Michael and Rosemary Knighton did not contest the proceedings, brought by the Department of Trade and Industry, and an agreed statement of facts set out the brief, sorry history that made the couple 'unfit to be concerned in the management of a company'. It stated that from the late 1980s – the time Knighton said he made his fortune from property and was looking to buy the country's biggest football club – he had 'ceased to be involved in the educational operations of the school but remained responsible for financial management'. In that role he was evidently not a resounding success. Rosemary Knighton, it said, was the school principal and 'had little responsibility for day to day management'.

Knighton told *On The Line* that the recession of the early 1990s particularly affected the ability of Huddersfield's bourgeoisie to pay private school fees for their children. The court papers baldly note that the Inland Revenue were owed PAYE, National Insurance contributions and corporation tax totalling £297,854, going back to the tax year 1992–3. They had been seeking payment of arrears since at least December 1992.

From January 1993 to November 1996 Knighton had made 16 proposals to clear the tax arrears, offering payments by instalments and sending post-dated cheques. In October 1994 the Inland Revenue threatened to wind the company up but were persuaded

not to by further promises of payment. The court document that set
out the disqualification, a 'statement of facts not in dispute' signed
by the DTI, and the Knightons' court papers stated that:

> Of these proposals, four were rejected as being unsatis-
> factory ... in seven cases no payment was made by the
> company and in the remaining five cases the company
> failed to make more than one payment. Throughout the
> period from January 1993 until August 1995, the arrears
> to the Inland Revenue continued to rise.

The allegation, which the Knightons did not contest, was that the
arrears to the taxman had run up to £288,463, although other creditors had been paid, and so the Knightons had 'caused St David's
improperly to retain monies totalling £288,463 due and payable to
the Inland Revenue'. Effectively, they agreed, they had used the
taxman to provide working capital for the company.

In August 1995 the Knightons sold the school, which was the
company's only business, clearing £369,278. At the time, 'in preference to the Inland Revenue [owed nearly £250,000 by then] and
other creditors', they paid £203,379 to Knighton Holdings – the
holding company through which Knighton owned 93 per cent of
Carlisle United. Knighton Holdings had loaned St David's £365,312
and this debt was substantially reduced, while the taxman and
others were left unpaid. On 23 May 1997 St David's finally went
bust, owing nearly £500,000. Knighton Holdings' debt had been
reduced to £161,933, while the Inland Revenue was owed £288,463.

The Knightons accepted that these two irregularities, the
'retention of Crown monies' and payments to Knighton Holdings in
preference to the taxman and other creditors meant that ... the
Court can be satisfied as to their unfitness to be concerned in the
management of a company and that it would be appropriate to make
orders against them'. Directors' disqualifications are legally enforce-
able orders and if they are breached, that is, if somebody acts as
a director or 'directly or indirectly in the management of any
company', it is a criminal offence, punishable by up to two years
in prison.

In mitigation, Knighton had blamed the school's collapse on the recession; he asked the court to take into account his good character and said that there were no allegations of dishonesty against him. He also said he had personally lost £175,000 when St David's went bust. Shortly afterwards he said: 'All the funds from the holding company were used for the football club because that had become my principal interest.'

The court judgement meant that he had to resign from the club as a director, losing his £100,000-plus a year salary as a consequence. The deadline was December 2000. Almost immediately, his son Mark, a 23-year-old who had at one time been a trainee footballer at Carlisle, then worked on the programme, became a director of the club, and Knighton Holdings, in his place. Andrea Whittaker, an administrator at the club, became a director as well.

Albert Doweck took over as chairman and he tried for some time, together with other local directors, to buy the club from Knighton, but without success. Eventually, the old board resigned, leaving Mark Knighton and Whittaker as the only directors. The fact that Knighton still owned the club and had a son on the board of directors led to persistent rumours that he still had a hand in running the club. He and his son always vehemently denied this but the *Carlisle News and Star* obtained one of Mark Knighton's mobile phone bills that showed constant calls to his father – 58 in a week. Both denied that they talked club business: 'I do not talk about Carlisle United to Michael Knighton,' said Mark Knighton.

Local MP Eric Martlew, became increasingly drawn to the campaign by most of the fans and the local paper, that seemed to take over the culture of the whole city. In the summer of 2001 Martlew called for an investigation and he told *On The Line*:

> One of the allegations I have heard from a number of people is that Michael Knighton is still basically running the club. And as he'd been disqualified as a director, it seems he was going against the rules and the law of the land, and therefore I've asked the DTI to investigate that part of it.

On The Line was also handed a document, which purported to be board minutes, in which Andrea Whittaker seemed to suggest that Michael Knighton was still involved in Carlisle's financial affairs. But the document was false; Albert Doweck, chairman at the time, said the minutes were not genuine, and they were not signed. Knighton scoffed at the document, describing whoever wrote it as 'pretty sad and desperate people', and always rejected any suggestion that he was still involved in the club. Later he said there had been an investigation by the DTI that cleared him; certainly no proceedings were ever brought.

In January 2001 came another twist. Knighton finally announced – the news the fans had been pleading for – that he was to sell Carlisle. A quarter of the club was going to an individual, Stephen Brown, for £700,000, and 60 per cent had been sold to a company based in Gibraltar, Mamcarr, whose backers wanted to remain anonymous. Sceptical as ever, the Carlisle rumour mill was soon on to it. It took barely a moment for the city to speculate that Mamcarr was an anagram of the first letters of the Knighton family's first names: Michael and Mark, Chevonne, Rory (the younger son) and Rosemary. Knighton laughed at the suggestion that Mamcarr was really him, situated offshore: 'The anagrams you can put to Mamcarr are endless,' he said. 'All I will say is that this is a genuine vehicle and deal to transfer the ownership from Michael Knighton.'

Almost immediately, Stephen Brown went missing. The newspapers would later have it that he was 'exposed as a former curry house waiter with a beat-up Vauxhall' but neither of these actually qualifies as an offence or wellspring of personal shame. It did seem unlikely, though, that Brown had the cash to land him a quarter of Carlisle United, and he was never heard from in connection with buying Carlisle again.

The Mamcarr deal began to unravel. Knighton said he was waiting for 'clearance' from the Football League and the Inland Revenue. The League had simply asked who Mamcarr were, and received no reply. The Inland Revenue did have to be satisfied that the transfer of the shares to an offshore tax haven was a genuine commercial deal and not just a vehicle for avoiding tax. As it turned out, the deal never went through. He said the Stephen Brown affair and the League's request had scared Mamcarr away. Even as the deal died, he continued to say that Mamcarr had been genuine purchasers of Carlisle United, operating through Gibraltar, determined for their own reasons to remain anonymous.

On The Line interviewed Knighton in the summer of 2001 in Manchester. We had wrangled over the terms of the interview and eventually agreed he could be involved in the live radio discussion following the programme. He turned up in Manchester with a bumper-sized briefcase, his trademark smile, two or three stone heavier than we had seen him before. He doesn't drink, he told us, is still a workaholic and finds it hard to switch off. At times of stress, he said, he turns to food.

He had in his briefcase a pile of front and back pages, going back months, from the *Carlisle News and Star*. He said repeatedly that he had been victimized by the paper and was consulting his lawyers about suing them. 'Let me show you this one,' he said, then spent nearly an hour rifling through his papers, in his briefcase and plastic carrier bag, looking for a paper which he said was key to the whole thing.

When we finally began the interview, he talked through his time at Carlisle. He argued that his promise of success was realizable at first but over the decade the financial requirements of football clubs – most centrally players' wages – had mushroomed. He was, he maintained, genuinely trying to sell the club.

Speaking of his disqualification as a director, the events at St David's were, he said, a 'technical breach' of the law that he had decided not to defend.

Knighton was adamant that Mamcarr was a genuine deal. He waved a document triumphantly, saying, 'This is a share and purchase agreement.' He offered it to us and we had a quick look. It did indeed show that Knighton was going to transfer his Carlisle United shares to a company called Mamcarr, but inside, there appeared to be no payment for the sale. Instead, Knighton was to receive shares in Mamcarr. According to the document, therefore, Knighton was not finally passing on the club to somebody who might make a better job of running it but transferring it offshore to a company in which he would still have a substantial shareholding. Knighton said this was wrong, that after he took possession of the Gibraltar shares he would cash them in, selling for £3 million the club he had bought for £75,000. 'What you've focused on, I'm afraid,' he said, 'and my lawyers did warn me, is a technical point.'

When we tried to probe this 'technical point' a little further, asking who Mamcarr were and whether there was anybody else involved but Knighton, he became agitated and turned the mini-disc recorder off. He would only say, when we had all recovered a mood approaching normality, that Mamcarr were 'some pretty high-powered people', whose 'desire for a degree of confidentiality was to avoid precisely the sort of debacle and embarrassing saga that Mr Brown caused'. Figure that one out.

Both Chris Green, the reporter, and I, had interviewed Knighton before, years back, mostly about his Manchester United episode. We got on well with him, and found him, as most people do at first, engaging, articulate, a visceral storyteller. After this strange interview, which took over three hours, we were left close to disturbed for him. His enormous weight, the briefcase with piles of old local newspapers, the pressure weighing on him – he had the aura of a man almost completely alone, yet still he declaimed with the same bombast justifications, the refusal to admit any fault. We felt a weird semi-detachment long after he had left, at 7pm, to drive all the way back to Carlisle.

The Football Association, acting on the persistent rumours, sent in its Financial Advisory Unit to examine Carlisle's books but, 14 months later closed the investigation. They confirmed, according to the club, that no charges were to be brought against the club, its directors or owner. In fact, they found a pristine set of accounts and legal documents, produced by prestigious firms. Doweck had always believed that Knighton was misguided in his ideas for Carlisle but never improper. 'Michael loved his lawyers and accountants,' he said.

This was a telling observation, we felt. Knighton's juggle on the Old Trafford pitch had announced to the nation – self-destructively as it turned out – an ego with an appetite. It went beyond the need for fame or acceptance by a game with which he longed to be associated. A PE teacher in the late 1970s, owner of a fee-paying school and property buyer and seller in the Thatcherite 1980s, the decade which formed him as an adult, Knighton's self-esteem appeared to rely above all else on his idea of himself as a business-man. There was the 'fundamental absolutes' jargon, his relish in dealing with lawyers, accountants, bankers. Even his fat salary, if you listened to what he said about it, was more about the 'rate for a qual-ity chief executive' than a desire for the good things money can buy. Doweck, a man who loves his own pleasures, remarked on how little Knighton spent, never going on holiday or buying clothes or eating out. His weight, Knighton told us, was the result, mostly, of comfort-eating at the chippie.

The tragi-comedy of Knighton's tenure at the proud little Cumbrian club lasted barely weeks beyond the promised decade. There was no sign of Real Madrid or Lazio at Brunton Park, but the inspired management in adversity of Irishman Roddy Collins in 2001–2 meant there was no need for a last game of the season escape. But after seemingly interminable negotiations to sell the club, first to a businessman, Brooks Mileson, then to Collins's Irish friend John Courtenay, things broke down in acrimony and Collins was sacked. There was time for another last roar of defiance, another strange episode, when Knighton contacted Mike Corry, chair of the Carlisle and Cumbria United Independent Supporters' Trust, and Labour peer Lord Clark, a lifelong Carlisle fan, threatening to take the club out of the Football League as a reaction to all the hostility.

The trust organized a boycott of season tickets for the 2002–3 season and in the House of Commons Eric Martlew raised the sub-ject of Carlisle's mounting tax arrears. Courtenay and Collins fumed. Then, in May 2002, the Inland Revenue, owed over £400,000, finally issued a winding-up petition against Carlisle United. From there, it was a short jog to the end. The club went into administration – the chosen route of insolvency for the many foot-ball clubs going bust. Two months later, proposals were put to Carlisle's creditors and Courtenay bought Carlisle from Knighton.

It was an ignominious end for Michael Knighton's 13 years in football, from his first sun-kissed dance in Manchester United kit to his exit, a banned director from a traumatized Third Division club sunk in administration. His time spanned an historically crucial period for the game, from Hillsborough – football's lowest ever point – through the optimism of ground rebuildings and new business thinking, to the clutter of insolvencies for lower division clubs in 2001–2. Knighton, a dreamer, an egotist, a painter of grand visions, was there throughout this time, on the wilder side of football, yet somehow embodying the core of its events.

A remarkable crowd of 10,000 gathered at Carlisle's first home match in 2002–3 to celebrate his going. Unbowed, he wished the club well. He always looked back at his deal with Martin Edwards and said that Edwards had plenty to thank him for: 'I'd have made an absolute fortune if I'd taken over Manchester United.' That is one of English football's more tantalizing what-might-have-beens: what would have happened to Manchester United, trophy-less for 22 years and in need of investment, had Michael Knighton taken them over with a £24 million overdraft in 1989? One for United and Carlisle fans to ponder, perhaps, over a pint.

CHAPTER FIVE

European Community
How the Legal Eagles Thwarted Europe's Biggest Club Collectors

Clubs with the same owner are playing in the same European competitions, threatening the whole integrity of the game and highlighting issues that will concern all football fans and possibly undermine the very reason they support their team.

It was more of a hesitation than a stumble, a momentary lapse in concentration perhaps, rather than a slip; either way, it let in one of the most prolific goal scorers in the League, and within a split second the ball was in the back of the net.

That slip, or hesitation, by Tottenham's talented defender Ledley King, allowed Andy Cole his chance and gave Blackburn Rovers the Worthington Cup. More importantly, though, it meant that they were now guaranteed a place in Europe. It could have been so different. If the predatory Cole hadn't latched on to the loose ball and hooked it past Neil Sullivan – it could have been Spurs waiting to be drawn out of the UEFA Cup hat to face Bulgaria's CSKA Sofia.

Lausanne, Switzerland, March 1999: some of the biggest hitters in European law are gathered before the Court of Arbitration for Sport. The case they are there for is 'AEK Athens of Greece and Slavia Prague of the Czech Republic v UEFA.' The evidence they were to hear and the judgement to follow was considered so important by European football's governing body that they claimed the whole integrity of the game rested on it. For whatever the outcome of a match, the fans need to be 100 per cent certain that the result has been decided on the pitch and not in the boardroom before a ball has been kicked.

Although it was in the name of AEK Athens and Slavia Prague, the case was brought by their owners, Enic PLC, which also holds substantial or controlling interests in four other European clubs – Glasgow Rangers, Vicenza Calcio of Italy, FC Basle of Switzerland and their latest acquisition, Tottenham Hotspur.

The rule that Enic wanted to challenge in court was simple: clubs with a common ownership were not allowed to play in the same competition. But if they were to prosper then it was vital for Enic to have all of its clubs playing in the lucrative European club competitions. They were determined to get the rule overturned.

In August, after nearly six months' deliberation, the court returned its verdict, which was, in their opinion, that UEFA was within its rights, and the rule stood. Enic's whole ethos as Europe's biggest collector of football clubs was now in serious doubt.

Enic's story begins in the paradise setting of Lyford Cay in the Bahamas, where huge, sprawling mansions overlook the clear blue water, giving not-so-subtle clues as to the financial clout of the people who live there. The word 'Bahamas' means shallow waters, but it's been the deep pockets of one man that is behind the Enic dream.

Joe Lewis is a billionaire currency dealer and he bought Enic in 1996, slowly building it up. Journalist Dominic Prince has been following Lewis and his business dealings for some time:

> It is a real rags to riches story. Having graduated from catering, Lewis bought a company called Hanover Grand, and they did outside catering. One of the things Hanover Grand had was a series of cashmere shops, including one in particular, based in Hanover Square in London. What Lewis realized was that lots of Japanese tourists were coming in and looking to buy his cashmere, and by the time they had to go out again to change their money they had changed their minds, so he started a bureau de change in the back of the cashmere shop, so he made more money from the back of the cashmere shop than he did on the actual cashmere.

Joe Lewis's name is a regular fixture in the top ten of the *Sunday Times*'s 'Rich List' but estimates of this secretive man's fortune are in fact just that: estimates. Even educated guesses can only hover at somewhere between £2 billion and £4 billion. His main business, according to Prince, is trading in foreign currency from his palatial Caribbean base:

> At his house in Lyford Cay he has a dealing room that is like something from a Bond film. He has 20 people working for him, dealing currency, with machines spewing out bits of paper with reports from Wall Street, Tokyo and all over the place. It is very much an active business and he also acts with others for and against currencies. He has absolutely huge firepower.

Why Lewis decided that football should be his next venture is a mystery to Prince, who says that he didn't even know that Lewis knew anything about the game; but the circles he moves in may provide the necessary clues.

His friends include millionaire Irish racehorse owners and gamblers John Magnier (of the ultra-successful Coolmore racehorse stable and stud) and J.P. McManus, who have both built up a significant stake in Manchester United, and Dermot Desmond, who owns 20 per cent of Celtic. Neighbours on Lyford Cay are former Irish rugby international and now publisher Tony O'Reilly and actor Sean Connery, who, it is rumoured introduced Lewis to David Murray, the former chairman of Rangers – the first club to come under the Enic umbrella.

Football in the mid-1990s was the city's blue-eyed boy, but like many a high profile love affair, the city and football soon drifted apart, though never quite splitting up with bilious acrimony. Justin Urquhart-Stewart, an analyst with Barclays Stockbrokers, has watched the turbulent relationship closely. With the hive-like trading room floor busy behind him, he explained:

> The city get bored of new toys very quickly and last year's fashion tends to be this year's tank-top, so what you saw is people being rather dispirited by it – not so much that they didn't like football any more but they didn't exactly see the kind of returns that they had been expecting.

Prince thinks, therefore, that it was no surprise that Lewis wanted in:

> His real interest is making money. He sees that Rupert
> Murdoch is prepared to invest or buy Manchester United
> for £600 million and that it's worth £1.2 billion. In fact
> he once got involved in a muted bid for Manchester
> United, along with Magnier, McManus, and another
> friend, Michael Tabor. He sees owning a football club,
> especially one like Rangers, as a commercial opportunity.

To those in the know, it certainly seemed a peculiar time to buy into football, and Enic's share price bore this out. For example, as Tottenham kicked off their 2002–3 season with a 2–2 draw at Everton, their share price stood at 32.5p, which was less than 10 per cent of its highest price.

Shortly after Lewis bought Enic in 1996, he appointed family friend Daniel Levy as managing director and put him in charge of the day-to-day running of the company. Levy was a city high flyer and a Spurs fan. On the first day of that season Enic's football portfolio looked like this:

> Glasgow Rangers, Scotland – 20.2 per cent
> Vicenza Calcio, Italy – 99.9 per cent
> FC Basle, Switzerland – 11.8 per cent
> AEK Athens, Greece – 42.8 per cent
> Slavia Prague, Czech Republic – 96.7 per cent
> Tottenham Hotspur, England – 29.9 per cent

In 2002–3 AEK Athens and FC Basle qualified for the lucrative group stages of the Champions League and Slavia Prague and Glasgow Rangers were contenders for the UEFA Cup. After the court ruling that clubs with the same owners couldn't participate in the same competition, Enic-owned clubs were once again doing just that.

In 1999 Enic wrote a letter to UEFA to try and persuade them to overturn the rule, saying: 'We feel that the proposed rule change banning teams with common ownership from competing in the same competition would be extremely damaging to Enic. Its implementation would be very harmful to Enic and it would materially impact on the clubs which we currently own.'

If the share price of the company is an accurate indicator they were, of course, correct.

On nearly every one of the 69 pages of the involved and sometime turgid ruling, the phrase 'integrity of the competition' crops up. One of the army of lawyers who sat before the three-man court of arbitration in Lausanne was Alisdair Bell, who represented UEFA. Sitting in his office opposite the Bank of England, he explained why they defended the rule so vigorously:

> There is a UEFA rule that would prevent two or more clubs controlled by the same entity participating in the same UEFA competition. And the reason why we have that rule is because we believe that there is an inherent conflict of interest, an unavoidable conflict of interest, if you would have two clubs controlled by the same person playing in the same competition.

If two clubs controlled by the same company face each other on the field, can fans be certain that the winners and losers are decided on the basis of what happens on the field within the 90 minutes and not in the boardroom on the basis of commercial considerations?

An internal UEFA memo stated:

> How could UEFA guarantee sporting competition if two clubs of the Enic group met in the same competition? Who would win? Would Enic or its management decide or would the winners be decided on the pitch, in a purely sporting encounter as desired by UEFA and its public? UEFA must take all legal measures possible to guarantee clean competition. The interests of clean competition in sport are at stake.

Bell helped argue this very point to the court:

> We feared that there would be a public perception that

clubs owned by the same person might not be playing to win, to put it bluntly, and that's a situation which we felt should be avoided in order to maintain the integrity of our competitions. I mean, there have been situations in the past; probably the best one known in the UK is that of Robert Maxwell, who tried to take control of Derby County and Oxford United. He was prevented from doing so and I would suggest that his subsequent business record strongly supports that it was a good idea to prevent him from owning these two clubs.

No one is suggesting that Enic or any other company buy football clubs to fix matches or to undermine the integrity of sport and no one could, of course, compare them to Robert Maxwell. Every fan watching, though, expects a fair contest to be played out – it's at the very core of the game. As Bell points out however, transparency is an absolute must.

Dr Bill Gerrard agrees. He is a lecturer at Leeds University Business School and an expert in the business of football:

If Enic had been successful it would have had grave concerns for UEFA. It would have allowed a corporation to build up sizeable indeed full ownership stakes in a number of clubs then compete in the same competition, and that could have very well brought into doubt the very legitimacy of that competition.

Dr Gerrard, a softly spoken and engaging Scot, played out one of the possible scenarios:

If you have got two teams owned by the same club, competing on the same basis, and if one of the teams has no way of getting through and the other does have a chance of getting through, there would always be the suspicion that the other team would throw it. That's why UEFA was concerned and battled hard to get that upheld. Certainly the court put a great deal of weight on the importance and legitimacy of contests, and the belief that these are true athletic competitions and that they are not being rigged through common ownership.

The court concurred, stressing that it was not so much a judgement against Enic but a judgement to maintain the legitimacy of contests. Its final ruling stated:

Due to the high social significance of football in Europe, it is not enough that competing athletes, coaches or managers are in fact honest: the public must perceive that they try their best to win, and in particular that clubs make management or coaching decisions based on the single objective of their club winning against other clubs.

Ultimately, the absolute aim of the court of arbitration decision was to eradicate any feeling that the fixing of matches could take place; in fact, one of its conclusions was that although there have been instances where matches have been fixed, it is rare, and when it has happened, the guilty have been brought to book. But, it continued:

Even assuming that no multi-club owner, director or executive will ever try to directly fix the result of a match between their clubs or will ever break the law, the panel is of the opinion that the question of integrity must still be examined in the broader context of a whole football season and of a whole football competition.

The court found that the main problems lay across three issues, namely: 'The allocation of resources by the common owner among its clubs, the administration of the commonly owned clubs in view of a match between them, and the interest of the third club.'

In an attempt to match UEFA's firepower, Enic put together an impressive and powerful team of their own, including the architect of the Bosman Ruling, Belgian lawyer Jean-Louis Dupont, and top London QC Michael Beloff. They also enlisted the support of Glyn

Ford, MEP for Southwest England and President of the European Parliament's Sports Intergroup. He argued that UEFA's fiercely defended regulation was contrary to EC competition rules on free movement of capital – the backbone of the Union. Sitting in the huge, impressive glass parliament buildings in Brussels, he asked:

> What is the rule put in place for? The rule is put in place, we would agree, so that we have a competition, and so we can rely on both teams playing to win rather than one team lying down and dying because it's more convenient for the revenue stream or the TV rights.

As Ford recognizes, television is the important factor. The introduction of the Champions League was at the behest of the television companies, who didn't want the biggest clubs, and therefore the biggest audience pullers, being knocked out early in the competition. Hypothetically, if Spurs were to face Slavia Prague in the UEFA Cup, which of those teams progressing makes most financial sense in terms of potential audiences and advertising revenue to the owner they have in common? Not the biggest economic brain-teaser.

Ford feels strongly that the bureaucrats of Brussels were being over-zealous and that some sort self-regulation was far more appropriate:

> My advice was that they had to find a way of dealing with that by some kind of independent arbitration or some kind of self-imposed rules, so that the EC could say this was not necessary to protect the sporting side of what is a multi-million pounds business. The question is whether it is a proportionate response. The argument is not that the EC is going to say, 'You are not allowed to ensure sporting integrity on football,' they are saying, 'Is this the only way in which it can be done?' or 'Are there other ways that actually avoid you seeking permission to breach the competition rules of the EU.

Bell disagrees:

What the Enic case is about is really, whether sports bodies can take proportionate measures to protect the integrity of the competitions that they organize, and UEFA is pleased to see that the European Commission also seemed to have recognized that that is a legitimate thing to do and it doesn't contravene any provision of the EC treaty.

As it stands, the UEFA rule is clear enough, as it was when the deal to buy the controlling interest in Spurs from Alan Sugar was ratified by the Enic board in the spring of 2001.

Looking at the varying stakes of each of the six clubs that Enic has, it is difficult to argue that they do not have some sort of influence on them. What forward-looking company, having paid out millions of pounds basing its corporate policy on building up its football stable, would not want a say in how its course is steered?

From his University of Leeds office Dr Gerrard asked himself some similar questions:

There is concern, what exactly is Enic? What is its vision of itself five or ten or fifteen years from now? And what do the City see in a company that has located itself in the entertainment and leisure business with stakes in several businesses, which are football clubs. There is concern that outside Manchester United and one or two others, there has been very little sign of significant shareholder return from football.

Also, according to Dr Gerrard, the clubs they have chosen could hardly be classed as Europe's footballing elite; on the whole they are involved in small to medium clubs who require relatively small investment:

There is no investment cost up front and those clubs run on a tight budget with the expectation that they can do reasonably well in domestic competition and have a run in European competition to generate a return on their investment. What they didn't want to do, and have never said they will get involved in, is a bidding game to acquire big stakes in big clubs. That would be very expensive and very difficult to generate any return on.

If these tactics are to bear any kind of fruit, then UEFA and the European Commission will have to make a remarkable U-turn, which they have not done as yet. According to MEP Glyn Ford, it is down to how 'integrity' is defined, and Enic need to persuade UEFA that their interpretation is wrong. As it stands UEFA have the power to decide exactly how it is defined so any change is therefore unlikely:

> Enic is going to have the right at some stage to challenge this in the European court, and I guess that when it gets to the point where it is costing them serious sums of money they must be tempted. My advice would be to deal with the problem UEFA claim they have, which is, 'What is it that UEFA claims is sporting integrity?' Once that could be dealt with, then the rule will be one which is comparatively easy to overturn. I would have thought that unless they come up with some way of dealing with this issue, then the Commission will call in UEFA's favour. However, if someone comes up with an alternative then UEFA is in trouble.

In June 2002, though, the EC's competitions commissioner, Mario Monti, did rule on the case after Enic appealed, coming down in favour of UEFA and their interpretation and upholding the decision of the Lausanne court. In announcing his decision, he reiterated its importance:

> The main purpose of the UEFA rule is to protect the integrity of the competition, in other words, to avoid situations where the owner of two or more clubs participating in the competition could be tempted to rig matches. Although the rule could theoretically be caught by Article 81 of the EU Treaty, it is intended to ensure that sporting

competitions are fair and honest, which is in the interest
of the public and football fans in particular.

But as the 2002–3 European campaigns began, only Tottenham and
the relegated Italian club, Vicenza from the Enic stable, missed out.
The full UEFA rules are there for everyone to see:

> 1. *No club participating in a UEFA club competition may,
> either directly or indirectly:*
>   *a) hold or deal in the securities or shares of any other club,*
> *or*
>   *b) be a member of any other club, or*
>   *c) be involved in any capacity whatsoever in the manage-
> ment, administration and/or sporting performance of any
> other club, or*
>   *d) have any power whatsoever in the management, admin-
> istration and/or sporting performance of any other club*

What is also clear is what should happen if two clubs with the same
owners are to play in the same competition:

> 2. *In the case of two or more clubs under common control,
> only one may participate in the same UEFA club competi-
> tion. In this connection, an individual or legal entity has
> control of a club where he/she/it:*
>   *a) holds a majority of the shareholders' voting rights,*
> *or*
>   *b) has the right to appoint or remove a majority of the
> members of the administrative, management or supervisory
> body, or*
>   *c) is a shareholder and alone controls a majority of the
> shareholders' voting rights pursuant to an agreement
> entered into with other shareholders of the club in question.*

In the opening groups of the 2002 UEFA Champions League, FC
Basle were drawn in the same group as Liverpool, while AEK Athens
were placed in a different group with the Italian giants

Internazionale. In the UEFA Cup, Rangers faced the Czech side Viktoria Zizkov and Slavia Prague took on Excelsior Mouscron of Belgium. UEFA's response to *On The Line* was to say:

> The ruling of the Court of Arbitration for Sport on 23 August 1999 was in favour of UEFA's stance and declared UEFA's rules prohibiting multiple ownership in European club competitions to be lawful. The modifications to the UEFA rulebook carried out following this decision and implemented according to the orders of the Court of Arbitration for Sport, and subsequently endorsed by the European Commission, were in accordance with the Court's decision and reflected their view of a controlling stake. We have to be in line with the law in order to have workable rules.

This displays all the elements of a classic UEFA fudge. Just because Enic don't have a majority shareholding or a 'controlling stake' in their clubs, it doesn't mean they don't have any influence – it would be difficult to imagine a company as focused as Enic not wanting some sort of control for their large outlay.

As it turned out, UEFA were fortunately spared having to confront this, as Rangers were disappointingly knocked out in the first round on away goals by Viktoria Zizkov.

Enic's 29.9 per cent shareholding in Spurs isn't a random figure: if they owned just 0.1 per cent more they would be obliged by the City to bid for the remaining stock. They clearly do not have majority control of the club but there is no doubt that they are pulling the strings at White Hart Lane where Enic's managing director, Daniel Levy, is Spurs chairman.

The governing body has acted against Enic in the past; in 1998 they threw Athens out of the UEFA Cup because Prague were also in the competition. Alisdair Bell says that at the start of each competition UEFA asks the clubs to declare who controls them and to confirm whether or not they are in compliance with this rule:

At a certain moment at the beginning of the competi-

tions we have to trust the clubs that they are in con-
formity with this rule. If it would transpire that there was
an individual who was influencing the management or
sporting performance of two clubs playing in the same
UEFA competition, they would have to investigate that.

Every single club across the continent starts off the domestic season
knowing that if they do well a European place is up for grabs, so
UEFA must recognize that qualification for their competitions is an
incentive. Bell accepts that this is a tantalizing carrot to dangle in
front of the clubs:

Oh absolutely, it is definitely there as an incentive and I
can't necessarily deny that it would be for a club if it
knew that performance in a domestic competition would
not result in eligibility for UEFA competition, because a
club owned by the same entity is already in a UEFA competition. It is inevitable that with a rule like this there are
unfortunate situations that arise, but what is the more
important objective to achieve? I think most people
would agree that protecting the integrity of the game and
protecting against conflict of interest situations is a kind
of higher objective than the fortunes of one particular
football team.

As Enic's interest in Spurs was announced, the chairman of AEK
Athens publicly denounced the company for the way they have run
the club. He told the Greek media:

In this context, I am curious to see what difference Enic
will make to Tottenham. Their investments in football
clubs have failed, with the exception of Vicenza, thanks
to an exceptionally clever manager, and all largely
because of an inability or unwillingness to fund in accor-
dance with their stakes.

His admiration for Vicenza couldn't have lasted too long, though –

they were relegated to Serie B.

Christos Zeir belongs to the AEK fan club 'Original 21' in London. In the years leading up to Enic's investment he says, they celebrated three consecutive championships, but the success has dried up recently:

> We have the best team in Greece, I don't know how they got to such a bad situation, it's very dodgy. Enic have spent a lot of money but the chairman is changing every couple of months.

Christos knows that success for an English team will be more profitable to a company than success for a Greek or Czech team. It's clear to him where AEK stand as far as Enic are concerned:

> Maybe the lowest priority, maybe not a priority at all. I can recall two years ago when we were calling Enic in London to express our disappointment with the team. There wasn't someone to speak with us and once we sent a three-page letter expressing all our feelings on the way they manage the team. They did a couple of transfers and the next day it was in the Greek press that the fans from London were threatening Enic, but that wasn't the case at all.

Unfortunately, Enic is a PLC and such is the nature of that particular beast that it is the City who are answered to first, with supporters some way down the list. The company also has a duty to provide a profitable return for its investors, which is something that the court of arbitration had recognized in its final judgement. It is also conscious that priorities should be concentrated where there is more chance of a profit; this is common sense of course, but of no comfort to the smaller clubs. The court stated that it was:

> ... of the opinion that such differentiated allocation of resources among the commonly owned clubs is in itself perfectly legitimate from an economic point of view, and

can even be regarded as a duty of the directors vis-à-vis the shareholders of the controlling corporation. In situations of common ownership the fans of either club would always be inclined to doubt whether any transfer of players or other management move is decided only in the interest of the club they support rather than the interest of the other club controlled by the same owner.

Enic are without doubt the biggest club collectors in Europe. The other high profile multi-club owner is French TV company Canal Plus who, at the start of the 2002–3 season, were looking to sell their stakes in Paris St Germain and the Swiss team Servette, no doubt influenced by the EC decision as well as their own massive debts and PSG's perennial inability to win the French championship.

In the vernacular of the competition they run, UEFA have that precious away goal and Enic's firepower has been snuffed out by a well-organized defence with the help of a sympathetic arbiter.

Multi-ownership is off limits, for the near future at least, but can Enic, having built their reputation on this philosophy, afford to back down and let UEFA have their way? Daniel Levy, bullishly, still believes they can sneak in a late equalizer.

You're never going to stop people that want to do dodgy things, particularly in football. You know some of the things that go on within the football market, and what UEFA should be doing is trying to really encourage transparency, and the only way you encourage transparency is to allow transparent public companies to be involved in the sector.

It's an optimistic view. UEFA not only have the European Commission on their side but, more importantly, the moral argument, and even with all the legal brains of Europe, Enic will find that difficult to overturn.

CHAPTER SIX

Sorted!
Why Drug Tests in English Football Help to Paint a False Picture of Drug Abuse Within the Game

The FA claim their drugs testing system is the most comprehensive for any sport in this country. In fact it is so ineffective that a player would have to play for over 400 years before having half a chance of being tested. Footballers have the means, the motive and the expertise at their disposal to take advantage of the finest performance enhancing drugs. In ten years of Premiership football not one first team player has been caught using any drug of any description. And as things stand, they are not likely to.

In the past decade and a half there are few sports that have not experienced the fallout of a positive drugs test. Runners, jumpers, throwers, cyclists, weightlifters, rugby players, swimmers and the rest have all at one time or another hit the headlines as a result of performers popping pills they ought not to have popped. Specifically pills that aid performance, so-called performance enhancing drugs.

Odd then, isn't it, that even though athletes from almost any sport you care to name have been done, in by far the biggest sport in the country – football – there is yet to be a positive test for a performance enhancing drug. Even though it tests more people than any other sport football is, according to the testers, as clean as a whistle. Every now and then there's bit of marijuana, ecstasy or even heroin but of performance enhancing substances, not a trace.

Do the drugs not work with football? Are footballers naturally squeamish when it comes to taking them? Or is it that the system set up to catch them has so many opt-outs and caveats that a player would have to be monumentally unlucky or staggeringly stupid to get caught? It is a rhetorical question, of course!

In the ten or eleven months of a year that football clubs are in business there are some players who have more reason to loathe

Mondays than others. It is the day, custom would have it, that the doping doctors, if they are coming at all, arrive at the training ground.

When they do turn up it works like this. They report to training ground reception or, if it is match day, the stadium. Dr Richard Higgins, club doctor for Sheffield Wednesday, knows the score:

> They turn up unannounced and as I come off the pitch I am told two players have been selected for a drugs test. There is a room at the stadium and training ground set aside for the purpose and the players are taken straight there without being allowed to go into the changing room. They stay there for however long it takes to give a sample.

(This can sometimes be quite a while as footballers are generally pretty dehydrated after running around for a couple of hours.)

In the nine years up to August 2002 since the Premier League was launched there have been 3,465 matches featuring getting on for 2,000 players, but so far there has yet to be a single positive test indicating the use of a performance enhancing drug.

Dr Higgins does not find this odd. He believes British players just don't go for it: 'I have difficulty even convincing the players to take a complex carbohydrate drink because the mentality in the British game is that you don't take supplements. We still have to convince players that drinking tea at half time is a bad idea!' (It makes you wee and causes you to dehydrate alarmingly during exercise.)

The perception within the game is that there is no problem with enhancers but there is a bit of a problem with inhibitors – booze and the so-called recreational drugs. And it is these that most concern the Football Association. Michele Verroken, the drugs control officer at the Sports Council, who runs the programme on behalf of the FA, explains:

> We have noted the prevalence of socially abused drugs. It has been worthwhile to target that area and say, look,

there is a zero tolerance towards these substances by the
FA so don't waste people's time, money and your careers
by using these substances because there is a high chance
you will be caught.

Actually, there is not. There have been 62 positive tests for recreational
drugs in 14 years. And, it bears repeating, none at all for performance
enhancers since the Premier League was launched. They have only
ever caught one player over the driving limit for alcohol. Not a good
strike rate given the reputation of footballers, and the scope of the testing, which not only covers the four professional leagues but also the
reserve, youth and academy leagues and the women's Premier League.
During the 1999–2000 season the FA carried out 1,066 tests in and out
of competition (match day and training grounds).

They visited 32 matches and 261 training sessions, which
breaks down in theory to an average of two visits by a tester in a
season. Not that it works out like that in practice, as the youth coach
at a professional club in the Midlands told *On The Line*:

We always give out the FA's information on drugs and
what have you and lecture the players on the damage
drugs can do, particularly the younger ones. We tell
them about testing but I have to say in the seven years I
have been here I have never seen a tester.

By contrast, a London club was visited 14 times in 1998. According
to popular anecdote, Premier League clubs get at least one visit a
season at the training ground but as far as match days go it is a different story.

The 32 matches visited by testers in the 1999–2000 season represented less than 1 per cent of the 3,500-plus league games played
that were subject to testing. Factor in the rule that on each visit two
players from each side have to give samples and statistically you
would have to play professional football for 432 years in England
before having a 50–50 chance of being tested at a match.

Greg Moon is a professional drugs tester and he works for the
World Anti-Doping Commission (WADA). It is an arm of the

International Olympic Committee and Moon and his colleagues are charged with keeping tabs on Olympians all over the world and, when they feel like it, they test them. He thinks the football testing in England is pretty weedy:

> If a club is done one match a year they can pretty much rely that once the test is out of the way they can go along on their merry way regardless. The way to catch people is randomness. Appearing one day and then very shortly afterwards to catch people with their guard down. Thirty matches does not seem like a very big sample to me and one in which you could have reasonable confidence of avoiding a drugs test, certainly if the testers have been early in the season.

Not only do footballers run an extremely low risk of being tested in the first place but, as I mentioned earlier, it seems that as far as training ground visits go, players are pretty confident about which day of the week the tester will pitch up. One club even gave the dope tester his own parking space before the good doctor realized what an early warning message he was sending out!

Matt Yates, the former international middle distance runner, who now works as a part-time fitness consultant with a number of football clubs, finds the situation risible:

> I do know it is a standard joke in football that the testers will be in on Monday morning because they would be looking for social drugs that expensive footballers might have been consuming on the weekend. But that is the least of it; the testing in football is pretty much a joke.

The thinking behind the Monday morning visit is that a drug like cocaine can be out of your system inside three days so Monday is the last chance to catch a Saturday night user. But the players know this and if they have indulged it is easy for them to avoid Monday morning training, reporting in sick, or perhaps indulging their habit midweek when they know there is little chance of being asked to give a sample.

Little wonder then that a doctor told a contact of *On The Line*, 'They always seem to know when I am coming.'

So not only hardly ever and not quite unannounced but also football has managed to negotiate another 'get out' – no home visits for random testing. Indeed, no testing of any kind outside the club's training ground and the stadium on match day. Compare and contrast this with the experience of an athlete like Yates:

> I have sort of semi-retired but even I still get tested. In my career I imagine I was asked to give a sample on around 100 occasions. Typically the phone would go and they would say they were parked around the corner, could they come and do a test? It could be especially intense in the run-up to a major event like the Olympics or a European championship. Basically, the British Olympic Association did not want the embarrassment of being caught out with a doped athlete in the full glare of competition.

You get the impression that Michele Verroken would love to run a similar system within football but the reality is that she knows the clubs would not wear it:

> The present situation is that we do work in partnership with the sports but that does make us reliant upon them to want to participate in the ultimate aim. Admittedly one cynical view may be that some sports are guiding us away from where we should be looking.

Because the FA are not obliged to test for drugs – or opt into the UK Sport programme, the Sports Council have little choice but to negotiate terms. Football has the upper hand here because it does not receive any grants from the Sports Council.

Effectively it is a compromise between best practice and what the clubs will put up with. And what they won't put up with is the prospect of their expensive assets being knocked up in the middle of the night and being asked to wee into a sample bottle.

Howard Wells has worked in professional football at Watford and Ipswich and used to be chief executive of the UK Sports Council. He explains that football is not alone in being able to negotiate opt-outs:

> I think the protocols range from one sport to the other and while we may think there are standard procedures, there are not, and there is a considerable amount of integrity placed on the governing bodies to determine their own rules. Therein lies the problem.

In yet another of its arrangements with football, the matches to be visited by the drugs testers are agreed with the FA before the season kicks off. *On The Line* were unable to find out how much notice the individual clubs get, if any, of an impending visit because neither the FA nor the clubs that we asked would tell us. But at the very least, a precise programme of testing agreed up to nine months in advance would seem to further compromise the all-important unannounced element of a dope test.

On The Line asked WADA's Greg Moon for his opinion about the various opt-outs relating to football and drugs tests:

> Well that is just worthless. You might as well not bother going. My definition of 'unannounced' is that you are sitting at home, I knock on your door and it is now. It is not 'Oh, can you come back tomorrow?' It is now. And if they happen to be going to the airport, then I will arrange to go with them and if they get on the plane, I arrange for someone to meet them at the other end.'

As nothing like this ever happens in football you have to treat the FA's assessment of its programme as the most comprehensive in British sport with caution if not scepticism. Football may have doubled the number of tests from 500 to over 1,000 between seasons 1998–9 and 1999–2000 but then it is our biggest sport and compared to the 796 tests carried out in 1999 on athletics in the UK there are massive windows of opportunity for drugs cheats to avoid or prepare for tests.

Frankly, clubs cannot afford to have their star players being caught for using drugs. Unlike many sports subject to dope tests, a positive result in football would have ramifications far beyond the individual player – it could have a catastrophic impact on the team, as Verroken acknowledges: 'It is a liability on their assets. These players are assets to the club but what we try and do is encourage them to be open in their accounting of the testing programme.'

We already know that no player has been done for performance enhancing substances in the last ten years but no *first* team player in the Premier League has ever been positively tested for a recreational drug either.

The majority of the miscreants paraded before the FA disciplinary committee for drugs offences are youth team players or women. The others are all from the lower leagues. Between 1994 and 1999, for example, the clubs involved were West Brom, Reading, Tranmere, Leyton Orient, Huddersfield, Barnsley, Ipswich and Charlton, at a time when these last three teams were not in the Premiership. The only team in the top flight to suffer the embarrassment of a positive test was Newcastle and then the player in question was a youth. The only two high profile players ever to have tested positive (both for marijuana) were Lee Bowyer and Chris Armstrong, and that was at a time when neither was playing in the Premier League.

The fact is that the tabloids have a better record for uncovering drug and alcohol abuse in football than the FA does. Football clubs have every reason to want to wash their dirty linen in private, of course, and there is evidence that some are doing just that, much to the irritation of Verroken:

It has been reported to us that private testing is going on and all I can do is warn clubs that they have to be absolutely sure that first of all these methods are as effective as the screening methods we use. It is difficult to gauge how widespread private testing is. There are a number of highly successful companies out there and so someone is making money.

It is possible that when players undergo these tests they believe they are sanctioned by the FA. This came to light when a regular England international claimed in an interview with a football magazine in 1999 that he must be the most tested player in Britain and he had no idea that he was spilling any beans.

When they read this at the Euston HQ of UK Sport it was of keen interest because they knew they had never tested him. It must have been someone else. Someone else like the company that wrote to Howard Wells when he was chief executive at Watford during their spell in the Premier League: 'I received a letter from a commercial operation offering services to drugs test our players, which I realized was in conflict with the work being done by UK Sport.'

Howard would have been especially conscious of this because he had left the chief executive's post at UK Sport to take up his job at Watford. How many other clubs received similar letters and what they did with them can only be guessed at. Wells forwarded his letter to the FA but heard no more about it.

Clubs are clearly aware that banned drugs are being passed around dressing rooms or being taken in treatment rooms, on or off their premises, and they would rather find out in private than have their highly prized assets dragged through the press. What makes this all the more galling is that you and I, the taxpayer, help fund this malarkey.

The agreement to allow testing to happen in professional football is that the Sports Council, i.e. the public, pays for the first 250 tests every year. With each test and its associated costs now running at over £500 a pop, which amounts to £100,000 of public money subsidizing drugs tests to little effect in Britain's biggest and richest sport.

On The Line contacted the FA for comment on the drugs issue in football. PR supremo at Soho Square, Paul Newman, said they were 'totally relaxed' over the prospect of any criticism of the FA's drug policy and saw no reason why they should enter into a dialogue with us about it.

This is just the sort of crass arrogance we have come to expect from the FA, who have a distinctly patchy track record when it comes to attaining the kind of high operating standards we have the right to expect. Instead, they typically tend to dismiss attempts to hold them to account as 'troublemaking'. Of course, they are not alone in adopting this defensive 'don't be ridiculous' attitude to criticism.

The Italian football authorities felt the same way about their drugs testing programme in 1998 when the then coach of Lazio, Zednek Zeman, came out and said he believed the Italian game was rife with dope. Zeman knew a thing or two about dope, being from Czechoslovakia – a country whose history lay within the drug-fuelled sports regimes of those eastern European countries where the appliance of science in pursuit of victory was explicitly sanctioned by the communist regimes.

Zeman was slaughtered in the Italian press, dismissed by the footballing authorities as barking mad and pilloried by the fans for daring to cast such an aspersion on their heroes. But not everyone thought he was insane. A Turin-based magistrate decided to launch his own investigation. He discovered that Zeman was probably right.

The problem lay within the International Olympic Committee accredited laboratory that carried out and processed all the dope tests in Italy. The magistrate discovered that it had been common practice to dump tests results in the bin. He was also appalled at the lax system of testing. Firstly, there were not many tests taken in football at all and secondly, of those that were, there were instances of players and clubs being given prior notice.

The upshot of the investigation was that the laboratory was closed down. For the start of the season 2000–1 a new testing regime was established. So now, in addition to random tests at training grounds, two players from each side are tested at every Seria A and Seria B match. The findings of this new system paint a very different picture of Italian football. Zeman, it seems, had been telling the truth.

Paddy Agnew is the *Guardian* correspondent in Rome and he followed the story: 'We had players from the lower division testing positive for the steroid nandrolone and it came to light in a spectacular way when you had two of the biggest names in world soccer, Edgar Davids and Couto of Lazio, also testing positive.'

By the end of the season over a dozen players had given positive samples. So what does this tell us about soccer and the proclivities of professional players to take drugs to boost performance, or perhaps, more importantly, to recover from injuries? That the sport is rife with them? Possibly. That it is clean and the positives are the result of contaminated supplements, a fashionable defence among athletes of every ilk? Again possibly. That it only happens in Italy? Definitely not.

Concurrently there was a clutch of positive tests in Greece, the Netherlands, France, Germany and Spain. Greg Moon has a good perspective on drug use in a range of different sports:

> It does vary from sport to sport. Some you don't expect many problems and in others we are racing against the sportsmen concerned. Some are cooperative and some are not. The type of drugs will vary from sport to sport. But I find it difficult to accept that any sport, never mind a huge one like football, is completely free of drugs.

On the face of it, nandralone (the substance that most of the positive tests identified) is a curious drug for a footballer to use. Athletes have traditionally turned to steroids to help them produce explosive bursts of power but this is not something that offers a special advantage in football. However, they are also used to put bulk on to slight frames and, more importantly, they are used in general medicine to help people build up strength after illness or surgery. 'One of the aspects of steroids,' explains Moon, 'is they aid recovery from hard matches, so someone who has had a hard match on a Wednesday could take them to ensure a peak performance on Saturday or Sunday.'

Steroids would also help players to get going in the pre-season when most of the strength and conditioning work takes place. A lot of pre-season work is done abroad, where there is zero chance of being tested (the dope testers don't travel outside the UK) and if the drugs were used during this time they would no longer be detectable when the main fixtures start in August.

Sports medicine has grown on demand. The need to get expensive players back to the same condition or better than before is one of the challenges that has informed much of the progress in sports science in the past decade. Hand in hand with these developments, the profession's understanding of how drugs can help this process has also improved.

For Matt Yates the natural drug of choice for a footballer would be EPO (Erythopoietin), which is rife in endurance sports such as cycling:

> EPO would be great, especially for a midfield player. You would get 90 minutes out of them flying all over the place and then they would come out again and play a brilliant game three days later. With the right doctor you could have a programme with very few side effects as well.

EPO increases the number of red corpuscles (the agents that carry oxygen to the muscles) in the bloodstream, and extra oxygen in the body improves a person's ability to perform endurance tasks. The other attraction of EPO for a professional player is that it does not show up in the urine – and a urine test is currently the only one that British footballers are subject to – so you would have to analyse a blood sample to detect it. EPO is administered by injection, and while Spanish and Italian footballers are used to vitamin injections, there is no similar culture of using syringes in the British game, which may explain why it does not appear to have caught on.

But the times they are a-changing. A few years ago only a handful of top flight clubs bothered to hire so much as a full-time qualified physiotherapist but nowadays all of the Premier League clubs maintain a team of medical experts. And an inevitable by-product of this greater expertise and application of sports science to the game is that it brings the dopers ever closer to their subjects. And as knowledge expands, so does the opportunity to apply it, legitimately or otherwise. Until very recently it was unheard of for club doctors to do blood tests on the players in order to determine their pre-season fitness levels. Not so now.

At the start of the 2002–3 season the number of foreign players on the opening day of the Premier League season equalled those of the home-grown variety for the first time. So it is no longer true that the players in our top flight are naturally antagonistic to scientific assistance. Every dressing room has players from environments where there is a more sophisticated approach to fitness and performance.

Tony Banks is an orthopaedic surgeon in the north west of England. He frequently operates on footballers and has wide experience in the world of sport. His own sporting pleasure is weightlifting, an activity where drugs are often thought of as endemic. He has also acted as a medical officer at a number of major international multi-sports events:

> The public attitude in track and field athletics 15 years ago was that there was no problem with drugs. That it was a peripheral problem, but of course athletes were taking drugs. We knew it then and we know it now. It would be very odd indeed if football, the world's biggest sport, could legitimately be singled out as a sport with no drugs problem.

Banks knows footballers use drugs. A club physiotherapist once approached him brandishing a bottle of injectable steroids that had been found in the dressing room.

Clubs on the continent are usually attended to by a sports medicine practice on a contract basis. We do not have any such arrangement because sports medicine is not something you can qualify for within the NHS. There is no royal college to set the standards and train the specialists as there is for other areas within medicine, such as oncology, cardiology, orthopaedics and so on. The result is that our home-grown expertise in these matters is, by comparison, limited.

Sports medicine practitioners in Italy, France Spain and elsewhere will not only deal with footballers but also cyclists, athletes and everyone else. Consequently, a doctor who works with cyclists, for instance, a sport widely believed to be at the cutting edge of performance drugs technology, will have the knowledge to apply, should he or she choose to do so, to athletes from other disciplines.

'You know what is going on with some of the big European teams,' says Yates, 'because I know people from athletics who visit these same doctors who are known for advising on performance enhancing drugs.'

It is doubtless still the case that most footballers would not think of using drugs to boost their performance on the pitch, but when it comes to recovering from injury you can see how a little chemical assistance suddenly becomes a very attractive option. Injury is particularly traumatic for a footballer, especially if you are a fringe player or under pressure for your place in a competitive team.

The point about football and drugs in Britain is that the expertise is available. There is the motive and the money to pay for the best dope doctors in the world and not much chance of getting caught. Like the rest of sport, football exists in its own global village. Footballers play and mix with colleagues from every continent on earth. Word gets around and the temptation, particularly if you do not believe you will caught, must be great.

No sport has managed to keep the dopers at bay. As long as the rewards for success are so great and players have the money to pay for the best chemical assistance and the masking agents that can cheat tests, then there will always be those who will use banned drugs.

The only defence is a robust testing system. The heart of any effective testing programme is random unannounced testing. Anything else is a waste of money. In the case of the FA and its testing programme, a waste of *our* money. And what is worse, it ensures that the structure for accessing and using drugs will grow and become more sophisticated. Every other athlete in the UK has to suffer the indignity of a knock on the door from the dope tester, so what is so special about footballers?

CHAPTER SEVEN

The Friendly Club
Cosy Deals and Abuse of Trust at Stockport County

You would love to love the lower division club battling for attention in the shadow of its giant Manchester neighbours. But Stockport County's rise to the First Division was accompanied by inflated invoices, struck-off companies applying for grant-aided work on the ground, and an industrial tribunal's damning judgment of its treatment of the club's most celebrated manager.

Stockport County is English football's self-styled 'friendly club', a sobriquet which smiles on the public face of a club battling doughtily for its identity, much like Stockport itself, which resists being absorbed by the sprawl of Manchester, ten miles to the north. For much of the club's 120-year history there was not too much for County's fans to celebrate, other than being friendly and local; the club scudded around the bottom of the Football League, giving the odd ex-Manchester City or United playing legend a final pay packet on their way down and out of football.

This small town inferiority complex began to change after 1988, when the local professionals and businessmen who made up the club board stood aside for a new major shareholder and chairman. His name was Brendan Elwood, a landlord from Sheffield, who had been looking for some time to invest in football. For all the rancour and bitterness that would ultimately blacken Elwood's time at County, his chairmanship produced the club's most successful ever spell on the field, achieved through his initially inspired recruitment of managers.

Elwood's first appointment to the manager's battered office in County's rundown Edgeley Park ground, in 1989, would furnish future pub quiz compilers with a nice teaser: who was the first foreigner to manage a club in English football, the first to work with an England team? Not Arsène Wenger, the future pub quiz teams should conclude. Nor Ruud Gullit, nor Sven-Goran Eriksson. In fact, it was a little Uruguayan, who had clambered indefatigably through the jungle of English football since, speaking little English, he hustled his first coaching job at Luton Town when he arrived in Britain in the 1970s. His methods, rooted in obsessive work on players' individual technique, had been recognized on coaching courses by the Football Association and in 1980-2 he was asked to work as a coach with England youth sides. He has the squad picture in the scrapbook of an extraordinary career, featuring him, the first foreigner to line up for an England team picture, standing proudly with three lions on his tracksuit chest – Danny Bergara.

An enthusiast, a life force, Bergara moved to Sheffield United but lost his job in favour of bigger names, appointed by chairmen to curry favour and headlines, if not enduring success. He settled in the area but was out of work and coaching Sheffield, the famous amateur club, believed to be the world's oldest, when Elwood saw him at work and spotted his winning way with players.

Bergara managed to land his first manager's job in 1988, at Rochdale, another club not lounging in the glamour end of the North west's family of professional clubs. He tells a laugh-out-loud story about mice in his Spotland office eating into his kit bag and munching the chocolate bar he had salted away for a long away trip. The following year, Elwood, by now Stockport's chairman, offered him the manager's job there and he accepted. 'It was my chance,' he said. 'I'd worked so hard for it, and I was determined to be successful.'

The plan to turn Stockport around began with what might be termed the infrastructure, as Bergara remembers:

> The dressing rooms were disgusting, filthy, there were nails sticking out. I said I wanted them repaired, painted. The players had too little respect for the club and themselves; they were walking around the showers barefoot and I insisted they wore flip-flops to stop them slipping.

He introduced changes to the playing methods, training practices, and tactics. Briskly, defiantly, he insisted that Stockport was not a suburban dumping ground in the shadow of its Manchester giant neighbours but a club with its own history, dignity and a few thousand loyal supporters who deserved self-respect too.

Two years later, having occupied the Fourth Division for 21 years, Stockport won promotion. The following years, 1992 and 1993, they went to Wembley for the final of the Autoglass Trophy, although, as with two Wembley appearances in play-off finals, they trudged back up the M6 as losers. Bergara became a hero, loved by the fans for his enthusiasm and his passion for the game, communicated in a unique Manc-Uruguayan accent. He showed a talent for finding players who were underachieving elsewhere, coaching them into unprecedented form and, given Stockport's place in football's food chain, selling them at a profit to bigger clubs.

Kevin Francis, the 6 foot 7 inch centre forward signed from Derby, also became a cult figure for the fans, pulling apart lower division defences, who couldn't cope with his size. He scored freely for Stockport before the club sold him to Birmingham City for £800,000. Bergara wrought exceptional performances from other players, such as Andy Preece, Alun Armstrong and Paul Williams, who had never previously excelled, earning handsome transfer fees for Elwood's Stockport from bigger clubs. It was a measure of his coaching skills that many of the players never really achieved much when they left him.

For the first time money came to Stockport County, and as a coach Bergara felt that not enough was spent to improve a bumpy, rutted pitch. The money was spent on the ground. Elwood set about rebuilding Edgeley Park, a job required following the 1989 Hillsborough disaster and subsequent Taylor Report, which called for wholesale improvements to Britain's crumbling football grounds.

A man who would be key to the rebuilding of Edgeley Park was another director, Mike Baker. He is a builder, whose company, Ellenby Construction, a small firm based in Bolton, was to carry out almost all the work on the ground. As recently as 1991 Ellenby recorded an annual profit of only £990 but the work awarded to him at Stockport was to make Baker's name as a builder of football grounds – and his and his company's fortune. *On The Line* went to see him in his bright new two-storey office block in Bolton, which is decorated inside with pictures of the new stands Ellenby have built at Stockport and at several clubs since, including Mansfield Town, Bradford City, Rochdale and a handful of others across the North.

Baker told us that his route to the Edgeley Park boardroom was not quite the usual one of supporter-made-good sending a few quid the way of his beloved club. Ellenby had in 1987 carried out some routine work on the railway end terrace at Edgeley Park and the struggling, pre-Elwood club hadn't been able to pay for it. Baker had threatened to put them out of existence. 'At one time I was in possession of a winding-up order against the club,' he said. As a device to fend off liquidation, the club suggested he become a director: 'I was approached by the then chairman, Josh Lewis, to see if I would be prepared to join the board almost as an overseeing role until the club were able to pay us.'

Baker said that after going along to Edgeley Park for a few matches he became a fan: 'I was hooked and have been hooked on Stockport County ever since.'

It was to prove a happy addiction for Baker and his small building firm. The improvements to football grounds insisted upon by the government after the Taylor Report were helped by some £200 million in public money, made available in grants by the Football Trust. Many people believe in retrospect that too little was asked of the clubs in return for these grants. Some now argue that the money should have been paid in the form of low interest loans, which could have been repaid by the clubs when they landed in richer times. As early as 1992 football had its commercial bonanza, with Sky TV paying millions to the Premier League, yet the clubs, even the richest in the country, who would soon make millions floating on the stock exchange, were still given grants to build the new stands.

The Football Trust counter any such reservations by pointing out that their prime concern was to improve safety following the horrific loss of life at Hillsborough, and that the timescale for improving ragged grounds at most of the 92 professional clubs was too urgent for too many bureaucratic safeguards. The system was nevertheless intended to be reasonably tight, to procure the rebuilding at reasonable prices and thereby ensure that the public money was responsibly spent.

The clubs had to show on their grant applications to the Trust that the work was necessary to improve their grounds or that it would allow them to comply with post-Taylor Report regulations. They also had to provide three 'properly authenticated competitive tenders' for any job and the Trust's rules required them to disclose any connections between a director of a club and a building contractor; the Trust would take such associations into account when assessing the tenders. As long as the Trust considered that the tenders were genuinely competitive, they awarded the grants according to the lowest quoted price. This basic system was intended to allow the grounds to be rebuilt quickly while protecting the club and the public money administered by the trust. The point of the tendering process was to ensure that pricing was competitive and that there was no question of fixing a price that would increase the amount of public money spent.

At Stockport more than £2 million, much of it subsidized with grants from the Trust, was spent converting Edgeley Park from a crumbling old Fourth Division ground to post-Taylor Report respectability. The bulk of the money was paid to Mike Baker's company, which was awarded all the serious work. The key project for him was the rebuilding of the all-seater Cheadle end, the home fans' favoured position behind the goal. Baker, speaking of his company, described it as 'our breakthrough' – the major stand that helped Ellenby win other work at northern football grounds. For that job, Baker's company did indeed come in cheapest in a competitive tender with two large building companies.

But *On The Line* learned that for two of the jobs, one for re-seating Stockport's main stand, the other for extending a car park, Baker's company won the work with tenders that were pitched against two other companies well-known to him. On neither occasion, we were led to understand, were either of the connections disclosed to the Football Trust. Of the other two firms whom Stockport invited to tender against Baker, one was based in Bolton. Baker knew one of their senior staff: 'They have a director who once worked for me,' he admitted. Both he and the company denied they discussed the contract before tendering.

Behind the other company, which was called Field Acre Construction, lay a more intriguing tale. Baker told us, quite openly, when we interviewed him, that the owner of Field Acre, who put the tender in, Tony Marland, was known to him. 'I was at college with Tony Marland,' he said. 'We went on the same course.'

Not only that, but Baker actually called Marland to tell him he had suggested Field Acre to the club's architects. He even gave Marland a rough figure, 'less than £100,000 or something of that order', and then personally enquired if he would bid – for a job against Baker's own company. 'I think I told Tony, "I've put your name forward",' he said. "Do you want to price a job of this order?"'

The Football Trust received tenders for both jobs, in 1995 and 1996, from Ellenby, the Bolton company and Field Acre. For the re-seating job, the Bolton company's tender was for £89,000 and Field Acre's was for £86,000. Ellenby came in at £79,000 and so, according to Trust rules, the Stockport County director was awarded another piece of work at Edgeley Park, for which his company was paid.

The most curious point of all was really quite fundamental. Marland's company, Field Acre, which had been so narrowly thwarted in its attempt to win this work, did not in fact exist. It had packed up, ceased trading. It had even been struck off the company register in 1987 – eight years before bidding for the work. So when Baker invited his old college mate to tender against him for the re-seating contract, Marland did so on behalf of a company that he knew had been dissolved some years before.

Baker and Marland both deny there was anything untoward in this. Marland said that the company was trying to get back into busi-ness in the mid-1990s and had gone after a few contracts then. Baker said that he had not known Marland had ceased trading eight years earlier: 'I had not spoken to him for some time. When I rang him to say that I had put his name forward to the club's architects, he told me that Field Acre had not been trading but he was looking to restart Field Acre.'

The Football Trust, administering public money to repair grounds after 96 Liverpool supporters were killed in the terrible crush at Hillsborough, asked for three 'properly authenticated competitive tenders', and for connections between directors and contractors to be disclosed. The clubs, private companies, had only to comply with these basic requirements to have cheques written out to them. It was an almost uniquely generous system, set up after football's own neglect had produced such tragedy. At Stockport, the company of one of the directors was paid for work after bids were received against his – one from a company with a director who used to work for him, the other from an old college mate, in the name of a company struck off the register eight years before.

On The Line put it to Baker that what had happened could sound like collusion – precisely what the Trust's rules were designed to prevent. 'Well, I hope it does not,' he said, 'because there has been no collusion. We are submitting our prices in a bona fide way and they are there to be beaten or not ... I am not going to apologize for being successful.'

In another case involving work at Stockport, *On The Line* found a flagrant breach of the Trust's rules and procedures. The Trust had agreed to pay 75 per cent of the cost of installing a new PA system, an important safety feature. A local firm, Delta Communications, sitting on the A6 three miles from Edgeley Park, were, to the delight of its proprietor, Alan Ratcliffe, invited by the club to tender for the job. The price, confirmed by Ratcliffe to us, was £41,750. This included, he also confirmed to us, very clearly, the cost of the work and, in a competitive market, Delta's profit. It was by far the lowest bid submitted and so Delta were given the job.

Then Ratcliffe was invited down to Edgeley Park to discuss the detail with Stockport's then chief executive, David Coxon. Ratcliffe told us that Coxon suggested that Delta should increase their invoice, but the extra money, it was made clear, would be paid back to the club, not go to Delta.

Ratcliffe said Coxon asked him to lay the figures out in a memo, which he did. *On The Line* obtained a copy of it. It showed that the price eventually put in was £59,999, a penny short of £60,000, nearly £20,000 more than the true price of the job. The application Stockport sent in to the Football Trust stated the higher price, £59,999. This was still the lowest tender and the Trust duly paid Stockport County 75 per cent of it: £44,999. The grant awarded, therefore, was £3,000 more than the real cost of the job. Stockport paid Delta the full £59,999 but Ratcliffe was immediately required to pay back the difference of just over £18,000. This, the club said, was for 'sponsorship'. Ratcliffe confirmed that the club gave Delta hoardings round the ground for two years, scoreboard advertising, a lounge facility and 'various other small items over a period of time'. He admitted that the invoice for the work was inflated beyond its true value – which included his profit – but said he did not know where the club was getting the money from and certainly had no idea that they were going to apply to the Football Trust for a grant, or that their application for the money had been successful.

David Coxon told us *On The Line* that he could not remember the incident and that all his files were at the club, so suggested we contact the club secretary, Gary Glendinning, who issued the following statement: 'Three independent tenders were submitted of which Delta Telecom were the cheapest at £59,999; this amount was paid in full. Delta Telecom subsequently re-invested their profit on the project by way of a two-year sponsorship agreement worth £18,315, which was their perogative.'

But Ratcliffe insists that this was simply not the case, that the original price of £41,750 included his profit, 'a low profit margin', and that his invoice was inflated at the suggestion of Coxon, the then chief executive of the club. *On The Line* asked him, 'The actual price of the job was £41,750, is that right?', and he replied:

> It was at that particular time, yes. I was concerned about the increase in price, about the way it was put to me. It was an increase in profit although that profit never came to us. I do remember a conversation with Mr Coxon. It was suggested to me that our profit was very low in the first place, there might be room for manoeuvre and because of that, yes, we did inflate our profit if you like, which was turned back to sponsorship.

We asked Ratcliffe to confirm how this worked, that when Coxon had said 'room for manoeuvre', he meant that the price for the job could be inflated.

> 'Yes, if you like,' he said. 'It's a question of how you inter-
> pret it. Inflate the price or increase your profit. Yes.'

And we asked again for confirmation:

> 'But you weren't getting any more profit because you
> were only getting the price you'd already quoted?'
> 'Yes,' he replied, 'that is correct.'

There was no question that the original price, £41,750, included profit. The £18,000 was an inflation of the whole job, and the grant came in at 75 per cent of it. This was enough to cover the total actual cost, even though Stockport were required to meet a quarter of the cost. They even received £3,000 extra, then paid Ratcliffe £18,000, which he was required to pay straight back to them. He was, he said, 'quite angry and upset' about the affair.

This is not the image of the 'friendly club' that Stockport have sought to portray under Elwood's chairmanship, differentiating themselves from the Manchester clubs that have become corporations (one more successful than the other perhaps) through England's 1990s football boom. On the field, Danny Bergara had coached, cajoled and crafted his ragbag collection of signings into a serious lower division force, although the four Wembley disappointments, in 1992 and 1993, may have suggested he had taken them as far as he could.

He had, though, salvaged the self-respect of Stockport County and its fans. One lifelong fan told *On The Line*: 'He is a hero of mine. There are people here who would give their right arm to save Danny. He was held in such high esteem by a lot of people here.'

But not, ultimately, by the people with most reason to thank him – the chairman and directors. By 1995, Bergara, according to his contractual entitlements, was being paid close to £90,000 a year. He still lived near Sheffield and so had agreed with the club that he could stay in modest digs near Edgeley Park on odd late working nights. The club made available an accommodation allowance of £50 per week. As an arrangement for a successful football manager it was painfully unextravagant. In March 1995 Bergara agreed with Brendan Elwood that at the end of the season they would review the accommodation allowance.

Shortly afterwards, on 16 March, Stockport had a board meeting. Bergara was not there. He had asked if he could be excused from it and asked the chief executive, David Coxon, to speak on his behalf about playing matters. At that meeting, Elwood told the board, falsely, that Bergara had agreed that his £50 weekly accommodation allowance would 'cease forthwith'. Quite apart from the fact that this was untrue, nobody, according to Bergara, communicated this to him. Two weeks later he put in an expenses claim for the heartbreakingly petty sum of £64 with no idea that he was about to lose the job at which he had toiled for two decades.

The romantic involvement of the man from Uruguay with the club down the A6 ended in a foul split, an industrial tribunal hearing and a subsequent appeal, both of which Bergara won. After hearing the evidence, the tribunals reached their conclusions about what had happened. The club refused to pay the expenses claim, and Bergara lost his temper. He was abusive to Coxon and said that Elwood and David Jolley, the finance director, were 'bastards' for withholding his expenses. He referred to the two directors 'again in bad language' when speaking to his two deputies, John Sainty and Dave Jones. (Jones subsequently replaced Bergara as manager on a third of his salary.) The club's vice-chairman, Graham White, testified that when he met Bergara at a sponsors' dinner he heard him describing the chairman and finance director as 'fucking gangsters'.

Bergara accepted the tribunal's judgement that the swearing was 'out of order' and said that if he had been given the opportunity he would have apologized for it. But he had not been given the chance. However, the tribunal found that at the sponsors' dinner, at the Alma Lodge Hotel in the leafy Cheshire suburb of Altrincham, Bergara had behaved 'quite properly' in spite of statements to the contrary put forward by witnesses for the club. But Elwood did not do the same in the foyer after dinner: 'He swore at Mr Bergara, he sought to assault him by striking at him on two occasions and told him not to bother to turn up for work as he no longer had a job.'

The record of finance director David Jolley's behaviour was equally damning:

> [He] poked [Mr Bergara] in the chest and issued him with a tirade of swearing and abuse which he, Mr Jolley, described as a 'Sheffield volley' and then Mr Jolley said that [Bergara] was to come to a meeting at his office the following day and at that meeting he would 'tear up his contract and shove it up his arse'.

The tribunal further noted that 'It is suggested on behalf of the club that that was a very proper invitation to a disciplinary committee at which these matters would be fairly heard,' but dismissed this explanation. Had the consequences not been so serious for Bergara, the whole shabby story would have had its comic elements.

On 31 March Elwood told a board meeting that Bergara had assaulted him. The tribunal came to the opposite conclusion, but the story that Danny Bergara had hit his chairman went round the footballing world like wildfire and is the single biggest reason why Bergara has struggled to find another manager's job ever since. Here is a coach with rich experience, who who has spent most of that time underemployed at home near Sheffield. Yet the tribunal was unequivocal about what has since been accepted as a true piece of football gossip: 'That was clearly an untruth. It was Mr Elwood who tried to assault Mr Bergara.'

Acting on Elwood's version of events, which followed Elwood misleading the board about Bergara's expenses, the board voted to sack Danny summarily. In the end the industrial tribunal judged Bergara to have been 25 per cent to blame, for his 'intemperate, derogatory and vulgar remarks' and for not attending the meeting at which Jolley had promised to 'tear up his contract and shove it up his arse'. This meant that they considered the club to be 75 per cent to blame, declaring them to be 'an employer who, so far from being reasonable, had treated this employee, this manager, with a complete lack of frankness, in a disingenuous way, which must have been exceedingly provocative to him'.

Bergara won his case, and was paid damages, but not until August 1997 – nearly two and a half years later. When *On The Line* saw him, he declined to talk about it; the papers were there to see, he had won, he had nothing further to say. He talked only about football, about his record at Stockport and his work on the technique of the raw players he had brought to Edgeley Park, whom the club had sold on as lower division stars.

Bergara was a kid from a footballing family and his career began with Racing Club of Uruguay, then continued in Spain with Real Mallorca, where his coach was Cesar Rodrigues, his first mentor. He also met his wife, Janet, there, in Mallorca; she is English and was working in the travel industry. His next club was Seville, in the Spanish First Division, and he played against Barcelona and the Real Madrid of Puskas, di Stefano and Santamaria.

Sitting in his living room, frustrated, he came alive talking football. He had to quit playing because of injury and he and his wife decided to move to England. When he arrived in 1973 he could speak little English but a cousin of Janet's introduced him to Harry Haslam, who was then managing Luton Town. From this fragile link, Bergara carved out a career that touched many people, like Ricky Hill, the graceful Luton Town and England midfielder, who says he has Bergara to thank for making him a player. A career great in its unique way. And it all effectively ended with a seedy piece of out-manoeuvring over £64 living expenses, an attempted assault by Elwood and chest-poking and foul abuse from Jolley.

One close friend of Bergara's told *On The Line* that she laughed ruefully even at the 25 per cent fault attributed to him for the intemperate remarks made in the maelstrom:

Danny is a gentleman, a lovely man, totally opposite to the people running that club. The fact is that he had to learn to swear to fit in in English football, which is a crude and brutal place to work. It was just so laughable that he ends up being criticized for a way of behaving and language that, as a foreigner, he was taught by the English.

We learned that Bergara was not the only Stockport employee who had felt the need to make a claim to an industrial tribunal for unfair dismissal. Three others, accounts assistant Lyn Porter, lottery manager Tony Constance and safety officer Philip Collister, brought cases to the tribunal and had them settled by the club. Four instances in five years for a club that employed fewer than 20 nonplaying staff is a record that David Cockburn, a solicitor and vicepresident of the Employment Lawyers Association, told us indicated a nasty regime at the 'friendly club':

> I'd say that is a high number but it's not only a high number. I think it discloses an approach to a style of management which has little to do with modern management techniques. It's more a macho management where they will hire and fire at will, where they think they can develop more obedience than team spirit.

David Jolley has since left Stockport County but Brendan Elwood is still there, still chairman. His company, City Estates in Sheffield, was paid huge amounts of money by Stockport for 'construction and repair work for the ground and restaurant', £384,538 in 1998 and £612,715 in 1999. The club's accounts for 1999 show them owing City Estates a total of £1.2 million. There is nothing illegal with a club doing business with its chairman or a director, especially if no public money is involved, but *On The Line* asked Stockport what work was done for figures on such a scale. They replied:

> The figures referred to are totally inaccurate. The chairman's company has undertaken work for Stockport County purely to finance projects. All transactions are done at arm's length and are correctly reported as related party transactions in the club's accounts. The chairman has a substantial amount invested in the football club which is completely interest free.

The club did not explain what the projects were.

We broadcast our findings about Stockport County's breaches

of the Football Trust's rules on Radio 5 in August 2000, then immediately passed our file to the Trust and to the Football Association, which, as the game's governing body, has a responsibility to investigate. The FA announced it was formally investigating Stockport in January 2001 but since then very little has been heard. In September 2002, more than two years after the serious findings we broadcast, the Football Trust (now renamed the Football Foundation) told us: 'Stockport is on the FA's desk awaiting their decision to charge or not to charge.'

The FA told us: 'The investigation has still not concluded. We have had some new arrivals into the organization. It is not too far from a conclusion now, so it's a question of watch this space.' The FA has consistently insisted that it is committed to upholding its laws and clamping down on wrongdoing by football clubs. In the case of Stockport County, Greater Manchester's 'friendly club', it has been a long wait to see if the governing body will be true to their word.

CHAPTER EIGHT

Caring for the Community
How Football Clubs Pay Lip Service to and Exploit Their Own Grass Roots

The refusal of multi-million-pound-a-year turnover football clubs to fund their Football in the Community schemes, whose workers are often paid pitiful wages to promote the clubs' interests, sits uncomfortably against ubiquitous photographs of the smiling faces of participants. So what really lurks behind the beguiling phrase 'Football in the Community'?

The dominant image of Football in the Community is one of jolly bonhomie – of football clubs sending teams of smiley employees out among the local populace to run a variety of happy-go-lucky courses out of the goodness of their hearts. Why would it appear any different? After all, most match day programmes proclaim the benefits of this sterling work. In a game often plagued by headlines about the behaviour of players, greedy chairmen, dodgy agents and ailing clubs, the apparent charity and goodwill of Football in the Community should be a good news story. But the reality is not quite that simple.

In the summer of 2002 *On The Line* revealed that many clubs view their Football in the Community programme as little more than a commercial opportunity and that most of them put virtually no money into the scheme. Despite the massive amounts clubs are willing to spend on players' salaries and transfer fees, Football in the Community's willing army of workers are generally paid well below the national average wage.

Late on a Wednesday night, in the Black Country town of Bilston, 25 teenage boys compete intensely in a five-a-side tournament organized by staff from Wolverhampton Wanderers' Football in the Community programme. These are players aged 12–16 in the Twilight League, which, along with a similar scheme for older youths up to the age of 21, called the Midnight League, is a regular football coaching session arranged specifically in areas with high rates of crime and teenage pregnancy. The aim is to give youngsters something enjoyable and constructive to do.

'This is our second year,' explained one of the programme's workers, Rob Williams. 'We've got four venues running, we started with two, and from September 2002 we'll have six.' Wolves' community team operate the schemes on Monday and Wednesday nights – the Twilight League from 7 p.m. to 9 p.m., the Midnight League, as the name suggests, from 10 p.m. to midnight. The appeal of football allows Wolverhampton's youth workers to deliver more serious health advice on the risks of drink, drugs and teenage pregnancy. 'Football is the vehicle to engage the kids,' says Williams. 'The lads here wouldn't come if they didn't want to play football. We stress from the start that the health input is important and that's part of it and if they're not going to do that they're not going to turn up for the football.'

Williams admits the main draw of the scheme is the club's name and the old gold and black tracksuits of the coaches: 'It gives it a lot of credibility. In this area, although there's the odd Manchester United shirt, they're 99.9 per cent Wolves fans.'

The problems of Bilston are no different from those of many other urban areas. For teenagers there simply isn't enough to do. When the local youth club closed a couple of years ago Wolves effortlessly moved in to fill the void, if only for a couple of nights a week. The kids are appreciative. 'It's free, it's enjoyable, the time is not too bad, and it's regular,' said one player. Another felt that local adults didn't understand the lack of facilities around. 'If you start playing football in the street people come out on the doorstep and say: "Move on!" So you come down here and no one can shout at you.' But another player projected a more sober image: 'It's something to do on a night rather than dossing about on the streets.'

Some of the Twilight and Midnight League players have been referred to the scheme by the police or social services. Williams and his colleagues are often working with, at best, difficult, hyperactive youngsters. 'What do they do on the other nights of the week when we're not here?' he asks. Williams explained another incentive of the programme – that players are rewarded for regular attendance with free tickets to matches and the chance to play on the hallowed turf of Molineux by participating in special Midnight League matches prior to Wolves' home games. All the Twilight and Midnight League players are also encouraged to drop into the Wolves' community office to receive advice on a range of health issues. Even though the scheme has only been running for a couple of years, some players have been spotted and joined local non-League clubs, although this is not an aim of the project.

Statistics suggest these imaginative twin projects are working: teenage pregnancies are down and the police say there is less trouble in areas where the Twilight and Midnight Leagues are operating. In 2001 Wolves won the Sportsmatch Community award. Sportsmatch is the government's grass roots sports lottery funding project, and Wolves collected their trophy at a prestigious presentation at the All England Tennis Club at Wimbledon. It was rich reward for the efforts put in by their workers in less salubrious surroundings. 'It's just a nice added something in respect of the work you're doing really,' said Williams.

Most of the credit showered on the scheme has gone to Wolverhampton Wanderers Football Club, a major business backed to the tune of £50 million over the past decade by the Bahamas-based businessman Sir Jack Hayward. Their ground, Molineux, has been rebuilt and the club have signed several million pound players. In 2001 Wolves' turnover was £16 million – most of it spent on an unsuccessful push for promotion to the Premier League. Their Football in the Community programme, insisted the club's chief executive, Jez Moxey, is about garnering good publicity:

'Because football is very big business, the Football in the Community department is also there as a PR arm to show the caring side of us as a responsible organization within the community,' said Moxey. Not that Wolves' community programme has been set up to be funded by Wolves. Like the vast majority of clubs, it has to be self-funding, which means it has to make its own money, by finding sponsors, and charging for children's coaching courses and even birthday parties. He continues, 'It is not designed to make a direct profit for the club but it needs to be self-funding if at all possible.

Like every department, it has to be able to stand on its own two feet and I'm pleased to say that our community department does very well'.

The award-winning Twilight and Midnight Leagues are not directly funded by Wolves but operate with public money: £200,000 from Wolverhampton Health Action Zone, £30,000 from the government's Sportsmatch grant programme and £30,000 from a local sponsor, the Birmingham Midshires Building Society. Moxey told *On The Line*: 'The Twilight League and the Midnight League are initiatives which we sold to local and central government and indeed Sportsmatch. They saw a huge benefit in what we're trying to achieve so in terms of raising funds to support community initiatives, there is an ability to raise money.'

Moxey insisted that in underwriting the costs of their community programme Wolves were effectively funding the Twilight and Midnight Leagues, but reiterated that the main aim of the community department isn't charitable, it's commercial: to attract youngsters to coaching sessions bearing the Wolves name and convert them into long-term customers:

> First and foremost, from the club's perspective we want to encourage children to come to Molineux and become supporters of the club, that's the primary objective of the Football in the Community programme. If a supporter stays with us and buys season tickets, shirts, pies and programmes over a period of 70 years, with inflation built in, it's going to run into tens of thousands of pounds.

When asked whether he saw the Football in the Community programme as a sales and marketing operation, Moxey replied, 'No, I would call it more of a PR department for the football club.'

This view is not out of kilter with many of Moxey's colleagues at other Football League clubs. The nationwide Football in the Community programme was presented to them free of charge. It arose out of the sport's darkest days in the mid-1980s, when the charitable arm of the Professional Footballers' Association (PFA), the players' union, sold the idea to the clubs as a way to improve their public relations and to bring them closer to their communities.

Football in the Community's senior administrator, Roger Reade, who has run the programme since it began in 1986, says:

> If you recall going back to the mid-80s, football had its own share of difficulties and society had a huge unemployment problem, and included amongst the unemployed were a number of former players. There were also the difficulties of hooliganism. I think attendances reached an actual all-time low in 1985 and it was against that backdrop that we recognized that football has the power to play a bigger part in society.

The PFA, understandably, had the interests of its members at heart. The scheme's two aims were clear; to build the clubs a presence in the community and to provide work for unemployed former players. Brian Kidd, the ex-Manchester United, City and Everton striker, was one of the first to be appointed. It was a step on the ladder to his current job as assistant manager at Leeds United. Many other former players have found Football in the Community an ideal way to stay involved in the game.

Some clubs were worried that Football in the Community would cost them money and it was Reade's job to convince them of the benefits:

> We spoke to clubs and we said, 'Look we have this concept, the idea is that you will be able to play a bigger part in the community and to a degree you will probably benefit from that involvement.' Some of the clubs were reluctant, they resisted the change. I think the cost was a factor. That was why in our early research we said, 'We can explore funding resources to be able to make sure that we can introduce the schemes without fear of any cost to you.'

The scheme was to be funded centrally by the PFA, with whatever money they could raise, and the clubs, who stood to benefit, were asked to provide nothing more than office space and a telephone. Yet even this basic request was deemed too much for some of them. Reade met chairmen who would loudly pronounce at the start of a meeting that they would not be interested in setting up a Football in the Community office at their club if it was going to cost them a single penny. The long-term success of the scheme is testimony to Reade's persistence, tact and diplomacy in persuading clubs to get involved. Many only yielded through a childish sense of envy: when they saw that rival clubs had adopted the scheme they wanted one too.

The hardened objections to spending any cash often continued once the schemes had been set up. 'Whenever we had any ideas we were literally told time and time again, "If that's going to cost us anything, then we'll close you down",' recalls Ivor Gumm, an ex-professional player who ran Swindon Town's Football in the Community Programme from 1993 to 1996. He felt that he and his colleagues were trying to boost Swindon's image in the community almost in spite of the club:

> It's very difficult to explain. We weren't costing them any money, we were creating our own funds. We were self-funding in the schemes that we ran. The only thing I could think was a problem was that we would from time to time ask for bits of kit and freebies. If you got a really good player in a coaching session over a week you'd want to give them something to get them involved within the club. I could only see positives from the whole thing, but it was just a negative approach from the management.

Gumm even resorted to drumming up interest by taking club merchandise and selling it to children on local housing estates:

> We had a van and one of the girls out of the club shop would bring some bits and pieces down on a Thursday or Friday lunchtime and we would sell things out of the back of a van for them,' he said. 'The club got the money. The club lent us the kit and we paid the club whatever

the retail price was for that kit. We didn't get anything out of it. All it was for us was to get people along to the scheme and involved with Swindon Town.

This desperate measure to attract people to Swindon Town's community programme – which Gumm insists had the full support of the players and management at the time – stretched the intended nature of his department's work. The club got the benefits from merchandising sales and any associated publicity, but gave the very little back to the scheme. Gumm's summary of football's venture into becoming a community friendly sport wasn't a happy one:

> We got an office but it was underneath the stand. You had to bend down to go through the door. It wasn't ideal. It was very poor. You get the backing from the players, you get the backing from the PFA, but you didn't seem to get the backing from the club itself.

Gumm eventually left Swindon Town to start his own coaching business. Swindon assured us that its community programme is not as crude as that now, and nationally Football in the Community has come a long way. Most clubs now have more than one officer involved, which is all most of them had in the 1980s and early 1990s, and some have recognized their potential and allowed their schemes to expand, which is something that Roger Reade is happy to acknowledge:

> The funding we were able to generate in 1990 literally was nil. It was marginal. It was incidental funding that was generated at that time. In 1995 we reached the point where Football in the Community schemes collectively were generating £3 million from a variety of different sources. By the year 2000, from the accounts we've had from the schemes that we have to date, the figure had risen to about £9 million.

Football in the Community has grown into a mini-industry,

employing around 600 full-time and 2,000 part-time staff at the 92 Premier/Football League clubs. They all receive some funding from the PFA, the football authorities and national sponsors. Although many clubs are involved in other community work – such as running the government-backed Study Support Centres – with a few well-regarded exceptions only a handful of clubs provide any of their own money to fund the programmes that carry their names into the community.

Reade accepts that very few clubs pay their way but he insists that this is due to the way Football in the Community developed: 'I would say a large number don't contribute but don't forget that's against the backdrop of the way we've established the schemes, which is as separate organizations.'

Football in the Community is part of the PFA's Professional Footballers' Further Education and Vocational Training Society. Although the PFA provide their own funds they also raise money from national sponsors which they pass on to their schemes around the country. In reality this is a very small sum per club, as Reade admits: 'The PFA have always given us half a million pounds a year which is rising this year (2002), our Railtrack and Adidas deals are worth £300,000 to £350,000 a year, so collectively they're quite beneficial. We then offer funding to support each club worth a minimum of £6,000.'

This small amount of guaranteed income means that the individual Football in the Community programmes need to raise extra funds just to exist. An easy way is to concentrate on money-making activities, with the ubiquitous holiday coaching courses proving a stable source of income. But there are many people who believe that this is a timid version of the potentially inspirational work Football in the Community programmes could do.

The headquarters of the Football Unites, Racism Divides (FURD) organization, based in the Sharrow area of Sheffield, overlooks Sheffield United's Bramall Lane ground. FURD was set up in 1996 to counter racism at the ground but also to increase the participation of ethnic minorities in football locally. They work with a number of clubs in South Yorkshire and alongside Football in the Community workers in particular. Project coordinator Howard

Holmes told *On The Line* he thought they could do better:

> Beleaguered is a word I'd use to describe them. With a
> few exceptions they have to raise all their own funding
> with help from the PFA and sponsors that the PFA might
> be able to bring on board. At Sheffield United the people
> there have to basically earn their wages by running
> coaching schemes, which they have to charge people for,
> so that immediately then mitigates against the participa-
> tion of large numbers of people, not just ethnic minori-
> ties but people from poorer white communities as well.
> They're forced to do that because the clubs, with very
> few exceptions, don't they pay them any real money
> other than providing them with premises.

Holmes believes that without reliable funding and clear aims and
objectives, community programmes are ill-equipped to tackle more
complex social problems like racism, which has remained a blight
on British football: 'They don't, as I see it, have an adequate ration-
ale as to what their work should be, in terms of the theories and
principles which might underpin that, rather than just having
schemes which attract kids that can afford to come to them.'

While most clubs have kept faith with Football in the
Community's original purpose – to raise their profile in the community – a few others have given them an altogether more ambitious philosophy: to harness football's mass appeal into a powerful
force for good. Although they may lag behind most clubs in many
other ways, Third Division Leyton Orient have led the way in using
football as a vehicle to address deeper social issues, as their community programme coordinator, Neil Watson, explains: 'I don't necessarily think the Football in the Community scheme should be a
marketing tool for the football club. What we're not about is looking to recruit new fans. What we're about is looking to work with the
very diverse communities of north east London in all their glory.'

Watson has developed a far more challenging aim for Orient's
community scheme – to reach out among as many of those communities as possible, whether they are likely to be fans of the club or

not. One of the programme's regular schemes is held on Monday afternoons at Walthamstow's Lowhall Sports Centre, run by senior development worker Ose Albangee:

> This particular project is where we try to get people who have a history of either drug or alcohol misuse into various leisure activities. We get a lot of our clients from the probation service or some of them are just unemployed guys who come and have a kick-around. What we're trying to do is get them into playing sport and feeling a bit more about themselves and trying to raise their self-esteem and improve their fitness. It's easy for us to attract people into doing some sort of meaningful activity which isn't anti-social, which they'll get something out of and it's quite rewarding for us working here as well.

This is the power of football in full swing. The training is intense and taken seriously – no one is trying to sell anything, least of all club memorabilia. The 30 or so players here are learning a range of skills; in one session the pitch is divided into thirds and the players at one end have to keep possession for a limited number of passes (while being hunted down by a defender) and then successfully chip the ball over the heads of the middle group to the other third of the pitch. It demands skill and attention – and it's fun.

Like the Midnight and Twilight leagues in the Wolverhampton area, you can see the immediate appeal of football and the local professional club in particular. I chatted to a few players at random. One was a Palestinian refugee on probation for stealing a loaf of bread because he was hungry. There was a teenager who had fled to London from the bitter civil war in Sierra Leone. He was desperate to get a professional or semi-professional contract so he could stay in Britain. He didn't know where his parents were or even if they were alive. Football was a level playing field because in his kit, unlike street clothes, he didn't stand out from native north Londoners.

Another player was Santos Perreira, a local man, who had served time in prison. 'I'm not ashamed to say what I went in jail for, I went in jail for robbery,' he told me. He described how people from his background in this corner of north east London drifted into crime through boredom: 'Some young kids get stuck in the crime life but they don't really want to be in the crime life.'

Perreira admitted to being initially sceptical about the aims and intentions of Leyton Orient's scheme but said it was helping him turn his life around. He insists his 'crime life' days are over – thanks to football coaching.

> I have been here for two years, I started playing football
> for them and they got me interested in football coaching.
> That's what I want to do – get some coaching qualifica-
> tions and take it from there. I think this Leyton Orient
> project is very good for people from the street, especially
> people into drugs or people doing robberies and that sort
> of thing. I think this is a very good way of coming out of
> it, if you have a love of football, it's never too late to play.

In the mid-1990s Leyton Orient took the bold decision to make its community programme completely independent, re-organizing it as a stand-alone charity, free from any agenda that the club or Reade's national Football in the Community scheme might try to impose. They secure their own funding from public bodies and business donors, and they employ specialist staff, whose training is more appropriate for the challenge – it's no longer enough just to be a former professional footballer.

This new approach has allowed them to redirect their efforts wholly into what Watson believes to be true community work, using the power of football to help people in all sections of society, as Watson explained:

> Until then we had defined the community around young
> people generally who were interested in playing football
> and had the abilities, or rather their parents had the
> ability to pay for the kind of activities we were offering.
> From 1995–96 onwards I think we totally redefined our
> community and started looking at it very differently and
> realized there are young men out there who are maybe in

drug treatment programmes, on probation orders. There was a travelling community, a refugee community, a homeless community and a huge community of 13–25-year-olds living on inner city housing estates who just weren't able to access some of the activities we were offering at that stage. So I guess we learned a new business.

Watson believes the appeal of football and the prestige of professional clubs provide a unique means of reaching out to people in all communities. In his view, Football in the Community should be far more than a recruitment agency for the next generation of fans. He fears that too many clubs have a short-sighted idea of what their community actually is:

Fundamentally it is unusual for a club to understand the nature of the communities where they are based. So often, they take the easy way out and define their community around some of the activities they are, maybe, undertaking at that particular time. For example, a Football in the Community scheme can start becoming a branch of the marketing department or it can help sell tickets or it can go and scout young footballers for academies and really that is not the business of a genuine community programme.

The government and the football authorities have both noted the success of Leyton Orient's scheme and via the FA's national game department, the re-formed Football Foundation and a number of central government departments they recognize that the power of football can help to meet a variety of official agendas on health, crime and education. This is something that Watson is well aware of:

I guess it's the glamour of professional sport and professional football in particular. Two or three people with a bag of footballs can roll up onto an estate with a difficult group of people and be able to engage them so quickly and actively. They can then sustain that interest over long periods of time by forming football teams and providing competitive opportunities and staying with them, letting that community and these client groups know this isn't a fireworks display, we're not going to fade away – we're going to be around in their lives as long as we possibly can be.

It isn't just Leyton Orient or Wolverhampton Wanderers who are involved in ambitious social-work-style community projects. There are many similar schemes at other clubs around Britain engaged in similar work. But the community officers attempting to organize these challenging programmes are not necessarily trained for the purpose, as Reade admits:

There isn't really a training course to offer for particular developments but we are looking now at the possibility of offering workshops, training days if you like, for particular areas. All Football in the Community staff, personnel must, if they are going into an environment where they are coaching young people or children, must have FA recognized qualifications, but also we ensure that all people who are appointed to work in the community have gone through the appropriate child protection screening measures, so to say they haven't had no appropriate training is not quite correct. You might see that as limited, but they have had some background.

Workers in this field are not trained to access all the potential funds to help them, whether it is local or national government, commercial sponsors or other potential funding agencies. As such, many Football in the Community schemes are selling themselves short because they don't have the expertise to tap into vital resources.

And despite the massive rise in most clubs' turnover and the huge wages demanded by players, Football in the Community staff have not benefited from football's increased affluence. Hundreds of workers carrying out this valuable, often difficult work are poorly paid. According to the last published national report, for 1999, the average assistant Football in the Community officer was earning £9,517 – £183 per week. Well below the national average.

'We have a minimum wage for community officers which we strongly recommend the clubs to adopt,' insisted Reade. 'Somewhere in the region of £13,500 to £14,000 at this moment in time.' Many, it seems, fall well short of that figure and, of course, their wages remain a world away from the multi-million pound salaries clubs readily pay their players. In today's football world, the £500,000 that the football authorities and the PFA give to Football in the Community looks pretty paltry: it is only roughly similar to the salary of the PFA's chief executive, Gordon Taylor, for instance. So does Reade feel the football industry is doing enough now for the credit that it receives?

> I think we've been grateful to receive half a million pounds a year. We have been able to generate other funding from other sources. We're in talks about our plans to develop and allow community schemes to have access to those resources that they are asking us for, or saying to us they need. We have got exciting plans for the future. If more funding comes our way I certainly won't say 'no' to it.

If football clubs won't provide the resources, there are those who question whether Football in the Community should be linked to them at all. Many rural communities, for example, are untouched by professional clubs' community schemes. The FA's new equity department is looking at how these sectors of society are being excluded from the national game.

There are two conflicting visions for how Football in the Community should develop. Jez Moxey, the chief executive at Wolves, is typical of the majority of club executives who see it as a marketing or PR operation of the club: 'We have not conducted detailed research to say that our community programme is delivering X number of supporters every single year and the natural progression would be to say how many extra supporters over and above the ones that we've got have been created by this initiative.'

But Neil Watson is demonstrating another view at Leyton Orient. 'I think this area of work is too important for football clubs to guide and manage,' he says. 'It should be in the hands of community development people who understand the nature of communities and the glamour and ability of football clubs to engage with them.'

Although some clubs, like Leeds United, for example, are prepared to commit themselves to £250,000 a year to run their community programme, there are people within football who will demand a direct financial return before investing similar sums – and that won't come from the sort of activities being run at Leyton Orient.

Since 1985 football clubs have had a good deal from Football in the Community. They use it to find the fans of the future and to revel in the endless, priceless, free PR it has provided – earned, mainly, by underpaid, hard-working people. Football has never been more high-profile at the top level. It has never been richer, yet it seems reluctant to use the undoubted power it has for the good of the community rather than seeking to boost its own income.

CHAPTER NINE

Blue Moves
Manchester City's Spanking New Stadium and How You Paid for It

The Commonwealth Games were widely regarded as a great success for all concerned, but the deal to hand the stadium to Manchester City after the tournament stretched the outer reaches of Lottery regulations – and the patience of the long-suffering locals, whose swimming pool was being closed down by the local council.

The 2002 Commonwealth Games in Manchester were the biggest multi-sport event ever staged in Britain. Awesomely well coordinated and enthusiastically covered by the BBC, they were unanimously reckoned to have been an exemplary national success in the Queen's Jubilee year. Also – and in Manchester this was felt to be most important – it was held that they were a great advert for the North, for the capabilities of England outside the metropolitan South, and for Manchester itself, the post-industrial city which had worked so hard to win and then stage the Games.

As a PR vehicle for Manchester – which, along with 'levering' public money to regenerate clapped-out east Manchester, was in fact the main purpose of the event – the Games were successful beyond imagination. They could have been tainted by cynicism; ingrained scepticism about major projects like the Millennium Dome or Wembley, allied with the overwhelmingly London-based media's agoraphobia north of Watford, could have trounced the Games, but in fact they worked in their favour. The media used the event's success as a new stick with which to knock London; basically, if crummy old Manchester could organize so much honest fun, what does this say about the capital? So, leading back naturally to the fiascos of the Dome and Wembley.

Manchester City Council, which underwrote and ran the

Games, actually benefited from this oblique form of London-centric prejudice; a patronizing pat on the head for a provincial city as a means of fuelling furious capital navel-gazing. One columnist on a national broadsheet actually said the Games had made him admit 'there is life outside London'. Another, an athletics correspondent, wondered at Manchester's renaissance, cooing that it now had more entries in the *Good Food Guide* than any other city outside London.

This did rather give away the priorities of London-based hacks forced to encamp up north for several days for the first time, and the wide-eyed accounts they filed were mostly of a piece. From the perspective of their hotels, a handful of *Good Food Guide* restaurants and the new stadium and press centre, the media judged that, through the Games, Manchester was regenerated, the shiny new £90 million stadium, as one hack put it, 'a symbol of the new east Manchester'.

Forced up north, the media gave it a superficial thumbs up. The Games over, they all left, and few will be back to see if any of it was true, if the expense of the Games was indeed justified, if the 'legacy' matches the hype.

World-class athletes Jonathan Edwards and Paula Radcliffe pooped the party a little by objecting to the ripping up of the best athletics stadium Britain has ever had, because it is to be converted to Manchester City Football Club's home ground. This provided a brief talking point to fill half-hours between triathlon and badminton, bowls and hockey, but when the Games finished, it was a non-issue. The track on which English athletes had thrilled full houses, crowds who seemed hungry for this entertainment, was dug up. Manchester City issued a press release which said excitedly that the track was now being 'ripped up'.

What was missing was a look beyond the undoubted fun of the ten-day Games to a serious assessment of their impact. Manchester City Council had famously bid for two Olympic Games before and these, the renamed Empire Games, were its consolation prize. They bid for two main reasons: firstly, they had a conviction that the future for industrial cities, when industry has rusted up, is to become centres of culture and living, and secondly, the structure of local authority funding leads cities to such bids. Years of cuts to their revenue budgets, which fund social services, education, road-sweeping, parks maintenance and the other everyday bread and butter of local authorities, has been accompanied by pots of money being made available for specific projects or initiatives. Public money is simply not available to fund even adequate local sports facilities, yet £493 million was spent on this event for elite athletes from around the world. The Games, particularly the construction of the stadium on an old contaminated gas site, were used to 'lever in' more public money – although it was difficult to see how far the funds had depended on the Games, rather than simply being available to help regenerate east Manchester, one of the most deprived areas in Britain.

Manchester City Council argued that the Games would 'prime-pump' the regeneration of east Manchester, and the media, so used to crying 'waste' at all public expenditure, took them at their word. And it was mostly for image enhancement: council leader Richard Leese told *On The Line* that the Games, and the new Sport City cluster of facilities, were 'a way of promoting Manchester as a major international city'.

Manchester argued fiercely that they needed a prestigious stadium to house the event, not a temporary one as was first mooted. The idea of mounting a northern games, and using the facilities built in Sheffield for the 1991 World Student Games that continue to be a millstone round that city's neck, was never considered. Indeed, Manchester beat Sheffield in rival bids to host the Games because Manchester claimed – insisted – in a signed letter to the government, that they would break even, while Sheffield acknowledged the Games would require a public subsidy. Manchester's claim, particularly after they were bailed out with £105 million barely 12 months before the Games, still provokes bitterness across Snake Pass in Sheffield.

Once the authorities – particularly Sport England, the Lottery distributor – agreed in principle to build a stadium with public money, Manchester had to find a continued use for it after the Games were over. The council's chief executive, Howard Bernstein, said they had offered to build a national stadium with retractable seating, which would host athletics, but were turned down in favour of London's ill-fated Wembley bid. Instead, they turned to the local football clubs and found that Manchester City, lurching through another of their perennial crises, would be prepared to move to the new state of the art stadium – but on their terms, as City's chairman, David Bernstein (no relation), explained:

> We were approached by the city council. They basically asked us if we were interested in occupying this stadium. If we couldn't do it, then it would not be possible to build a major permanent stadium. We said we were interested and there were three basic underlying conditions. One: it had to be a football stadium, not an athletics stadium. Secondly, it had to be a proper long-term home, and thirdly, we said from the beginning that any income sharing could only be above the Maine Road capacity because below that, frankly, we didn't need a new stadium.

It was an astonishing statement of bargaining power: City, who would tumble into the Second Division for the first time in their history in 1998, nevertheless held the whip hand. They didn't need to move; they had a perfectly good home at Maine Road in Moss Side, for 34,000 fans, which had itself received over £2 million of public money to develop it. The city council desperately wanted a stadium – and the Sport England money they could attract to build it – and needed City to give it the ongoing use which Sport England required, so City could set their requirements. They wanted the track removed for them, and to pay nothing, no rent, up to the Maine Road capacity. The council were prepared to deal with them even on that basis, because without them they wouldn't get a stadium at all, as Leese acknowledges: 'If we didn't have a permanent tenant for the stadium, then we would be left with the city council picking up the revenue costs of that facility and other than the other odd major sporting occasion, perhaps, not a great deal of use. It would be a white elephant.'

With City in, paying to fit out the stadium's corporate entertainment facilities and, crucially, paying the ongoing maintenance costs, Sport England gave them £77 million Lottery money towards building the stadium. The city council, hard-pressed and serving deprived communities with desperate claims on their funds, put in the £13 million required to convert it to a football stadium after the Games. In other words, the ripping up of the athletics track was done by Manchester City Council at council tax payers' expense, replacing the track with seating to make it City's new 48,000-seater home.

Since the beginning of the 1990s major football clubs have been reacting to the requirements of the Taylor Report and the game's commercial revolution by renovating their grounds or building new stadia. For this, limited public money was made available by the Football Trust – itself controversial enough, as the clubs were soon feasting on millions of pounds from BSkyB. Otherwise, the clubs have had to finance the stadia themselves, via share issues, if they were lucky enough to have people wanting to invest in them or, more usually through bonds and loans. The stadia – Sunderland's Stadium of Light, Derby's Pride Park, Southampton's St Mary's – were a great deal more modest, and necessarily cheaper, than the one being gifted to City.

Leicester City moved into their new stadium in 2002 – awful timing, because they had just been relegated from the Sky-blessed Premiership to the Football League, which had just been walloped by the collapse of ITV Digital, costing First Division clubs £4 million. Leicester faced serious financial problems compounded by the stadium they had built themselves. The parallels with Manchester City are interesting: Leicester's stadium houses 33,000 seats – the same capacity up to which City pay nothing for their new stadium. Yet Leicester's cost £28 million and, with interest on the loan, secured against the stadium and future TV revenues, which have now collapsed, they are committed to paying £2.4 million per year for 25 years.

Other clubs might be expected to complain at Manchester City's Lottery win, which freed their money to buy players, a fact rubbed in the summer of 2002 when City became the second highest spenders on players in Europe. The £13 million lavished on the single, moody talent of Nicolas Anelka was the same price as the city council was spending ripping up the track for them at the stadium. But English football, like the English way of bidding for sporting events, does not work like this. There is no requirement for a level playing field and little overall planning: it's every city, every club, for itself, and Manchester have played this new game better than any other provincial council since the funding straitjackets were buckled up in the mid-1980s.

City and Manchester signed the deal, an arrangement summed up by David Bernstein:

> It's a tremendous move for the club. It's giving us the chance to move to a state-of-the-art twenty-first-century tremendous home for our supporters and we're very excited about it. But that doesn't mean it isn't a great deal for the city of Manchester as well. I do think this is a win-win situation.

What was more difficult, even though the stadium was built entirely with public money, was to find out from the respective bodies what the deal actually was. *On The Line* asked Richard Leese how much the move was costing Manchester City, and he said, 'You'll have to ask Manchester City.'

David Bernstein was quite circumspect, claiming commercial confidentiality. All gave a general description of a profit share above Maine Road's current capacity, which Leese said was on a sliding scale. Derek Casey, then the chief executive of Sport England, was more forthcoming, accepting that publicly funded projects, by definition, had to be transparent: 'The arrangement we've got is that of ticket sales up to 40,000; that's the difference between 32,500 and 40,000, we get 50 per cent of the ticket sales income and above 40,000 that rises to 60 per cent.'

Casey was also clear that the rental income was to be applied very specifically, into maintaining the new facilities, also built with Lottery money, at Sport City:

> What we're going to do, is establish a new trust; effectively that money will go into the trust, which will have responsibility for running those facilities – the Velodrome, the tennis courts, the squash centre. And that is the method of obtaining subsidy for maintaining those facilities in the longer term.

We asked the council to confirm some of those details but they were surprisingly unfamiliar with them. Leese said he didn't know the deal in detail and told us to contact Howard Bernstein, the council's chief executive. We finally spoke to him and asked him what the deal, particularly the profit share, actually was. He said it was around a 50-50 share and that City could deduct their costs before paying the money over – in other words, they are not equally splitting the face value of the ticket. We asked for more details (this is crucial information) about how much exactly is coming back to public facilities from the £90 million spent providing Manchester City with a new home. Bernstein refused to give any. We argued that the details ought to be publicly available, because the project is publicly funded, and Bernstein said, 'That's bollocks.' Which pretty much brought the conversation with Manchester City Council to a natural close.

One aspect of a Lottery project is clear, however. As laid down in the Lottery Act, any project must not be 'primarily for private profit'. This is why most applications are made by councils or community sports clubs. Manchester City, though known as and felt fondly by its supporters to be a club, is in fact a private company, mostly owned by a few very rich men. John Wardle and David Makin, the owners of retail chain J D Sports, own 29.5 per cent of the shares; the family of Stephen Boler, the late kitchen magnate, have 13 per cent; BSkyB, substantially owned by Rupert Murdoch, have 9.9 per cent; and Francis Lee, the former centre forward and chairman, has held on to 7 per cent.

If City were to make money out of the stadium move, as they surely would, then these five major shareholders, along with all the others, stood to make money themselves. We asked David Bernstein if City's shareholders would be in a healthy position as a result of the move. 'Our shareholders?' he replied. 'Absolutely. I wouldn't be doing it and we wouldn't have been in negotiations for four years if I didn't think this was the right thing for the club.'

Manchester City Council and Sport England both said they had to make sure they were abiding by the restrictions placed on private companies profiting from public money, but had slightly different accounts of their responsibility. 'We had to be very careful that Manchester City could not effectively profit out of the public subsidy that went into the building of the stadium,' said Leese. 'The deal has been constructed to make sure they can't do that.'

Not so, according to Casey, who said: 'What the Lottery Act says is that we must fund projects which are not primarily for private gain. So, in other words, we can actually invest in private clubs but have to make sure there is substantial public gain when we invest in facilities such as those.'

In other words, Manchester City could indeed make money out of the spending of public funds, but the public had to get something back too. The argument of all concerned is that the Games themselves were a substantial benefit to the public, and Casey was satisfied with the deal investing a share of gate receipts above 33,000 people, in the Sport City facilities. But he was very specific about that – contrary to reports that washed around Manchester after the athletes bemoaned the loss of the track, when it was said the money went back to the council, or into the wider community, the profit share according to Casey, was specifically going back into Sport City.

When we made the *On The Line* programme, in the spring of 2001, Manchester City Council faxed a helpful pie chart showing the cost of the Games at £222 million. Of that, £150 million was public money. At the time, the running costs were said to be £62 million, which were underwritten by the council. According to the Games chief executive, Frances Done, they were then £30 million short: 'If the Games didn't manage to fund the total cost then technically the underwriting of that is with Manchester City Council – so obviously we're doing our utmost to make sure there isn't any kind of problem.'

Leese said that the council were convinced the Games would benefit the city, but promised that the funding would not cut into the overriding duty to actually provide the basic, humdrum necessities for Manchester's citizens. 'There are two things that shouldn't happen with the Commonwealth Games,' he said. 'One is that we don't have to put up council tax to pay for the Commonwealth Games and the other is that we shouldn't be cutting other services.'

In 2001 *On The Line* talked to people living in the communities closest to the stadium, in east Manchester. We found desperately poor public sporting facilities, which were threadbare and in dire need of improvement. There were just two exceptions: decent, relatively modern swimming pools, one in Miles Platting, in the shadow of the stadium, and the other in Gorton, a mile or so away. The council had announced their intention to close them both down.

We went to a protest meeting, attended by Leese, organized at the Gorton pool on the morning when the pensioner group used it for their regular swim. We found east Manchester not exactly humming with party spirit.

'They're talking about saving money here,' said one old woman, 'but they're spending money in a ridiculous fashion for the Commonwealth Games. But the Commonwealth Games is only a short-term thing, isn't it?'

The closure of two pools in communities without much else to enjoy – or even knit them together – were to save the council just £150,000 a year. And at Gorton the community would lose a splash pool with the only disabled access in Manchester. One of the users summed up what the swimming sessions meant to her:

> 'We come twice a week for the over 50s swimming; it's fantastic. It's a social thing as well, we meet people, we talk before it opens, we have coffee afterwards and it's really good.'

The public meeting was angry, and it was moving to listen to the pensioners speaking from the heart about this, another downward trudge in the steady decline of their area. Gorton, like most of east Manchester, was originally developed to house workers from the nearby factories and engineering companies but since much of the industry has closed down, these tight, proud communities have withered.

'Gorton's gone from being a place to live to a place people just drive through,' said one man. 'We've got drive-in KFC and burger places on Hyde Road, and now another proper facility for local people is being closed.'

'This area at the moment is bleeding to death,' said another. 'We can ill afford to lose a facility like this, this is the only one that's left.'

These people did connect the cuts in their community with the gleaming new facilities being built for the Games. One woman, surrounded by friends glumly agreeing, told us:

It's a little bit of a sore point really. We think, "Are they doing all this for two weeks of glory?" Manchester's holding its Commonwealth Games but I don't feel anything about it. Even though I live here, I don't feel excited. Manchester [council] has said that they are interested in the people but they're not really. They're interested in profile – a higher profile.

Leese disagreed, arguing that the pools were inefficient, that Manchester had a surplus of them, and that the swimmers could use the superb new aquatic centre built for the Games near the universities in the city centre. This brought a scathing response from the pensioners, who said they would have to get two buses to the new pool. Many said, again without anger, that they would give up swimming and so lose the exercise and socializing which it brought them. A local Liberal Democrat councillor in Miles Platting, Marc Ramsbottom, was opposing the cuts:

There doesn't seem to me to be much logic in having brand new state of the art facilities at one end and closing local community swimming pools at the other. The amount of money needed to save this pool compared to what's being spent on the Commonwealth Games is infinitesimal, really, there's no comparison. I think the theory is that the Commonwealth Games and Sport City and the stadium and all the other facilities will act as a regeneration catalyst for the area. The reality is we haven't seen it yet.

David Bernstein said he did not know that local community facilities were being axed in the very neighbourhood in which his club were being furnished with a new £90 million stadium.

If City, consumed by the financial swirl of the Premiership, manage to take a look at the local football facilities in their new swathe of Manchester, even they will surely feel some humility. We went on a tour of the sporting wastelands of east Manchester with Alan Grafton, 56, a community stalwart who has lived all his life in Gorton. He is a director of the Manchester County Football Association and he ran the Gorton Sunday League, which boasted six divisions of local football clubs, for 27 years until it closed down when the clubs gradually faded away. He acknowledged that changing lifestyles and work patterns undermined traditional Sunday morning football but he was in no doubt that the dire state of the pitches and changing rooms had much to do with it. 'It's a crying shame that the League had to go, through lack of facilities,' he said. 'As a league you can't attract teams if you've no facilities.'

In total, four local leagues in east Manchester, including historic Saturday institutions, have closed in recent years. The parks on which they played have suffered from a generation of cuts to the council's revenue funding. Parks are not a statutory provision of councils, who are therefore not obliged by law to maintain them, so they are often the first to decline when budgets are shrunk. The council also admits that compulsory competitive tendering, a policy introduced by the Conservative government in the 1980s, has seriously undermined the quality of maintenance at parks, leading to what the authority itself described as 'roving gangs', who would turn up at a park, just do the mowing and other basic work, then move on to the next one.

Changing facilities for local amateur football have also decayed or been closed to the point where – and we found this a stark fact given the hype and expense of the Commonwealth Games – there are no usable changing facilities at any council-owned pitch in the whole of east Manchester – a huge area. Grafton wants this decline to be halted:

> They should be putting more money to grass-roots football, looking after the people who live in Manchester, the people that are paying their council tax to Manchester. Big money is out there, but unfortunately they're not looking after the areas they should be looking after. We,

> as people of east Manchester, should be getting some-
> thing back for it, and something back decently, not like
> this – dilapidated pitches.

After our dismal tour of east Manchester's ragged parks and football
facilities – the journey the London hacks didn't see – Leese made a
surprising admission. 'The pitches in north Manchester are actually
worse than the ones in east Manchester,' he said. Hardly the best
advertisement for increasing sporting participation in the city.

Grafton had some blunt advice for the council leaders:

> It's great to get the Commonwealth Games, great for the
> city and the council need patting on the back for that,
> but they need to come out and have a look and get their
> feet dirty, and see where the money is spent, because
> people in east Manchester, a deprived area, we're not
> getting anything, and that's where the stadium is going
> – east Manchester.

Of Manchester City's old home, in Maine Road, little has been heard
for some time. In exchange for the new stadium, City are to hand
Maine Road over to the council. Written into City's accounts with a
£28 million valuation, it is in fact worth very little as anything other
than a sports stadium and the council have had a forlorn struggle
trying to come up with a future use for it. In early 2001 they finally
announced that Maine Road was to be occupied by Sale Sharks, a
rugby union club whose 2,700 supporters were more used to their
charming little ground in loamy Cheshire than a 34,000 capacity
stadium in Moss Side. The council told *On The Line* that Manchester
City themselves had had a part in this decision. Stockport County,
the smaller Football League club south of Manchester, had expressed
an interest in Maine Road. They faced complete opposition from
their fans, for whom separateness from Manchester underpinned
their very identity and support, but Manchester City had also said
they would prefer their ground not to go to another football club
because this could undermine their support. Quite whether the
council should have been influenced by City at all seemed dubious,

but nevertheless, Sale Sharks got the nod and the council's leaders emerged to talk about a new rugby union policy for the city and the real benefits – and grant money – which this game would bring.

At the time, Sale Sharks were being run by a chief executive, Peter Deakin, who had spent time working in US sport and had brought his particular commercial vision to both rugby league and union at a mini-series of clubs. Sale Sharks had been saved from the perilous post-professionalism tumult of rugby union by a local mobile phone entrepreneur, Brian Kennedy, who with his partner Ian Blackhurst, ran 15 businesses with a total annual turnover of around 300 million.

Deakin foresaw a significant growth in interest in club rugby, believing that the Zurich Premiership, fuelled by TV money from BSkyB, would begin to generate 'mass audiences' at clubs like Sale. 'It's fantastic to be able to say that that stadium could be ours,' he said. 'That would be sensational for the club. I mean that would probably make us the biggest rugby union club in the world with its own facilities. So its a nice selling point – hopefully we could tap into that.'

The proposed deal was again unclear; it appeared to involve, as with Manchester City in their new stadium, zero rent up to a certain attendance figure, then a profit share. This was a windfall for Sale Sharks and Deakin acknowledged that their owner, Brian Kennedy, stood to reap the rewards personally. 'You're relying on his ownership to keep putting money into the club,' he said. 'Now if the guy makes money as a consequence of that, fair play to him. He's had to cash flow the business, for years maybe, to eventually get a pay day out of it.'

But Sale Sharks, with rather less fanfare than greeted their initial interest, withdrew from the idea and Deakin has moved on again. There has been no public announcement since about what is to be done with Maine Road. The latest rumour has it as a business park, in which the offices would be the entertainment suites Manchester City installed in the new Kippax Street stand, built with a hefty grant from the Football Trust.

A matter of weeks after we made our programme, and after the House of Commons Select Committee on Media, Culture and Sport was also told that Frances Done was confident of raising all the running costs for the Games, it emerged that this was far from correct. The running costs of the Games had been dramatically underestimated and Manchester were hugely over-budget. The government sent in Patrick Carter, a friend of Jack Straw's and a favoured troubleshooter, who went through the books in six weeks and came back with the devastating conclusion that a further £105 million was required if the Games were not to be a disaster, a national embarrassment. There followed intense arguments about where the money was to come from. Sport England were eventually forced to pay £30 million, which came out of their budget for community sport (Trevor Brooking, Sport England's chairman, declared publicly that he found this extremely frustrating) and the government itself contributed £20 million. This left Manchester City Council lumping another £50 million into funding the Games they had originally won on the basis that they would break even and require no money from the government.

By the time S Club sang and Tony and Cherie Blair boogied at the Commonwealth Games opening ceremony at the City of Manchester Stadium in July 2002, the cost of the Games had inflated to £493 million. This was overspending of Dome- and Wembley-like proportions but the perceived competence of the Manchester organization was only welcomed by the media – as a means to hammer London. Half a billion pounds spent, on a ten-day event of mainly domestic appeal. In one of the poorest areas of one of the poorest cities in England. The Games were hailed as a success in every respect: sporting, cultural, an 'advert for Manchester', and for 'the new east Manchester'. But when we returned to east Manchester we found it unchanged, except for the stadium, gleaming by the dual carriageway, and a massive new Asda Wal-Mart, the cut-price American superstore, which the council boasts of as the forefront of the regeneration of the world's once proud, first industrial city.

Looking at the worn-down, always basic provision for the community in east Manchester, we couldn't help wondering, in the light of the £493 million, what a difference a few thousand pounds here and there, patching up, might have made to the lives of the local people. Richard Leese was adamant the policies would bring long-term benefits:

> I remain confident that when we get to 2003–4, when it's all over and we've done the books, that we won't be putting council tax up, we won't be cutting services to pay for the Games. What we will be doing is reaping the benefits of what will have been the most successful Commonwealth Games ever.

At the public meeting in Gorton that Leese attended, one of the pensioners protesting the closure of their swimming pool (and one of Leese's council tax payers), had serious doubts. 'I feel so disappointed,' she said of the Games, the stadium and the whole idea, 'because we're the losers, aren't we?'

CHAPTER TEN

Another Fine Mess
The Tin-pot World of the FA's Disciplinary Process

Footballers are routinely fined vast sums of money for minor misde-
meanours – usually to public acclaim. But should we be cheering? This
chapter examines the amateurism and inconsistency of a kneejerk justice,
meted out by blazers behind closed doors. Footballers may not be perfect,
they may even be louts, but they deserve better than this.

Whatever Robbie Savage goes on to achieve in his football career, the
erstwhile Leicester midfielder is liable to be remembered for one
thing (other than his combative playing style) and that will be the
day he took a dump in the referee's toilet.

Savage claims he was caught short. The Football Association
decided it was a calculated act of disrespect against the referee that
brought the game into disrepute and they fined him £10,000. His
then club, Leicester, joined in the fun and docked him two weeks'
wages. All in all, a small mortgage for what at worst was a schoolboy
prank – and this in the nation that invented toilet humour!

Take a trip down any street, in any town, on any Saturday night
and you will see acts of wanton yobbery. (At least Savage used a
toilet!) But the perpetrators, when brought to book, will probably be
let off with cautions. If their misdemeanours warrant a fine or compensation, the chances are it will be hundreds of pounds.

A couple of years ago, for example, a man came before the
magistrate of a court in west London, where he admitted spitting in
another man's face during an argument in a Kensington wine bar.
Not surprisingly, the magistrate took a dim view of this and fined
him. The fact that the man was Chelsea centre-forward Chris Sutton
(now with Celtic), did not seem to enter into the calculations when
they fined him £300 for the offence.

A month or so later, Patrick Vieira also spat in a man's face. This time it was during a televised football match at West Ham. The recipient of Vieira's 'sample' was Neil Ruddock, a man not known for his gentle approach to defending. Vieira felt the full force of the FA's wrath. He was fined £30,000 and received a playing ban to boot. At heart, the same offence. Both incidents had involved highly paid footballers but Vieira's penalty was *one hundred* times greater than Sutton's.

Although there are many other walks of life where the 'glitterati' earn stratospheric rewards – rock stars, movie stars, movers and shakers in television, the law or business – no earnings provoke as much outright public hostility as footballers' wages. As with so many aspects of planet football in the UK, the notion of discipline is wholly outdated, applied with inconsistency and fundamentally flawed. Even though most Premiership players actually receive monthly wage slips, the image of an obscenely stuffed weekly wage packet is bandied about in the media almost as a provocation to the millions of fans whose own weekly reward is featherweight by comparison. Brad Pitt may earn $15 million per movie (great!) but Roy Keane earning £90, 000 per week? (Outrage!)

We live in a culture where, when it comes to footballers, the bigger the fine, the louder the cheer, but no sensible system of justice or disciplinary code of any worth is based on the mercies of the mob. Even so it is hard, even among those within the game who we may consider to be paragons of reason, to find people who recognize the FA's disciplinary system for what it is: an outmoded code motivated not by justice, but retribution and caught out now by the crazy inflation in the game. It is a disciplinary system that harks back to the patriarchal past of a game where clubs owned footballers, paid a maximum wage, and players called the manager 'sir'.

The disciplinary department at the FA is one of its busiest. Typically, it sits every week and in the course of a season thousands of miscreants from all levels of the game are dealt with. Over and above the law of the land, most organizations will have their own rules and regulations, with sanctions for breaking them. Mostly these rules and regulations relate to a list of offences that could result in the sack. But football is different. Players are never sacked, because they are the clubs' assets and no business would throw a valuable asset away without very, very good reason. So the purpose of the disciplinary code is twofold: firstly, to protect the rules and ethics of the game from thuggish erosion and secondly, to take account of the fact that if you can't or won't sack a player then there has to be an alternative to deal with the kind of behaviour that would usually end in a dismissal warning elsewhere in the world.

Discharging these dual duties through a code of discipline when it applies to highly-paid young men should, most people would agree, take some account of the likely impact of a fine, as lawyer and sports agent Mike Townley explains:

> A fine of [between] £100 and £1,000 might represent, for many types of offences in magistrates, a fairly heavy punishment. In football it clearly does not and higher fines are justified on the basis that they are proportionate in the context of what players are earning and what the governing body needs to do to manage its legitimate sporting aims.

But in seizing this right to impose such massive fines, which are far more than you would find in any other court, tribunal or company in the UK, then at least morally the FA has the responsibility to ensure their justice is applied consistently, fairly and openly. The problem with FA justice is that, routinely, none of the above applies. The evidence would suggest that they have no sensible tariff and the level of fines is arrived at arbitrarily.

Martin Wassik is a professor of law at Manchester University and he advises the Lord Chancellor on sentencing. He points out that the difficulty with this sort of approach is that it runs the risk of losing all sense of proportion between one offence and another:

> It is hard to imagine that a court would uphold a fine of £30,000 for spitting. The problem with imposing such penalty is if you do that for a relatively minor offence – and, unpleasant though it is, spitting is a minor assault – how do you deal with something that is much more

severe? You run the risk of losing the sense of justice and
the relationship between the offence and the penalty.

In fact, in a civil or criminal court a fine of £30,000 would almost
certainly be associated with a custodial sentence and would involve
the seizing of assets acquired through illegal activity. But when it
comes to antisocial behaviour in football, there are those who think
that most professional players are louts who ill-deserve the fantastic
financial rewards that some of them enjoy and therefore do deserve
everything that the FA can dish out to them. It is possible that many
footballers themselves believe they deserve everything they are
given, too.

The consequence of this line of thought is that footballers are
often hammered for actions that, in another context would draw a
mild rebuke or even raise a laugh. This perverse juxtaposition was
illustrated in the *News of the World* recently. The inside news pages
ran a spread of Zara Phillips, the Princess Royal's daughter, fooling
around with friends at a polo match. One member of her party was
snapped letting off a fire extinguisher in the direction of Ms Phillips.
In the same edition, a rueful-looking Stan Collymore was pictured in
the sports section after being sent home from a pre-season training
camp for doing something similar in a bar. He was fined £30,000.
There were no charges brought against Ms Phillips's friend as far as
I know.

While there may be little sympathy for such behaviour, are
footballers being judged fairly? The Professional Footballers'
Association (PFA) chairman Gordon Taylor, thinks not in all cases.
'Footballers are expected to set standards that do not apply to politi-
cians, churchmen, people in the legal or business professions,' he
said. 'Because some of them are highly paid there is this view that
they should be taught a lesson.'

Kicking footballers in the wallet is certainly a popular pastime
with the press and public – and playing the discipline card is an easy
bandwagon to ride when you are struggling to make an impact.

Before Adam Crozier started his first full season in charge at the
FA in August 2000, judging by his public pronouncements, it was
not the woeful lack of qualified coaches, nor the sometimes poorly

trained medical staff, not the drunken behaviour in the corporate entertainment suites, nor even the parlous finances of so many football clubs that vexed him. No: it was the lack of discipline on the field. And a promise that the FA was going to crack down harder on the miscreants was his rallying cry.

The spokesman on such matters at Soho Square, the FA's spanking new HQ, is Nick Coward, a lawyer by training and now effectively number two at the FA. 'We have to look at the profession as a whole,' he said, 'and what we do is speak to employers, the clubs, the players' union, and we have to have a consensus within the game as to what is right and that is where we have ended up.'

In other words, as a governing body, the FA have not looked at what is right, what is wrong, what is desirable and achievable and taken a lead accordingly, they have just drifted along tinkering with custom and practice and upped the financial sanction in line with football's crazy inflation rate.

In Europe, where they have taken the lead in most things when it comes to football, the disciplinary system is radically different. For example, in Germany and the Netherlands, all hearings are open to the public like any other court. The process is a direct mirror of personnel and procedure that you find in civic courts. Players will have a lawyer to represent them and there will always be legally qualified staff on hand to advise the football governors.

When *On The Line* presented him with the notion that the FA could follow this example and hold the proceedings of their disciplinary committee in public, Coward responded: 'If you look at the various tribunals there is debate whether you get better or worse justice in a public environment.' It is an unusual perspective from a lawyer, especially one who was no doubt taught in law school that a touchstone of English common law is that, 'justice must not only be done but be seen to be done'.

The penalties in the UK are also way out of kilter with the rest of the world. In Europe, penalties are in proportion with the civil code. Take the famous incident in the Brazil v Turkey match during the 2002 World Cup Finals, for instance. In the preamble to a corner kick, a Turkish player kicked the ball towards the Brazilian Rivaldo.

The player fell as if poleaxed, making out that he had been hit in the face when it had actually hit him on the thigh. UEFA officials fined Rivaldo £2,000 for cheating. British commentators could not believe it and many said so but it was wholly consistent with the sanctions that UEFA have handed out in their competitions before.

There was also the occasion when a goalkeeper playing in a Champion's League game cuffed a ballboy who gave him cheek during a game that was being televised. The incident was not so different in essence to Eric Cantona's famous kung fu kick. But this player was not dragged through the courts, banned for half a season and heavily fined – he was admonished and fined the equivalent of £2,000.

This is due in part to the fact that the football culture is very different in the rest of Europe, where the clubs and the fans tend to view their players as mature adults and treat them accordingly, and also because the players themselves tend not to get involved in high jinx as much as their English counterparts. Either way, there is little evidence to suggest that the swingeing nature of the fines in England leads to any significant improvement in players' 'behaviour' in England compared to elsewhere.

Former West Ham player Julian Dicks, who retired from the game through injury and now runs a hotel, spent more time in front of various tribunals than most. 'I was getting booked for dissent, and so I was fined by the club,' he told *On The Line*, 'but your points for bookings and sending-offs accumulate and if you go over a certain level you again get fined by your club and you go to the FA and they fine and ban you, too.' In the 1992–3 season he was sent off three times, and with a host of bookings to his credit as well, he claims that he ended up paying out more in fines to his club and the FA than he earned that year.

Mike Townley thinks that football's status as the number one sport means that it can get away with more than most:

> I have been a sports lawyer for 15 years and in that time sports governing bodies have been dragged kicking and screaming into the twenty-first century. I think it was the case that up until the 1980s most sports governing

bodies really did think they operated their own fiefdom and that they could sanction and operate on more or less any basis.

I think with various landmark actions that have gone on, some governing bodies have come into the real world and overhauled their disciplinary code, but the Football Association has certain luxuries in terms of its longevity as an association and in terms of its cultural and commercial strength, that allows it to operate fairly robustly and to take any challenges on the chin, which many other sports simply cannot afford to do.

Although the FA maintains that it has few complaints from inside the game, this must be seen within the context of a workplace culture where thinking for yourself is frowned upon. Players played, others made and enforced the rules. The 'schoolmasterly' approach to discipline is one that generations of players from their teenage years have grown up with. For Dicks this attitude and atmosphere was harder to stomach than the fines:

> They treat you like children. I was an adult. So, all right, I had broken the rules but I was still a grown-up, married, I had kids, and was generally treated as an adult in every other aspect of my life, but up there I was treated like a naughty kid. I thought I was back at school.

Football agent Jonathan Barnett looks after the affairs of a number of players who have been considered 'trouble' and whose exploits have led them into civil and criminal courts, but Barnett states that given the choice between the two approaches to crime and punishment, he would take the magistrates court over the FA every time. 'In court you are represented fairly, you are given an open hearing, you are judged by someone who is qualified and completely unbiased,' he said. 'I do not think you have that in the FA.'

What you have at the Football Association is basically three blazers, behind closed doors with little or no specific qualifications deliberating within a pseudo legal environment on issues of guilt, innocence and sentencing. In foreign regimes of dubious legitimacy we call that a kangaroo court.

It is not unusual for a case that is the focus of extreme media attention to arrive in front of the FA disciplinary panel. Given that those who hear these cases are primarily in football administration and not law, fairness can be a casualty from the off. Especially if there is a hue and cry and the person concerned has previous, as Townley explains:

> I don't think lay people find it easy to disregard the media, whereas a lot of people who have sat as judges do have the ability to park those issues to one side while they look at the facts between them. And that is not to be rude about people without such experience who do hear these kind of cases in various tribunals. But maybe the time has come to say, 'Look, let's hand this over to people who have experience in judicial matters'.

The prime example of this, perhaps, is the case of Eric Cantona, who went for a spectator in the crowd at Selhurst Park because he thought the man had shouted out an insulting remark about him.

Maurice Watkins, Manchester United's solicitor recalls life inside that particular circus:

> There were three processes: first there was a club/player disciplinary situation, then we had disciplinary proceedings by the Football Association and then finally we had the magistrates and, on appeal, the crown court. There was huge publicity when the bench sentenced Eric to two weeks in prison, which we immediately appealed. This was set aside and reduced to 120 hours community service.
>
> In the judgement the appeal court judge clearly emphasized that the decision of the magistrates had been made to make an example of a public figure and did not deal with the gravity of the offence. So the magistrates did get it wrong.

In the magistrates court Cantona was afforded due process to which every citizen is entitled. The proceedings were open to press and public scrutiny. The procedure and reasoning at each stage was clear. In contrast, the FA's decision to extend his ban from three months to six was taken behind closed doors, and how they arrived at that ruling remains a mystery. For the players who have grown up with justice FA-style, the attitude is one of resignation.

Julian Dicks was summoned to a disciplinary hearing to face the charge that he had deliberately assaulted Chelsea's John Spencer by stamping on him. Dicks attended the hearing with a lawyer, a video of the incident and a physicist who attended as an expert witness. After watching the video of the incident, the physicist asserted that it is difficult to stamp, at least with any force, while totally airborne, which is what Dicks was until he made contact with Spencer. Dicks says that although his lawyer put forward a strong case in his defence he never expected it to make any difference to the FA panel. He was right. 'Even before I went in there I think they decided what they wanted to do,' he said. 'My case took most of the day to get across but still they came to their decision within a matter of a couple of minutes. Guilty. Fined and banned. End of story.'

The FA may operate with all the paraphernalia of a court but when Mike Townley was called to defend two women players who had tested positive for certain recreational drugs he found their due process was decidedly sloppy:

> The Sports Council lay down requirements, and nearly every governing body has requirements that there will be confidentiality over the finding of a positive sample until the first instance hearing. Now in my case there was no attempt to observe that convention. In fact the FA press office put out a press release before there had been any hearing at all.
>
> For someone who was not making a living out of the game but was a professional in another capacity this was very damaging to have press releases issued before she had had a chance to put her case in mitigation and

explain her personal and professional circumstances, which in this case were very, very relevant.

During the summer of 1999 Nick Bitel defended Leicester City's Stephen Guppy who, along with four other Leicester City players, was up on charges that he had passed on tickets to Spurs fans who, as a result, were able to cause trouble among the Leicester fans at a Worthington Cup final. The picture of a thug punching a woman in the face during the game had been splashed across all the papers, making the case all the more emotive. In the end, four of the players were found guilty. Guppy was cleared but Bitel says the structure of the hearing was shot through with faults in procedure:

> In the case of Guppy's hearing, all three people who heard the case were FA officials and would have received tickets themselves and thus were sitting in judgement when they are involved in the very process that is being challenged. I think this is wrong. The people hearing the case have a vested interest in the outcome of the hearing.
>
> The trouble is there is no openness. Why were these players charged on this occasion? No one knows. Why were such swingeing fines handed out to some of them? Again no one knows. If you had an independent tribunal, if you had lawyers or outside people who were on that committee who were guiding the panel to their decisions, if there were people who were advising them then you couldn't complain.

It has to be said that the PFA, made up mostly of ex-players themselves and who therefore suffered the same treatment, do not feel the injustice, but chairman Gordon Taylor does admit that there could be greater clarity in the proceedings with perhaps greater fairness flowing from that. 'There needs to be openness so the public can see what the offence is, what is involved, previous penalties for that offence and to make sure that the people dispensing the justice are seen to be independent and taking on board what would happen in a civil or even criminal court.'

The key issue concerning the FA and its disciplinary procedure is not merely whether it is fair but whether it is sensible. Because the more wealthy and savvy footballers become, the less likely they are to take all this punishment lying down. 'Fining someone two weeks' wages could mean a sum in excess of £100,000,' Bitel points out. 'All that means is that footballers have been able to afford better representation.'

Agent Jonathan Barnett agrees. 'They have been brought up with this system, it is something that they live with and just accept,' he said. 'Pretty soon you will see a less pliant attitude. Players won't go like lambs to the slaughter any more.'

But if the FA are less than rigorous with their procedure, the situation is worse at the clubs. The majority of players are fined by the clubs. There is an agreement with PFA that the maximum fine is two weeks' wages although there have been moves to increase this to four weeks.

Quite apart from the fact that there is an obvious financial motive to have a robust system of fines at football clubs (and maybe the taxman would have something to say about it), such is the power of the manager at a club that on-the-spot fines are not unknown for offences such as missing training, turning up drunk, giving 'cheek' or generally larking around. Perhaps more rare these days, as top players surround themselves with a better quality of agent and advice, is the paying of fines, in cash, direct to the manager.

On The Line has learned of a club where this was almost standard practice. Players would settle smaller fines immediately with a quick trip to the nearest cash point and would hand over larger sums later in an envelope, in both cases direct to the manager. There was no explanation of where the money would end up but the players had their suspicions. All confirmed that after the manager moved on, draws in his office were found to contain dozens of envelopes – some still full of cash. Not that any player would have blown the whistle of course, for fear of damaging his own career. And anyway, you just don't 'sneak' in football.

Clubs caught in the media spotlight have been known to overreact, perhaps anxious to make an example and prove that they will not tolerate certain behaviour that has brought opprobrium down on the good name of the team. The result is that fairness goes out of the window.

A difficult and controversial example of this is the punishment meted out by Leeds United to Lee Bowyer in the wake of the trial in which he was accused, along with others, of beating up and horribly assaulting a young Asian man in Leeds city centre.

Bowyer was eventually acquitted, after an aborted trial that lasted ten weeks before being abandoned because of a prejudicial press report and a second trial lasting five weeks. But at the end of it all the club fined him six weeks' wages and ordered that he should involve himself in more community programmes than he might otherwise have been asked to fulfil.

This penalty, then, cost Bowyer thousands of pounds for essentially going out on a Saturday night and getting drunk. Granted, this is not something a footballer should be doing anyway, but the message the club was sending out was that they believed he had been up to no good even though he had been acquitted. This could be construed to be in contempt of the court and the jury's decision.

And that was not the end of it. The FA, by banning Bowyer from being picked for England, were swimming in the same murky waters. The upshot was that England went to Japan and the World Cup minus a useful player, who otherwise would certainly have been selected, and Leeds came within a whisker of finding one of their key players resuming his career elsewhere. It may be that you would not welcome a situation where the probity of team selection could only be questioned in the face of a criminal conviction, but nonetheless, the incident illustrates the subtleties and difficulties of running a disciplinary code.

If there is one aspect of the disciplinary code to which footballers (and indeed managers) are subject, which is the biggest affront to justice and fairness in this higgledy-piggledy system, it is the charge of 'bringing the game into disrepute'. This is the kind of law that in its scope and vagueness ranks alongside 'being rude to the leader' in dictatorships. It is the reason that no serving player would speak on the record to *On The Line* for this investigation.

Nick Coward at the FA, however, sees it as a legitimate offence to be prosecuted:

I think people have a misconception as to what disrepute is. Disrepute is a generally applicable standard which applies in any profession. If you look at professional life, be it an accountant or lawyer, the same applies to sportsmen. All sports governing bodies include a disrepute charge. We would never charge someone for an honestly held opinion but there have to be boundaries.

The problem with disrepute in football is that it is never really clear where the boundaries lie – surely a prerequisite for any law? For example, is Roy Keane bringing the Irish FA into disrepute by blowing the whistle on what are, in his view, inappropriate methods of preparation for major international matches? It is surely legitimate for him to criticize a team that indulges in a few drinks and pizza-guzzling before important games. Surely this all falls into an inalienable right in a democracy to freedom of expression. As long as it is true and not malicious in intent there can be no problem in law.

Likewise, a spectator or a newspaper can without fear of sanction express the opinion that a referee had a bad game or lost control. Why does it bring the game into disrepute if a player, manager or club official makes the same observation? It would probably be considered safe and within the law for one grown man to waggle his fully clothed backside at another grown man, so why on a football pitch does it attract thousands of pounds in fines?

For lawyer and agent Nick Bitel, the nub of the issue comes down to a lack of objectivity: 'I do not see how you can have a fair trial when the charge, and whether or not you have committed an offence, depends entirely on the subjective view of a tribunal and not on a standard set of rules.'

With disrepute you can commit an offence and not realize it until three men, behind closed doors, with barely an ounce of legal training, if any, between them, pronounce that you have a case to answer. The other aspect with disrepute is that in football it claims unlimited sanction – you can be fined anything for anything.

Lawyer, Mike Townley said to *On The Line*:

I think the concept of bringing the game into disrepute is one which will bring the game into disrepute. When that type of charge is continually laid against increasingly well-resourced players there is going to come a time when there is the prospect of the whole federation, the whole system, being taken to task in the courts.

Footballers, we are told, earn so much money that fines must be proportionate to their income. Otherwise anarchy will ensue. Not something we impose or expect from the courts when dealing with other highly-paid groups of young people, such as pop stars, actors, self-made millionaires or even well-heeled lawyers and accountants. In some cases the courts do take income into account and a resulting fine could be increased by a factor of two of three but never a hundred as was the difference between Vieira and Sutton.

In the lower divisions, where footballers are paid a lot less and two weeks' wages could have a swingeing impact, fines are less commonly used and can even be paid on terms! Yet there is no noticeable decline in behaviour from the Premier League to the Nationwide. The only difference is that Premier League players are paid a great deal of money.

Now it is possible to become overly forensic on behalf of rich young footballers, in laying out the inequalities of FA disciplinary procedures. It must be recognized that all sorts of internal disciplinary codes have considerable latitude in sanction available and that all players, when they sign their contracts, sign up to football's version. Also, while not looking to the 'mob' for direction, the law must take into account public attitude – and the public attitude toward footballers behaving badly, as indeed the attitude of the FA is that, as highly-paid young men, fines must bear some relation to earnings.

But this 'comeuppance' approach to justice is no excuse for imposing a system of discipline at both club and FA level which is punitive, inconsistent and illogical. Also, bearing in mind that the number of disciplinary incidents seems to vary little from one year to the next, it seems to have little impact on behaviour.

At the start of the 2002/3 season, the FA set up an appeal panel which is now chaired by someone with legal training. The court of 'last resort' seems to be an admission that the first instance procedure may make the odd mistake. It is a start, but why not extend it to all hearings? Why wait for appeals that only wealthy clubs and expensive players are likely to make use of?

Football's disciplinary system is the legacy of a time before millionaires and PLCs entered the game. Few groups of young men live their lives in the public gaze in quite the way footballers do, with television cameras trained on them when they are on the field and, in some cases, paparazzi when they are off. Sure, most of us would love to swap problems. They cannot claim the right to privacy – their careers are too public for that – but they can ask to be treated fairly and in line with sanctions suffered elsewhere in society when they fall short. Players are open to the closest scrutiny, unlike the people who run the game and pass judgement upon them.

CHAPTER ELEVEN

A League Apart
The Pitiful State of the National Sport of Wales (No, Not the One You Are Thinking of)

Cardiff City's rebirth under owner Sam Hammam and the glamour of the Millennium Stadium suggest Welsh football is on the rise. But behind the headlines we found a national league struggling for a sponsor, clubs threatening to break away from an old established governing body, a row over TV and a government inquiry. Enough to make an English football fan feel completely at home.

Cardiff has provided football with two conflicting images in recent years. There is the Millennium Stadium, a glamorous, formidable home for FA Cup Finals and a resounding lesson to Wembley about how to build a great modern sports arena. Then there is Sam Hammam's adventure since he left Wimbledon over £30 million richer and took over Cardiff City, a story of footballing recovery tarnished by bizarre nationalist rhetoric and notorious incidents of hooliganism.

Between these two extremes of success and squalor lies a fascinating story about Wales and football. For a start, it is the Welsh national game – for despite rugby's allure, many more people play and watch football. Somehow the game reflects the country at large, which is newly devolved with its own Assembly, but divided and uncertain, struggling to carve out a successful identity of its own.

In Wales, a country of only three million people, *On The Line* found crises and traumas at the professional clubs, a national league without a sponsor, widespread criticism of the governing body as 'a bunch of blazers', threats of a breakaway, accusations of rugby bias levelled at the BBC in particular and the media generally, and a political process intended to sort it out that turned into a soap opera in its own right. Among this morass, though, were people giving of their time, their lives, to improve the game, to drag it, with all its baggage, into realizing its potential and boosting the whole of Wales.

On our travels around Welsh football, we found committed people wanting to rebuild their game, a world away from Hammam's misguided nationalist rhetoric at Cardiff City. Yet, listening to Vince Alm, a spokesman for Cardiff City's Official Supporters Club it was also clear why Hammam's foibles have been tolerated, given the investment he has brought to Cardiff after so many lean years. Alm recalled the pleasures of the supporting life at Ninian Park, pre-Hammam:

> We had no money, no people willing to come in to invest, a dilapidated stadium and a poor team. Half the ground was shut because it didn't meet Football League standards, the terracing was falling apart. The toilets on the Bog Bank were just open toilets, no roof, you just peed up against a wall, basically. We were just treated as second-class citizens.

Hammam had been owner and chairman of Wimbledon since the 1970s, steering them up through the divisions to FA Cup victory in 1988 and over a decade in the top flight. Then, between 1997 and 2000, he sold the club to Norwegian shipping magnates Kjell Inge Rokke and Bjorn Gjelsten, who believed they could move the club to Dublin, and Hammam left with over £30 million. While Wimbledon were left without a ground, which Hammam had sold, the Dublin move was blocked, and the club torn apart by the planned move to Milton Keynes, he took over Cardiff City. Hammam saw the club as a sleeping giant, one which could attract supporters from all over Wales and compete soon enough at the highest level. 'Let's face it,' he said. 'Cardiff can go places. I'm hoping that in about 15–20 years we can aspire to compete with Liverpool, Arsenal and Manchester United.'

Considering the takeover, Hammam arranged a preliminary 'get to know each other' meeting with some fans at a hotel outside Cardiff. There he unveiled his vision of the club as Wales's club, wrapping it in talk of Celtic wars centuries ago, and the rebirth of the nation. He wanted to change its name, kit and logo to reflect Celtic colours and mythology and battles of yore. Most of the hard core fans were nonplussed by the history. They just wanted to win some football matches after the years of drought, as supporter Alm explained:

> I think he'd done a bit of research on the Celts, history-wise, because he came up with a couple of things through history when the Celts were united, and perhaps somebody told him that was the kind of thing that went on in Wales. He talked about everybody going up Snowdonia once a year as a big family. We thought he was off his head because he wanted to change the colour of the kit and change the name and that sort of thing, but he was definitely interested in taking the club forward. I could see where he was coming from, and it would be good for the business side of things.

After the meetings Hammam did go on to buy the club. He then issued his manifesto for it in an extraordinary – some would say irresponsible – pamphlet entitled *Follow the Dream*.

'It cannot be happening,' he wrote in his introduction. 'But it is. I am in a trance, dazed, swept off my feet, gobsmacked or perhaps hypnotised. In short I am in love with Cardiff City Football Club.'

Hammam said he would spend no more than £3 million on his new love, and challenged the fans to do the rest, in an appeal to the instincts of Welsh nationalism and Celtic mythology: 'This is a Welsh thing, a Cymru thing, a Celtic thing – not a Cardiff thing. There should be a feeling that every second week the Welsh Army is crossing the border carrying the flag high and proud. Remember this will take years and years to achieve.'

The idea of a 'Welsh Army' at a club with a hard-boiled hooliganism problem was hardly on the delicate side of sensitive. The idea that football is like modern-day warfare, that fans should come to Ninian Park to burn the shirts of English clubs, were base appeals to the idea of the Welsh as English-haters that misjudged Cardiff people's culture and attitudes. Alm said that these notions bemused most of the fans but he was still delighted that Hammam was coming in with big money and plans for the club:

> I was jumping with joy after the meeting, 'elation' was the word I want to use. Everybody wanted him on board. The only worry tinged with that at the time were the outrageous things he wanted to do with the football club. But it was unanimous, we would risk that, get him on board. And he's been fantastic.

The steady improvements at Ninian Park and on the field with new young Welsh players did not launch Cardiff into the national big time immediately. The remarkable victory over Leeds United in the FA Cup in January 2002 should have done so but Cardiff made the back pages for the wrong reasons that day. During the match, Hammam walked round the pitch to go and stand with the Cardiff fans, doing his 'Ayatollah' head-tapping gesture as he went. Some saw that as incitement, a charge denied by Hammam, and after trouble during the game, Cardiff fans invaded the pitch, coins were thrown and there was violence outside the ground.

Hammam would subsequently agree not to walk round the pitch during matches and the Football Association of Wales fined Cardiff for the trouble, but a siege mentality had it that things had been exaggerated by the English media. Alm felt this bitterly:

> The press ruined it, they ruined my day, they ruined one of the best days of my life, they ruined one of the best days of my family's life and I will never ever forgive any of the national media for the way they portrayed that. I believe the game was blown out of all proportion.

Cardiff's association with hooliganism was further exposed by an undercover BBC documentary, *Hooligans*, which travelled with the notorious Soul Crew, showing fans fighting and looking for trouble. Cameras captured some of the terror inside and outside Ninian Park for the Leeds fans that day – then filmed Hammam talking to some of

Cardiff's fans, saying, 'What violence? What fucking violence?'

As at Wimbledon, Hammam's shrewd rebuilding plans for the club on the field are matched by a commercial vision off it. Ninian Park is inadequate for his dreams of a Barcelona of Wales, and he is currently putting pressure on the council to approve a massive new stadium development with 500,000 sq foot of retail space. Football's realities are such that even lifelong fans no longer question the motivation of a chairman who stands to make money from his association with a club. Cardiff fan Alm acknowledges this:

> If he makes money out of it, I haven't got a problem with that. If he makes money out of taking us to the Premiership and giving us a brand new stadium, what have I got to complain about? He's put the money up front. It's his money, he's done it. He's seen a vision and he's seen it through, and I would be very happy with that, if he walked away.

So this was one version of Welshness and football: a rough ride, wrapped in atavistic images of nationalism and warfare. We found more engaging images elsewhere, but Cardiff fans' embracing of Sam Hammam becomes more understandable after a look at the recent plight of their nearest rivals, Swansea City.

Wales's second club had also sunk from heady First Division days in the early 1980s under manager John Toshack and they had slumped, in their clapped-out ground the Vetch Field, to the Third Division. Relegation in 2001, following promotion the year before, spelled the end for the corporate football dreams of Ninth Floor PLC, a windscreen replacement company based on the ninth floor of an office block on London's Marylebone Road. They had taken the club over in 1997, believing modern football offered a season ticket to TV-pumped millions. At Swansea, millions were spent, not made, propping up the club, while lower division wage inflation bit. Ninth Floor were still contemplating a flotation of Swansea City in early 2001 but a semblance of South Wales reality finally reached even the Marylebone Road and they decided to cut their losses.

The company's exit, when it came, was not without dignity:

they were still owed £800,000 by the club, but sent strong signals that they would not insist on immediate payment. The club was handed over to the commercial director Mike Lewis for £1, along with £200,000 cash flow. He was given three months to sell it, free of debt but with overheads looming over income. Lewis said that nobody firm had come forward locally and, with time running out before he himself would become liable for the club's debts, he passed Swansea on, again for £1, to a businessman based in Australia – Tony Petty.

Petty had no known Swansea connections and his business past was hardly bursting with promise. He had been a director of several companies which were still in business, but seven companies of which he had been a director had been dissolved and three were in liquidation. When he flew in from Brisbane, sacked seven players and told eight more he was dramatically reducing their wages, then immediately flew back out again, he ensured he would not be welcomed at Vetch Field with the kind of elation that Hammam had enjoyed at Ninian Park.

Leigh Dineen became chairman of the Swansea City Supporters' Trust, whose membership quickly swelled to 1,500 fans when they saw what they considered to be a violation of their club. 'What Petty was here for, nobody really knows,' Dineen told *On The Line*. 'Where he thought he was going to make his money, no one really knows. He was no different to many other people who've tried to come into football clubs, believing that there's money to be made.'

Football League rules forbid attempts such as Petty's to sack players on secure contracts (a little inconvenience experienced by one or two other lower division chairmen looking to cut their losses) and so the conflict deepened at Swansea. Then the players revolted too.

Nick Cusack was a senior Swansea City player at the time. He is now the club manager and is also national chairman of the Professional Footballers' Association. 'On Christmas Eve I was called into a meeting and told that the wages wouldn't be met,' he said. 'So you can imagine the disappointment for the players who'd been out and made arrangements to buy presents for their families for Christmas and under those circumstances it was very worrying and concerning.'

Players and fans united in a campaign to get Petty out. Eventually, after several months, which Cusack describes as 'very traumatic', Petty agreed to sell the club for £25,000 to a local consortium, backed by the Supporters' Trust, which now has two seats on the board. The salutary lesson of the Petty experience for Dineen and the Swansea fans, had been the opposite to that of their counterparts in Cardiff, with their charismatic London-based businessman owner. And Dineen is determined that they will never go through that again: 'Our job is to ensure the club will never ever be given out to a person who has no ties with Swansea, so anybody who's looking at Swansea for a property deal can forget it, it won't happen.'

Protecting the club will be a difficult struggle, though. In April 2002 Swansea avoided going into administration only by getting the creditors to agree to a two-year repayment schedule of debts of £1.7 million.

Elsewhere in Wales, the senior clubs are finding life no breezier. Wrexham, the country's only other professional club, was relegated in 2002; debts have mounted and they are now up for sale. Newport went out of the Football League in 1988, while Merthyr, a former League club, were relegated from the Dr Marten's Premier Division in England at the end of the 2001/2 season.

Since 1992 Wales has had its own national football league, complete with FIFA affiliation and European competition for its successful clubs. The League of Wales should be testament to ambition, a glue of sporting identity for a nation struggling to assert itself, yet in fact it only mirrors the problems in the country at large. You will struggle even to find its results, buried below England's non-League pyramid. For four years it had no sponsor, and wider respect is as hard to earn as thronging crowds.

Yet *On The Line* ventured into the League of Wales and we found a story of a club as inspiring as any in our journey round football in the summer of 2002, a heartening counterpoint to the excesses and deficiencies at Cardiff and Swansea. Housed in a proud little ground and clubhouse between the leisure centre and fairground on the sea front in the South Wales steel town of Port Talbot, it was a model community football club – Afan Lido, proud members of the League of Wales.

We saw Lido play Bangor City, a North Wales club with a little more money to spend, managed by the former Nottingham Forest and Manchester United striker Peter Davenport, who featured in his line-up former United players Simon Davies and Clayton Blackmore.

Blackmore, his hair bleached and styled with a mid-80s flick, looked the model of the flash ex-pro, but he gave a composed display at sweeper, in a game that Afan Lido won 1–0. The route for local footballers to compete in this company was constructed painstakingly by Phil Robinson, a wiry, intense man who started the club 35 years ago and is the director of football. Its roots are embedded in his desire to play and organize sport and had nothing to do with making money. 'In 1967 I was working in the Afan Lido Sports Centre as a weightlifting coach,' he said. 'Local boys were coming in playing football and wanting to play football. I enjoyed football myself so we decided to form the Afan Lido Football Club.'

It is a matter of fact account of what would be a remarkable story. Afan Lido were built from scratch, but on the soundest foundations, fielding teams in every age group, concentrating on coaching and nurturing their players – an object lesson that there are no magical answers, that football clubs are built on enthusiasm for the game and dedication to a cause.

The night before the game, we partook of time-honoured journalistic research, in the Afan Lido bar. Phil Robinson was in there, as we had been told he would be; he was serving drinks, emptying ashtrays, wiping tables, waiting for us to stagger out, late, into the South Wales night, to lock up behind us. The man is dedicated, if not obsessed.

The following day he told us more:

> We run U-18s, U-17s, U-16s, 15s, 14s, 13s, 12s – we start
> the babes at four years of age. Each team has a manager
> and a coach, or two coaches, all are qualified. We're very
> proud of the fact that we produce players from the club
> to play for the first team.

That day, all but one player was local and had risen through the ranks. When the League of Wales was formed in 1992, such was

Lido's progress to seniority that they became founder members. In 1995 they finished second and so, 28 years after they were formed, they played in the UEFA Cup. They lost, to Latvian club RAF Riga, but it was a great night for Lido and Phil Robinson. 'It was just a brilliant, brilliant experience,' he said. 'It's just a personal feeling. The whole town in Port Talbot got the football bug. Playing in the UEFA Cup, the Afan Lido Football Club, is just the ultimate.'

Yet for all this, and the benefits the club brings to its local community, running it is still a struggle, as Robinson says: 'The most difficult thing obviously is the financial side of things. It's very, very difficult to get the funding that you need because we're in the League of Wales and they can't get a sponsor, which is absolutely diabolical because they should have a major sponsor of the highest scale.'

It did seem extraordinary that a national UK league should be limping along, bereft of sponsorship and finance. Many of the people we spoke to in Wales blamed the governing body, the Football Association of Wales (FAW), believing them to be lacking.

The FAW is an old-established governing body, also running the Welsh Cup, with rich traditions, based in a Georgian terrace opposite the gleaming new Millennium Stadium in Cardiff. Inside their headquarters there are pennants, silverware, wooden panelling – and the unmistakably musty air of an organization under pressure in the modern era.

The League of Wales is wholly owned by the FAW, which set it up when national leagues became a requirement of international affiliation. The FAW's chief executive, David Collins, is also nominally chief executive of the League, and has his critics in the clubs, who claim that they are paid little attention and that efforts to find a sponsor have been inadequate.

One loud voice among the club chairmen is that of Mike Harris, managing director of an Oswestry-based company, Total Network Solutions (TNS). They were so impressed with the publicity they gained from sponsoring the shirts of League of Wales side Llansanfrei that they bought the club, which now bears their name. 'There is great potential here; it's a national league with routes into Europe,' said Harris. 'We've had tremendous exposure by sponsoring and owning the club – far better than if we had done a shirt sponsorship with one of the Nationwide clubs.'

TNS have, with some investment from the company, become one of the more successful League of Wales sides and have qualified for the UEFA Cup. But Harris is frustrated and he believes that the FAW should be doing far more. 'I believe that there could be more energies put into the development of our franchise,' he said. 'The League isn't getting as much attention as it needs, to take it from being what probably is seen as a burden to the FAW.'

He was openly critical of the arrangements for the League, repeating many times that it needed a full-time chief executive to drive it forward, find sponsorship and raise its profile, rather than a nominal chief executive like Collins, who did not regularly attend board meetings:

> I've been to several board meetings where the clubs have all been present but our chief executive hasn't been there. I don't have enough facts or first-hand experiences to say whether David Collins neglects the League of Wales or whether he has more important things to do with his time. Either way, there is a need to appoint a chief executive who has one remit and one remit only, and that is to develop the national league within the principality.

Collins rejected the idea that the FAW neglect the League, although he said that he personally left most of its day-to-day running to the League's secretary. He said the lack of a sponsor was a 'major concern' but that consultants taken on in the previous three years to help find one had failed:

> The major companies in business here are not Welsh. The one that was, Hydra, who we wanted to do a deal with some years back, were taken over by an American firm. The senior management that exists in Wales have to refer to London. And where you go out of the Principality and talk football, the only thing they think of is England and the Premiership.

He pointed out that the FAW had most to gain from finding sponsorship because they currently own and look after the whole League. 'We maintain all the general funding of the League: the secretary, his staff, the office here, all the travelling and the assistance which goes to the referees and the linesmen and to the clubs for travelling expenses,' he said. 'The funding is approaching between £150,000–200,000 per year.'

Harris had laid down a challenge, saying that he would spend half an hour a week looking for sponsorship and believed he would secure it for the League. He said he and other League of Wales chairmen were losing patience with the FAW and were considering breaking away as soon as next season:

> The League of Wales has to look and give the FAW an amount of time to get its house in order. There will come a point where there are forward-thinking chairmen out there of the League of Wales who will start looking at what we can do as a collective of 18 clubs. Ultimately, the clock will start to tick.

Restive clubs, an embattled old-established governing body, breakaway talk – you could almost be in England. But in Wales there is a particular reason for football's struggles – the shadow or, they would argue, the spectre, of rugby. *On The Line* heard from fans, chairmen, journalists, and most forcefully from David Collins himself, that there is a rugby bias in the Welsh media, particularly the BBC. Collins said funding was something of a catch-22: without substantial media coverage it is more difficult to attract sponsors but without the commercial boost of a sponsor the League is less attractive to the broadcasters. Collins explained:

> Football is the number one sport in Wales. We have approximately 1,850 clubs, something like 5,000 teams. On an ordinary Saturday, Cardiff City will have more people at their game than at all the senior rugby matches put together. But if you look at BBC Wales, heads of sport have been ex-rugby internationals so there's this bias

towards rugby. All our home international matches are transmitted, mainly on BBC2 Wales. We do not see, we believe, sufficient coverage of the League of Wales. The FAW Premier Cup gets very good coverage in its quarter-final, semi-final and final stages and the Welsh Cup itself gets televised live for the final with we believe not sufficient coverage in the early stages. And these are all parts of the discussion which are taking place between the FAW and the BBC.

A little known fact outside the country: the last three heads of sport at BBC Wales have indeed all been former Welsh rugby internationals – Gareth Davies, now chief executive of the Welsh Sports Council, Arthur Emyr and, currently, former flying winger Nigel Walker.

On The Line interviewed Walker about the perceived imbalance between the BBC's Welsh rugby and football coverage – and investment. He confirmed that the BBC pays around double for rugby than it does for football, money which amounts to the most significant funding it gets. But he denied that there was any bias at all. Rather, BBC Wales could not get the rights to show professional football clubs' matches, because Cardiff, Swansea and Wrexham were tied into the Football League's collective deal. He spelled out the difference this made:

The rugby contract S4C and the BBC jointly have is £22 million, our share is £11 million, and that's spread over five years – so just over £2 million per year. But for that we have all the domestic rights, we also have Heineken Cup, so it's good quality rugby. We have paid significantly less for football, but we don't have the rights for domestic league football, [or] Nationwide League football. We don't have the rights for Swansea, Cardiff City and Wrexham because those rights are held elsewhere.

Walker said he himself was an enthusiast for football and that the BBC was committed to the game and would like to show more of it:

Yes, I'm a former rugby international but also a former international track and field performer, and I played all sports at school and I've a love of most sports. Rugby does get a high profile in Wales but we're not the only broadcaster in Wales that gives it a high profile. I am just as committed to football as to all the other sports. We are a public service broadcaster and we have to meet the tastes of all the people in Wales.

Football people in Wales, though, are unhappy with the profile, status, funding and the general state of their game. It did not take long after devolution for this sorry tale to land in the in-tray of Jenny Randerson, the first ever Sports Minister in the new Welsh Assembly, who told *On The Line*: 'I think the subject which came through most of all in my postbag was concern, from ordinary people, about the state of football in Wales.'

Her response was to set up what she called the Welsh Football Forum, a body of 16 members that included what passed for the great and the good in the game, from Ian Rush to former referee Clive Thomas, together with no fewer than five members of the FAW. David Collins told us that the FAW had a list of requirements, including a national training centre to raise the standard of the national team and the game at large, and they had been unhappy with the idea of a football forum. The choice of chairman did not reassure him either: it was head of the Welsh Sports Council and ex-rugby international Gareth Davies.

'I'm certainly no expert in football,' Randerson confessed. 'It was obvious when I looked not just at the results but also the funding of Welsh football that there are things that needed to be looked at, and therefore I thought the best thing to do was to get together a panel of people who knew what they were talking about to represent a wide cross-section of people with a legitimate and wide interest in football.'

The Welsh Assembly and Sports Council wanted to see more funding go into football, particularly into youth development, but were concerned about exactly how their money would be spent. The FAW's accounts are basic. They don't explain where the money comes from, or how it is spent. £2.4 million comes in, £2.5 million goes out. If the Welsh assembly's football forum were to put public money in, they decided they needed to know more.

'The Forum,' Randerson said, 'has of course asked the FAW for a copy of their accounts and detail of their accounts and at this point I have no knowledge that they won't be supplying that.'

We found the answer rather more halting, and a resounding illustration of the knots in which sports politics can tie their much-loved games. With public money in the offing from the Welsh Assembly, but a simple request for financial details to answer, we thought the FAW would be falling over themselves to cooperate. But progress is not so straightforward in the FAW's wood-panelled rooms. There, somewhat affronted by the nosiness from the new Assembly, their response was a classic for the annals of sports blazerdom: they set up a sub-committee.

'The FAW council has set up a group of people to work on the request,' Collins told us, 'and those people are doing exactly that, they're looking at the response they will put together for that forum. They haven't provided it at the present time.'

Collins's frustration with the Welsh Football Forum sprang from more than what he and his council members perceived to be a Sports Council-led agenda that was concentrating too narrowly on youth development. The FAW were looking for help with a more top-down approach:

> Our major priority is to get the national team to a major final. Full stop. If there's any possibility. That will bring major spin-offs. We want to qualify for a major tournament and to do that we've said we need a national training centre and that's not even on the agenda. We've asked for other things: we want stadium grant-funding for the League of Wales to be restored, that's a major issue. Our people are not happy with the Football Forum. We think it's too led by the Sports Council and won't achieve anything it's supposed to.

It was surprisingly defiant talk from a governing body that looked in desperate need of help. With the Forum in danger of fracturing, they finally agreed to expand the agenda, to take note of the FAW's 'shopping list' and to present the case to the Minister, along with the Forum's recommendations on youth development. The national game of Wales is now waiting for the National Assembly of Wales to hear how promising its future might be. It is hard not to wonder whether the fates of both the game and country are intertwined, the one a symbol for the other.

Whatever: the man who rode into town flinging out rhetoric about the Welsh, Welshness, the Celts and their historic struggles, played no constructive part in the agonizing debate over the game's future improvement. Sam Hammam, the self-styled awakener of the Welsh football dragon, was invited and agreed to sit on the Forum, but then resigned without attending a single meeting.

Jenny Randerson did not criticize him. 'I was really pleased when he accepted the invitation,' she said, 'and then I was disappointed for a little while when he said he couldn't make any of the meetings. But I understood that, because he's an extremely busy guy with lots of other things to do.'

Hammam, who was at the time awaiting the FAW's disciplinary hearing into the trouble at the Cardiff City v Leeds cup tie, declined to give us an interview. We were told he was only ever in Cardiff on match days and he spends the rest of his time at home in London.

CHAPTER TWELVE

It's Academic
Why Non-league Football is Banned from Running Football Academies

Question: When is a football academy not a football academy? Answer: When the FA says so.

In December 2000 *On The Line* looked at the Football Association's staggering assertion that it had sole ownership of the word 'academy' – and its insistence that more than 60 college football academies in England offering hundreds of students a football education could not use the term. At the time they refused to recognize, license or offer a kitemark for academies or centres of excellence at non-League clubs and associated colleges. This is in stark contrast to those at Premiership and Nationwide League clubs, who are given huge annual handouts every season. When it comes to youth development in England, it really is a game of two halves.

On a chilly night in Staffordshire, Hednesford Town's academy team take on Shrewsbury Town's FA centre of excellence side in a Midlands Youth Cup game. During an evening of near misses, with the still night air broken by shouts from the players, in front of a small throng of parents and committed coaches assembled in the main stand at Hednesford's neatly appointed Keys Park ground, the home side have the lion's share of possession but Shrewsbury score the all-important goal to win 1–0. At the time, Hednesford were in the Football Conference, a league lower than Third Division Shrewsbury – but you would have been hard pressed to spot a difference in quality between the two teams. Yet there is one huge, significant difference between these two youth sides.

Every season Shrewsbury – like every other Football League club running an academy or centre of excellence – receive £138,000 from the game's governing body. Non-League clubs like Hednesford get nothing. 'It's barmy, isn't it?' fumed Hednesford Town's manager at the time, John Baldwin. 'We're all trying to do the same job and that is to develop our own young players. Just because we're not amongst the 92 Premier League and Football League clubs, we're not eligible for the same finances that they get. It can't be a level playing field, can it?'

Baldwin's frustration is shared by the club's youth development staff and academy players, who are also well aware of the disparity. 'We need better training facilities for a start,' one of them told *On The Line*. 'We were talking about getting an Astroturf pitch, weren't we?' he asks a team-mate. 'We've got a horrible pitch, ain't we?' says another. 'Once you've played on it a couple of times it goes all boggy. We need money, we need help from somewhere.'

Developing players has always been a time-honoured route to success and survival for small clubs. It is the only way they can compete against larger, better resourced clubs. You might have expected the introduction of FA licensed academies to help those best equipped to provide a football education for young players regardless of the status of the club. But non-League clubs – who have barely seen any of the money generated from any of the huge TV deals of the 1990s – have been systematically disadvantaged by an overhaul of youth development.

When the FA's technical director, Howard Wilkinson, drew up their blueprint for the future of youth development, the Charter for Quality, in 1997, the aim was to encourage Premier and Football League clubs to set up academies. Wilkinson's charter focused on: 'elite young players ... the quality not quantity of players'.

Understandably, the Charter for Quality was well received by the professional game. It instructed clubs to adhere to tight player/coach ratios, a high standard of facilities and the employment of qualified coaching, medical, education and welfare staff. Licences for academies and centres of excellence (there are differences in the level of facilities between the two) are only granted and maintained if clubs meet the regulations laid down in the charter. But there is virtually no mention of non-League clubs or the growing number of colleges of further education running academies and there is no access to funds that are readily offered to league clubs.

The charter states:

> *Independent Centres of Excellence must meet all the criteria*
> *for Centres of Excellence and will be subject to all controls,*
> *registration and inspection as Football League clubs.*
>
> *Applications for a licence ... will only be considered*
> *where a player cannot, within the stipulated travelling time*
> *per age, attend a Centre of Excellence operated by a Football*
> *League Club or a Football Academy.*

The minimum academy player's travelling time ranges between one and one and a half hours – depending on their age – but it's a vague interpretation. In theory, anywhere in England is within reach of a Premier/Football League club in that period of time so the case for the FA granting a licence to an independent centre of excellence on geographical grounds is immediately hampered. Yet such centres – usually run by non-League clubs in conjunction with a local college of further education – have mushroomed. Most Nationwide Conference clubs, for example, now run full-time academies but the FA simply ignore them. This means that the quality of coaching and the levels of football being taught in these academies is developing outside the remit or control of the game's governing body in England. Without licensing or recognition these academies cannot tap into the funds available to Premier/Football League clubs because without the backing of their governing body an application for Lottery funding is likely to be rejected.

'There was nothing in the Charter for Quality for clubs outside the Premiership and Football League,' the Football Conference's chief executive, John Moules, told *On The Line*. 'I think it was wholly designed to prevent clubs outside the Premiership and Football League from having schemes of a similar nature.'

Like many people in non-League football, Moules was incensed by comments made by Wilkinson and his number two at the FA's technical department, Robin Russell, who have both claimed that non-League clubs do not have the ability to develop quality players.

'The Charter for Quality had at its base the development of

elite young footballers and it is unrealistic and unfair to expect non-League clubs to make a contribution to this area,' Wilkinson told *On The Line* in a fax in December 2000. The FA's line is that there is no point in licensing, funding or approving non-League academies because the best 1,500 players at the age of 16 will already have been offered places at FA Premier League and Football League academies. Wilkinson's fax added: *'Any review over the last 5-10 years will indicate the realistic likelihood of players from non league football moving into the FA Premier league.'*

At a meeting with the Football Conference committee, the FA's technical coordinator, Robin Russell, went further, as Baldwin recalled: 'He stood up in front of, probably, ten Conference managers and said the Football Association want excellence and they don't believe non-League clubs will ever produce another England player. It's rubbish.'

Hednesford had recently had a youth team forward, Marc Richards, snapped up by Blackburn Rovers. He was soon selected for Howard Wilkinson's very own England under-18 team. Because non-League academies don't have FA status they couldn't claim the compensation that would have been payable between two academy clubs. John Baldwin told *On The Line*:

> If they had wanted to take Marc they could have had him for nothing, but they recognized that we certainly wouldn't be encouraging other members of our staff to go to Blackburn if they did, so an agreement was reached. We've had lots of our younger players pinched by Football League clubs. They want to play us in friendlies because they want to take our best players – and they do that all the time. It is not fair.

There is a long list of players who have reached the top in recent years who began their careers at non-League level. The list makes Wilkinson's and Russell's astonishing comments all the more remarkable: Kevin Phillips, Les Ferdinand, Warren Barton, Steve Guppy, Stuart Pearce, Ian Taylor, Lee Hughes, Barrie Hayles, Stan Collymore, Robert Lee – oh, and Malcolm Christie, who, at the time of our *On The Line* programme in December 2000, was centre forward in Wilkinson's England under-21 side, and had been at non-league Nuneaton Borough the previous season. Indeed, Wilkinson's own managerial career began at non-League level – as assistant to Jim Smith at Boston United in the late 1960s. John Moules of the Football Conference told *On The Line*:

> I don't think you can develop a foolproof system that says at 14–16 years of age we will spot every talented footballer in this country. When you have one weekend like we did a few seasons ago when the captains of England, the Republic of Ireland and Wales in Stuart Pearce, Andy Townsend and Vinnie Jones were all ex-Conference players, then I think no one can say that system will always be in place.

Although the charter has space to license non-League academies, in reality only one club, Yeovil Town has been successful. The rest failed to meet the FA's geographical test, much to Moules's annoyance:

> The charter says no boy can live more than 90 minutes from any accredited centre. So where is Dover, where is Morecambe, where is Scarborough, where are their nearest clubs? Who is offering boys in areas like Forest Green the opportunity to pursue their education while trying to develop their talents as a footballer?

The exception to the rule is Yeovil Town, who, at the time our programme was broadcast in December 2000, were on top of the Conference and had just knocked Third Division Blackpool out of the FA Cup. No one was surprised – it happens all the time now. The gap between the lower end of the Football League and the Conference has all but disappeared. Indeed, Yeovil's state of the art ground, Huish Park, boasts far better facilities than most lower Football League stadia. They wanted a centre of excellence to match their surroundings.

Chairman John Fry showed *On The Line* a 70-page document

spelling out Yeovil's case for an academy. 'We presented it to the Football Association,' he said. 'It's a geographical issue, a location issue. There's a lack of opportunity for youngsters in this county to possibly meet with the Football Association's quality criteria, which is a pity for the young people in Somerset.'

Yeovil Town are currently Somerset's biggest club. This rural county does not have a single Football League club of its own and although there are academies in Bristol, Exeter, Bournemouth, Swindon and Oxford which could arguably be reached within an hour or so, there is no local football academy.

In June 2000 the FA listened to Yeovil's unique case and granted them a licence to run a centre of excellence but this doesn't entitle them to access the funds that are automatically made available to a Football League club. 'A licence has been granted by the Football Association's Technical Committee,' Fry told On the Line. 'We've received a letter saying we've been given approval from a licensing point of view – but they could not help with any funding. As far as Yeovil Town are concerned the licence is no good without any funding.'

Yeovil estimate it would cost in excess of £200,000 a year to run a centre of excellence for the next five years – that is a total of £1 million on youth development. If they were a Football League club they could expect to recoup around £700,000 from Sport England and the FA Premier League. Without it, Yeovil cannot find the funds, so their plans are on hold.

If Yeovil won promotion to the Football League things would change overnight. At the end of the 2000–1 season they were pipped to the sole promotion spot by Rushden and Diamonds. Had they gone up, academy funding from the FA would have been theirs. But had they replaced the team at the bottom of Division Three at the time of our programme in December 2000, Carlisle United, a different, geographically huge and (football-wise) isolated part of the country covering the whole of Cumbria would have lost their academy status and their subsequent funding. Fry admitted:

If we manage to get promoted this season I've got all the

answers to my problems. But if we don't get promotion we've got to play the politics to get the money into this particular club. If we were in the League we would automatically, provided we meet the criteria, get recognition for funding as well the licensed approval for what we're doing.

This hardly seems a balanced approach to youth development, with schemes being funded on status rather than location. With such systematic resistance in place, it's small wonder non-League clubs have shown lateral thinking and have looked elsewhere for funds. An alternative route for many of them has been to follow the American collegiate system, where players mix football training with further education. The club looks after the football training and the college looks after the academic side. Education provides the bulk of the funds and everyone remains realistic: the chances of players becoming full-time professional footballers, though achievable, is slim. The college academies are looking to develop players who can earn a living at semi-professional level. But unlike the professional football club academies, much more is made of the education. Students get the best of both worlds.

Britain has been slow to follow the US model, where college sport is serious stuff – worthy of big funding, watched by huge crowds and shown on TV – and an important development route for elite players. By contrast, British football has virtually no track record in taking any notice of what the amateur game or academia have to say, either in terms of physiological theory and practice or as a recruiting ground. The age-old motto is: the pros know best – always did, always will.

There are 60 colleges of further education in England running their own football centres of excellence for 16–19-year-olds. Many are linked to non-League clubs. They fund their courses through education but none of these schemes is licensed by the FA. Not that that has stopped them from trying to lay down the law.

'The Football Association would wish to remind clubs that they should not seek to benefit from an association with the Programme for Excellence schemes ... without obtaining authorisation,' the FA's technical department wrote to one FE college. And Nigel Robbins, the principal of Cirencester College in Gloucestershire, told *On The Line*: 'The FA have written to non-League clubs and colleges telling them shouldn't use the term 'football academy'.

In 1995 Cirencester Town set up the country's first football academy – years ahead of Arsenal, Man Utd or any of the other top clubs in Britain – and two years before the Charter for Quality was published. The idea came from a club director who had seen this relationship work in the United States. Like so many ideas it is incredibly simple. Students mix football training with traditional academic work. Their ground was literally across the road from Cirencester College (although the club moved in the summer of 2002).

The scheme, which currently has 43 boys and 19 girls, has been remarkably successful. Not only have their teams captured the British Colleges Cup for four successive seasons, they have also won the English Schools National Under 19's competition for three years running and the South West League Cup by beating all the professional academy clubs in their region. The senior side have also progressed two divisions (Cirencester now play in the Dr Martens Western Division) and probably field the youngest side at their level in Britain – most of their players are either current or ex-academy players.

The FA were so impressed with the way Cirencester had established their academy that they went along to take a closer look. 'They came down for a number of weeks, looked at how we worked, at how we interacted with the college,' recalls Ivor Gumm, a senior coach at the academy. 'Then they went away, spoke to a number of the Premier League clubs and set up their own charter.'

When it was published the FA's Charter for Quality bore a strikingly similar resemblance to the Cirencester academy, but they were excluded from its criteria and were told not to use the word 'academy' any more as it now belonged to the FA. 'I feel disappointed that clubs like ours who do everything that the charter says – we have qualified 'A' licence coaches, we have doctors at games, we have full physio facilities, we have everything that they want,' said Gumm, who left Cirencester Town in September 2002. 'Yet we still get shunned and spurned and told you're not allowed to use the name 'academy'.'

Cirencester have ignored the FA and they continue to call their scheme an 'academy'. They are legally entitled to do so because they registered the name at Companies House but other colleges have not been so lucky, as Robbins explained: 'Threatening letters have actually been sent by the FA to colleges saying, "You can't possibly use the word academy, we've, as it were, copyrighted that. You're just deceiving people if you think you're offering anything like what we are sponsoring and supporting at the Premier and First Division academies".'

The FA claim that the college and non-League schemes confuse players and their parents and don't offer their students the chance of entering the professional game. The example of Cirencester Town would suggest otherwise. 'We have had five boys offered contracts by professional clubs,' argues Gumm. 'About 27 boys are on semi-pro contracts. Of the current Cirencester Town first team, out of a squad of 18, 13 players are ex-academy boys.'

Robbins claims the FA are simply being over-protective: 'Nobody could possibly mistake what colleges are doing with Conference or sub-Conference clubs in terms of developing young people and giving them a chance of getting into football through a different route with what's happening at the big clubs who have got their academies.'

And you could be forgiven for asking what right the FA believe they have to try to trademark a word which stems from Greek mythology as a grove where Plato used to teach. Or what right they have to impose regulations when they don't license, fund or recognize these academies in the first place.

'There is no official accreditation route for college football academies like ours,' said Robbins. 'There isn't a structure, there isn't a set-up, except what the colleges are doing themselves. And not one of those colleges has received any encouragement or support or financial assistance from the FA.'

Indeed, the colleges often cater for players who have had bad experiences at the hands of licensed academies at Football League clubs. At Cirencester I met Dean Gilewicz, who had been released when Swindon Town disbanded their centre of excellence side the previous season (1999-2000). Cirencester offered this local teenager a way of staying in football. 'The club went into financial difficulty and unfortunately our age group suffered the most, so I got letter saying they can't take anyone as a youth trainee,' said Gilewicz. 'I started looking elsewhere and thought Cirencester looked a good place to come to.'

Gilewicz's father, Tad, was impressed not only by the quality of coaching but also the emphasis on academic work at Cirencester:

> To me an education was important. YTS and a scholarship are two separate factions, YTS being polishing boots and playing the game. Scholarship meant college and football on the side. That to me and my wife was very important because if you don't get the education, even after the football – if you're lucky enough to get somewhere – if you don't get that scholarship, how are you going to make it after the football?

Another player, Jeremy Flowerdew, had been released by Bristol Rovers following a change of management. 'They suddenly wanted youth players to be able to play first team football at the age of 17,' he recalled. Like many teenagers, he had struggled physically to cope with a sudden increase in height which had sapped his strength. He was immediately released but felt much more at home at Cirencester.

Colleges like Cirencester have spotted the chance to offer football courses for an increasing number of players and parents with these concerns – and there are thriving leagues playing inter-college sport. Dewi Cook, who runs the British Colleges Sport Football Excellence league says:

> Traditionally, the further education sector has looked at opportunities of providing a service to the community. They see a niche market for youngsters who have had strong expectations of moving into the professional game but, because the cut-off point has eliminated far

more of those youngsters at the age of 16, there is
inevitably a potential market there for the further education sector.'

There are an estimated 1,000 students in college football programmes but they are unregulated and unlicensed by the game's
governing body, although in 2002 the FA began researching ways to
help the colleges. British Colleges Sport had tried to persuade the FA
to develop a kitemark for these schemes years earlier, as Cook
explained:

We do have our own system of evaluating those centres
where we look at the facilities that they have. We look at
the quality of the coaching that's going on in there, we
look at the back-up they have in terms of sports science,
we look at how the boys and teams conduct themselves
during games and the quality of refereeing, so we're
looking at the whole aspect. It would certainly be helpful
in our discussions with the FA if they could see the value
of what we're trying to do. If we were given that kitemark
and colleges could meet that kitemark there's a good
chance a commercial sponsor might be very interested
in coming in and matching any funding that the
Football Association might wish to make to underpin
this venture.

Talks have progressed since we made our *On The Line* programme in
December 2000 – but two years later the FA's technical department
have yet to develop the kitemark the non-League clubs and colleges
have been requesting. This has prevented them from finding funding from other sectors.

The Programme for Academic and Sporting Excellence (PASE)
is a scheme encouraging clubs and colleges to come together to provide a balanced education of sport and traditional academic work. It
is funded by the Further Education Funding Council and is run by
Bedford College. In September 2000 they joined forces with the
Nationwide Conference to form a national youth development

league – the PASE Conference. 'The scheme is intended to showcase the lads' talents as well as to give them the opportunity to improve their match-playing skills,' says Teresa Frith, the PASE project manager. 'We've been told it is already being scouted quite heavily by professional clubs. At the moment it is the third highest level of youth football in the UK.'

Funding for the league has come from many partners, including the Nationwide Building Society, and the National Conference have agreed to handle the administration. But PASE sought lottery money from SportsMatch, Sport England's grass-roots sport funding body. They were told, understandably, that their application would stand a better chance if it was supported by the FA. But when SportsMatch asked for more details about the league, the FA failed to offer their support – so the PASE Conference application to aid the development of 537 teenage footballers was rejected. Frith remembers:

> We were gutted. We'd put in so much effort, so much work and the Conference had been so supportive, all our clubs have been behind the scheme 100 per cent. The colleges that were involved have just been working really hard to get the whole thing set up and running smoothly. We really felt we'd done a great job, well worth sponsorship and obviously it was devastating to find that our governing body didn't feel able to support us even though the effort had really been put in.

SportsMatch don't give reasons why they reject a specific grant application but they told *On The Line* that if the governing body of a sport failed to support a bid for cash then it would stand little chance of success. The Sports Minister at the time, Kate Hoey, officially launched the PASE Conference in January 2001 and had asked the FA why they hadn't supported the scheme. The reply from the FA's technical department was that they had not known enough about PASE at the time of the Sportsmatch bid. 'We've since had meetings with the FA and explained exactly what the PASE scheme is, exactly how it works,' said Frith, 'and we now have an undertaking from them that we will develop an FA approval with them for these types of schemes at Conference level.'

The FA now approve arrangements for PASE to obtain sponsorship through SportsMatch, though it was too late for its initial launch. But as the PASE Conference entered its third season in the autumn of 2002 the FA had still not provided any funds or developed a kitemark for any of the competing clubs. 'We would like to expand the league to 32 non-League clubs but we cannot handle the administration without financial support,' said Nationwide Conference chief executive, John Moules.

You might have reasonably expected a body that is supposed to look after the game at all levels to at least have asked some questions before refusing to support a bid for potential funds. Indeed, you might think the FA would be more proactive in general. They knew PASE existed before drawing up the Charter for Quality, they knew that Cirencester ran a successful academy, and that non-League clubs, especially those in the Conference, would want to run licensed centres of excellence. But they've offered these groups nothing.

The dominant view within the professional game is that the non-League clubs and colleges do not have the infrastructure to meet the standards of the Charter for Quality: The FA's initial criticism of PASE was that they couldn't meet the 15 players to one coach ratio laid down in the charter and that the education options weren't broad enough,' recalls Teresa Frith, who said that PASE courses offer an 18:1 ratio. 'Who wouldn't want to run at 15 to 1 instead of 18 to 1 if they could? But we can't with our current financial situation, so some money to help support the scheme would go a long way. The FA have stated that they wish to support semi-professional training programmes through PASE. It would be nice to see that support not just come through the form of words but also through something slightly more tangible like cash.'

The colleges cry 'foul' when it comes to professional clubs looking sniffily down at them. They argue that the licensed academies at League clubs are still paying lip service when it comes to meeting the education requirements of their players.

At Preston College of Further Education they educate 120 players from five local Football League clubs. The programme is organized by the Professional Footballers' Education Society, whose chief executive, Mick Burns, is a passionate advocate of players looking at their chances of making it as a professional footballer realistically and in the long term:

> If you look at the programme we have on offer, it encompasses the whole framework of national qualifications from 'A' levels down to learning needs. It includes BTEC national certificates, diplomas, GNVQs, advanced or intermediate certificate, the new vocational 'A' levels, the trade courses through the NVQ framework and in a small number of cases, learning needs.

Yet rumours are rife that too many players, even in the revamped era of academies with education and welfare officers, are encouraged to take the easiest available course. In this respect they lag well behind the students in college football academies. Mick Noblett runs the Preston College football programme:

> We get them as part of their contract for a day and a half so we actually get them for ten hours. It means that they're not getting the same provision as full-time students, but what you tend to find is that the provision we offer them is in small special groups so we can fast-track them if necessary.

But when *On The Line* spoke to some of the players from local Football League clubs, they readily admitted that, though they do the work, they're here under sufferance. 'It's not as important as me football obviously. I put the effort in but if it came down to it I wouldn't be bothered,' said one player, who slouched across the table chin resting on his hands for an entire session. Another added: 'We're not really that bothered about college at the moment but in the future it might be something that we are pleased we did.'

This is a good scheme and the Professional Footballers' Education Society regularly monitors it. If players don't do their college work, they don't play football but that priciple also applies to the centre of excellence run by the college itself. Things might have improved markedly since youth traineeships were scrapped in favour of these sort of scholarships but Burns admits that getting all of the clubs to realize the importance of their players' education has been a problem:

> We've got the new programmes established at 86 of the 92 clubs. That was the difficult priority, to change the programme within football. The next priority is to change the culture of football and trying to change the way in which we look at the development of young people and that is going to be the big challenge. I have to say in some clubs it's worked really well and the cooperation has been superb, in others not quite so well.

Nigel Robbins at Cirencester College paints a more pessimistic picture:

> The feedback coming to the colleges' football centres of excellence from elsewhere is that three out of four leave professional football before the age of 21 and end up taking basic simple NVQ courses. That kind of education isn't going to allow you to progress very far, academically. I think we need a new charter for quality based on collaboration with the educational establishment with colleges and schools which points out different routes for youngsters going into football.

Two years after *On The Line* looked into these issues the PASE Conference League were still waiting for an approved kitemark from the FA. Although they have built up a much better relationship with the colleges, the FA has only awarded one small cash grant to the colleges, to be spent mainly on the development of female academies. Yeovil Town still have not received any money to help run an FA centre of excellence, and although Cirencester Town became the first FA Community Club in Britain (receiving £684,000 in funding

from the Football Foundation for their new ground) their academy
remains unrecognized by the FA.

CHAPTER THIRTEEN

Patriot Games
The American Ex-pat Who Was Let Loose on Chester City with Disastrous Results

In 1999 an American hero rode into town and saved its club from going out of business. Two years later he left – and not before time for the fans of the club, who had seen it become one of the laughing stocks of the game.

Terry Smith knew football, that much was evident – he had the championships and the medals, trophies and reputation to prove it. Unfortunately, the football that Terry Smith knew was American football. Still, that wasn't going to deter him from buying his own club, taking over as chairman, and then later as manager, and coaching the team himself.

Chester City were in administration and close to going out of business when Smith, the new messiah, arrived at the club's Deva Stadium in the summer of 1999. The saviour quickly built up a band of willing and receptive disciples eager to listen to his new message. Sadly, over the next few months, something seems to have got lost in the translation and it quickly became evident that, far from sharing a common language with his new Cheshire brethren, the 41-year-old American was speaking in incomprehensible tongues.

Like so many other clubs, Chester City have had their odd moments of glory but they have spent most of their near-120-year history in the lower half of the League. No wonder then that Smith, who promised the fans that they would have a say in how the club was run, was welcomed with such vigour.

In time-honoured fashion the new chairman made the usual fan-pleasing, season ticket-selling promises: the club would be playing First Division football within three years and the Deva Stadium would be filled every week. Les Smith (no relation to Terry) was a member of the Independent Supporters' Association (ISA), the group who had agreed to bid jointly for the club with his North Carolinan namesake. With his blue City baseball cap perched on his head, he explained to *On The Line* what happened:

> The first time we heard his name was in May 1999. We had a public meeting at the town hall and this was a last gasp attempt to save the club. It had been in administration for several months, the fans and some local business people were trying to put a consortium together to make a bid for the club. We had had many false dawns with other groups of people.

The situation was desperate and Les Smith knew they did not have long left to save the club. 'Terry Smith was at that meeting,' he said, 'and he was the first person to come along and effectively put his money on the table. As it transpired with the passage of time, it became a joint bid between him and us, the Independent Supporters' Association.'

Everything was going fine; the Chester City ISA had raised around £100,000 and all the right noises had been made about them buying shares in the club and being part of a real a partnership. But it wasn't long, though, before the honeymoon period began to sour.

They were only a few weeks into the new season when the club's manager and hero, Kevin Ratcliffe, suddenly left the club. Terry Smith took his place, though he had no experience whatsoever of coaching association football. In no time at all the American had the choice of two reserved spaces in the stadium car park.

Smith explained the move to the BBC by saying that his background was in coaching and so it made sense to him to utilize his skills. After all, he claimed, 80 per cent of all coaching techniques were the same, whatever the sport.

Soon after assuming the manager's role, Smith appointed three captains (a practice common in American football) and began handing out seven-page dossiers on the team's next opponents. It was as if he was talking another game.

Results were poor right from the start and the fans naturally became impatient. The ISA met in December and passed a vote of no confidence in Terry Smith as manager of the club. Naturally, this didn't go down too well, as Les Smith remembers. 'One of our committee told Smith of the vote, and his reaction was that the share issue was withdrawn,' he said. 'The next Saturday, in the Halifax Town match programme, there was a statement by Mr Smith that the share issue was not now going ahead with the ISA.'

This was all news to the supporters. They had their money returned and so Terry Smith turned his back on a valuable source of funds that could have helped the club stay in the League. It was to prove an expensive volte-face, though it was just the latest instalment in the Terry Smith saga of erratic behaviour.

In the mid-1980s a new craze was hitting Britain and names like the Raiders, Redskins or Cowboys were as likely to be slipped into the conversation as United, City or Rovers. Channel 4 started showing American football and suddenly, it seems, we were hooked. A domestic league sprang up and one of the first to come over from the States to try their luck, with the Manchester Spartans, was Terry Smith. According to Keith Webster, editor of *First Down* magazine, he quickly became a success:

> Terry arrived here in the late 1980s and it has to be said he had a decent knowledge of football, was a good communicator and managed to teach people, and there were many people in this country who benefited from Terry's teaching of American football. He made an immediate impact because up to that point most of the coaching had been done by British people who had some knowledge of the game but really didn't have the depth of knowledge that he brought, and he brought great coaching ability to the Spartans, compared to what they had before.

Webster recalls that honours quickly followed. 'Terry actually put the Spartans in a position to challenge for the title every year, and they won the championship more than once,' he said, 'Terry was largely responsible for that, and he also surrounded himself with people that were good communicators and good teachers as well.'

Word soon got around that back in the States Terry Smith had played at the very top – for the New England Patriots in the National Football League. He claimed that he had press cuttings, videos and programmes of his career, which was pretty good going because when *On The Line* contacted the Patriots they had to delve deep into the records to find his name as he had only actually played two pre-season matches for them. 'That was Terry's take on his previous experience, said Webster. 'At the time nobody was really ready to question it, you took these things as read.'

In the early 1990s the Spartans moved from Manchester to Sheffield and in 1995 Smith invited the people of South Yorkshire to sample a whole new sporting experience – American football, indoor-style. What the spectators actually saw, though, was not exactly what they thought they were seeing.

The Spartans of Sheffield were to scheduled to play the Munich Thunder in an exhibition match under indoor, or arena, rules. The posters were printed, the match was heavily publicized and tickets were being sold. The only thing missing was a German team, due in no small part to the fact that they had disbanded some months earlier. Undeterred and sticking to the old showbiz adage that the show must go on, Smith refused to cancel the match. Sheffield student Mark Bamford was due to play that night. Leafing through his scrapbook crammed full of memorabilia of an eventful gridiron career, he told *On The Line* what had happened:

> The night before the game, Terry said to a few of us, 'the Munich team are a bit short of cash and won't be able to bring a full team, some of you players will have to join them to make it fair'. Then on the day, it became apparent that there were no Munich players, and then no coach, so there were no Munich people at all.

As the hundreds of spectators filed into the Sheffield Arena expecting to see Anglo-German rivalries renewed under helmets and padding, Smith was handing out Munich team kits to members of the Sheffield University Zulus team, who, for the purposes of this match, were to pretend to be the German visitors. Bamford was one of those Zulus persuaded into playing against the Spartans, as a Thunder player:

> It was an arena game and he told us the rules of the arena game are that you have got to keep your helmet on at all time, because it was dangerous as someone can come over the barrier. We thought a-ha-ha! Yes, Terry, we have heard that before, all that kind of thing.

The accents under the Munich helmets were more Don Valley than Rhine Valley – it was a sham. But it didn't end there; the two teams lined up for the national anthems and as 'Deutschland Über Alles' blared out from the PA, Bamford stood hand on heart with his 'German' team-mates.

Big, burly forward Mike Jackson also played in that game, for the Spartans, and he remembers Smith announcing that Munich would not be playing, too:

> On the day of the game he just sort of said, 'Look, Munich have not turned up and we are going to play with some of our back-ups and some University guys. We are not going to tell anybody and no one is allowed to take their helmets off, we are just going to pretend these guys are German, and you're English, and we are just going to bluff it.

The match went ahead with the majority of the crowd oblivious to the charade going on in front of them. When the news inevitably spread back to Germany, Phil Hickey was one of those surprised to hear that the Thunder had been playing in Sheffield, or anywhere for that matter, and with good reason, for he had been the team's general manager when they disbanded:

> The very first time that I heard about the game was when somebody put an article from a newspaper in my hand and I believe it was dated a week or two after the game. If

the players had to be put back together again, I was the only person that could do it; the season was over, even if it was 15 players and not the 35–40 we played with which were needed to play an indoor game, and to gather these players I would have to know about it.

In a fax to *On The Line* on 15 February 2000 Terry Smith stated that the Thunder were never the intended opponents for the Spartans and the match was never advertised as such. Such an obvious and bizarre stunt did not go unchecked, and was extensively reported by the local paper the *Sheffield Star*. When an American football journalist quizzed him at the time about the game, Smith's enigmatic reply was, 'What is Munich? Munich is a state of mind.'

In a touching gesture of altruism, Smith kindly offered the Sheffield spectators refunds and season tickets. A seemingly magnanimous concession of that nature can only come from a man chastened by such an error of judgement, who is obviously keen never to make the same mistake again. Indeed, it was to be three years before Terry Smith was to involve himself in a similar adventure.

Keary Ecklund runs the Arena Football League in Neenah, Wisconsin. In 1998 Smith asked him if he would like to host an indoor match against a British team. Ecklund agreed but as the arranged date drew closer certain problems began to arise. 'Well, it was obvious that he didn't have players,' he explained from the offices of his haulage company, 'and he called us from Canada, and said he didn't have enough players and so we gave him coach's names to fill in his teams, but he didn't bring any players apart from himself and one other guy – I can't remember the guy's name.'

Smith's side played two arena games, one against the Green Bay Bombers and the other against the Madison Mad Dogs. One of the local players who turned out for 'Great Britain' was University of Wisconsin student Jason Crossveldt, whose college football season had just ended. He told *On The Line*:

I just played. I talked to a lot of people, they found it kind of funny that none of them were from Great Britain either, but I was kind of under the impression that this

was the team that went to Great Britain and they were
going to start their own league over there, that's what I
was told.

As Crossveldt waited to represent his new country he found out that
he wasn't alone:

> OTL: Did you know any of the players in the Great
> Britain team?
> JC: No, I didn't, I didn't know a single guy, but I know
> not one of them was from Great Britain.
> OTL: Are you certain? How do you know?
> JC: Because I talked to them, we sat around at practice
> and talked and guys tell you where they're from and
> where they have played.
> OTL: Where did the others come from?
> JC: What they told me when I was there was that this
> guy was recruiting people from around the US for a GB
> team, is what we were told.

Other players from the game support his story, as does a University
coach who recruited players for the match on Smith's behalf.
Crossveldt earned $200 for his trouble and landed himself a contract
with his opponents on the night – the Green Bay Bombers. League
owner Keary Ecklund had paid Smith $10,000 to provide the team
and had sold tickets to fans expecting to see Great Britain so he
couldn't let them down:

> Oh yeah, the games went ahead and they got beat pretty
> bad in both of them, because they had mix and match
> teams that had never played with each other. It wasn't
> what we were expecting, we were expecting to play a
> team from England who had played in one of your
> leagues over there.

By this time Smith had renamed the Sheffield Spartans the Great
Britain Spartans and they were playing in the newly formed Football

League of Europe. In 1995 they were due to play in Stockholm against the Nordic Vikings. Having been selected by Smith to play on opposite sides in the sham Munich Thunder game in Sheffield, Mike Jackson and Mark Bamford now found themselves reunited as team-mates in the Spartans.

Once again, as the fixture drew closer, the players started to pick up signals that all was not well, as Bamford remembers:

> We were at practice and Terry was talking, and he was saying, 'Well, we've got problems about not going to Stockholm because of the cost of flying there,' so initially he suggested we go by coach, cross the channel up through Denmark and get the ferry, but people wouldn't do that as it would mean having days off work. So everyone was saying they didn't want to do that, so Terry said if we are going to go to Stockholm by plane it is going to cost around £100 or something like that. I remember he even said he was considering cancelling the game.

Jackson also remembers discussing the travel arrangements to Stockholm with Smith: 'During the week he rang and said, "You can go but you have got to pay for your own flights, it is going to be £100 a piece," so some of us agreed, but some didn't, he let some go for nothing.'

The Spartans were now on shaky ground and it was to be on the dockside in Dover, en route to Sweden, where the foundations were to finally crumble. Mark Bamford was in the van:

> He said, 'I have rung round Dover; we can get the next ferry in the morning. There are no hotels available, everywhere is full.' He asked us if we were prepared to sleep in the vans, and we all sort of said, 'Yeah, I suppose so.' So we set off, and Terry went off in his van with some of the players and I went off in another van.

Bamford recalls that he and some of the other players got to Dover at 2 a.m. and they found Smith's van. 'It was full of players and no

Terry,' he remembers. 'It was like, where is he? One of the players said, "Well, he went in there with his girlfriend, he said he was going to sort her out and get her a room and we have not seen him since."'

While his team slept in their cramped vehicles on the dockside, Smith was tucked up in a nice warm hotel room. That was the final straw for many of the players, including Jackson and Bamford, who left Dover not by ferry but by bus back to Sheffield.

Despite the spirited Spartans' showing in Stockholm they were heavily defeated, but that was overshadowed by a bigger disappointment at home, at least for Mike Jackson, who was pursued all the way to court by Terry Smith for non-payment of the Stockholm travel costs. He was told by the court to pay £100.

All the American footballers we spoke to couldn't praise Terry Smith highly enough as a coach and his record certainly backs this up, but unfortunately for Chester City fans they were to witness one of the most embarrassing tenures in managerial history.

After Smith took over from Kevin Ratcliffe as manager, Chester City slid to the bottom of the Third Division. Halfway through the 1999–2000 season he appointed Ian Atkins, who couldn't turn the team around to avoid the inevitable last-day drop into the Conference.

Shortly after he took over, Smith invited a South African youngster, Craig Donaldson, for trials at the Deva Stadium. Donaldson was then at college in the USA, but craved a professional career in England. Smith answered his prayers and offered him a contract with the club. Now back at college in the States, Donaldson told *On The Line* about his dealings with Terry Smith:

> It was close to midnight and we had just got back from Port Vale and I wasn't too familiar with Chester as I was staying in North Wales in a hotel. Terry said he had arranged more accommodation close to the ground so I wouldn't have the travel problems I had been having. I was talking to him and he never actually said what he wanted to say, he was trying to make up stories about his wages being too high. Eventually I got off the bus, but my luggage was at the ground because I was supposed to

be moving to another hotel, and he just disappeared. I
had nowhere to go.

Twenty-four-year-old Donaldson, having been told to bring all his
possessions to the ground so he could move to a new home, was left
high and dry in a strange place thousand of miles from home. It was
his team-mates and an off-duty policeman, PC Paul Evans, who
came to his aid. Evans is a lifelong Chester fan and helps out,
unpaid, in the dressing room on match days. He is also the football
liaison officer for Cheshire Police. He told *On The Line* how he first
met Donaldson:

Craig had all the possessions he had brought into this
country with him. One of the players dropped Craig off
at my house to stay with me for a couple of days. He was
distraught, obviously, as he had looked forward to the
future in the English game. As far he was concerned he
had signed his contract and had a future in the English
game.

On The Line saw a copy of Donaldson's contract and can confirm
that he had indeed signed it, though the dotted line reserved for the
club chairman's signature was still blank.

In the fax that Terry Smith sent us he claimed that he had
arranged for Donaldson to stay at PC Evans's house but Evans is
adamant that this wasn't the case, and that it was only arranged as
the bus made its way back to Chester. Donaldson stayed with Evans
for two nights before returning to America, where he is finishing his
studies. He admits that his enthusiasm for the game has fallen away.

When Smith relinquished his car park berth early in January
2000 the team were firmly rooted at the bottom of the Third
Division. He carried on imparting his coaching skills, though, and
City fans were regularly treated to the sight of him, dressed in what
looked like uncomfortably tight tracksuit bottoms, putting goalkeeper Wayne Brown through his paces before every game.

It was to be a further 18 months before Smith finally left the
Deva altogether and it was a period littered with fallouts and

disputes, several of which found City embroiled in costly legal tangles.

The most expensive falling out was undoubtedly when former Everton defender Kevin Ratcliffe left the club in 2000, shortly after the American took over. A clause in Ratcliffe's contract meant that the club owed him around £500,000 in compensation. It wasn't until Liverpool boxing promoter Stephen Vaughn bought the club from Smith in 2001 that the claim was settled.

Two other appearances before the beak weren't as expensive for the club, but are illustrative nonetheless. In February 2000 chief executive Bill Wingrove walked out of a tribunal in Liverpool after winning a case for unfair dismissal and breach of contract against the club. Now commercial manager at Wrexham, he recalled the Sunday evening conversation he had had with Smith that led to him leaving Chester:

> I had phone call and it was Terry. He started with a 'Good evening,' and a 'How are you, Bill?' and he said, 'Have you had a nice weekend?' 'Yes, Terry, I said, have you?' He said, 'Yes,' and then he said, 'We had a meeting last night and we have decided to accept your resignation.' I said, 'Resignation, which resignation?' And he said, 'You know you said you would sort of consider your position and we accept your resignation.' I said, 'What are you telling me?' and he told me, 'We don't want you to come in to work again.' I said, 'Terry, what are you saying to me? You're dismissing me?' He said, 'We'd prefer you to say that you resigned.'

In court, the American football coach who had turned his hand to managing a soccer team had a go at legal advocacy and chose to represent the club himself. The tribunal chose not to believe his assertion that Wingrove and the previous chairman, Marc Guterman, had colluded to fabricate a contract of employment awarding him around £12,000. Again, it wasn't until Smith left the club that Wingrove recovered his money.

In December 2001 the actions of Terry Smith again found

Chester up before an employment tribunal after Graham Vile, the director of its centre of excellence, was sacked. The hearing heard that Viles's centre was funded by grants from Sport England, which reimbursed projects after they had proved that money had been spent. Vile said that Smith had wanted him to pre-sign the blank forms and hand them over to him. When Vile refused to do this, the tribunal was told, Smith wrestled him to the ground and stopped him phoning the police. The ruling was that the dismissal was unfair and Vile was awarded just over £17,000.

Events on the pitch faired as badly and, despite the best efforts of Ian Atkins, the club were relegated to the Conference. Atkins left soon after, joining another relegation battle, this time at Carlisle United. Smith's idiosyncratic approach to man management, though, was to rear its head once more, after a 4–0 FA Vase defeat at Canvey Island, when former Leeds, Sheffield United and Manchester City defender Paul Beesley was suspended.

The crime that warranted this drastic course of action was that the vastly experienced Beesley had, according to the former coach of the Manchester Spartans American Football team, stood in the wrong place at a corner. Smith told the newspapers: 'We had practised, as in American football, tactics of where to stand, and done scrimmages between the first team and reserves. In training, the first team had scored 10 goals, but Beesley stood in the wrong place, ruining it for everybody.'

Despite intense pressure, including a boycott of the club by fans, Smith refused to leave, only finally doing so after the club narrowly missed a further relegation. He sold the club to controversial Liverpool boxing promoter and the former Barrow chairman, Stephen Vaughn.

If marks were to be given for trying, Terry Smith would get a maximum ten. From his impressive-looking CV, which found its way into the *On The Line* office, he seems to have tried almost everything, including writing. He has a motivational book called *Hero Lives Inside of You* (Hero Inside of You Publications, £12.95) but, unfortunately, his methods of motivation, which included a prayer before every match, failed to work on his players at Chester City.

After leaving the Deva, Smith tried to set up a scouting company to find the best overseas players for clubs in England. *On The Line* applied for a place at his football school but we never heard anything back.

Smith's CV shows that he had also tried to make it as a baseball player, attending pre-season training with the Florida Marlins in 1985 – a fairly lonely experience it would seem, as the Marlins didn't play their first game until 1994.

Chester City, who weren't even Smith's first choice of club (he had enquired about buying another in the Third Division earlier), are slowly picking themselves up. They have put the Smith era behind them and have made a good start to the 2002– 3 season. But wider questions have rightly been raised about whether the football authorities should have tighter controls over who can buy into clubs.

Terry Smith was a trier and he probably still is. Unfortunately for the fans of Chester City, he chose to try at their club. Luckily, they have lived to tell the tale.

CHAPTER FOURTEEN

Suffer the Children
The Clubs, the Parents and the Agents Creating a Blooming Business out of 'Child' Transfers

At a time when the eyes of the football world were fixed on the 2002 World Cup in Japan and South Korea, On The Line *investigated a disturbing trade in young boys closer to home. Premier League clubs were paying six-figure sums to sign players as young as nine years of age and fighting fierce battles to sign boys as young as five or six. There has never been as much interest – or money – in football youth development.*

England's creditable display in the World Cup was achieved with a young team. The average age of Sven-Goran Eriksson's squad was 24. The FA and Premier League believe things can only get better when players start to emerge from the club academy system introduced in 1999, at great expense to all the top clubs. The clubs now have players from eight years old, which they insist they need to produce better footballers. But the results are yet to be seen and the new system has an ugly side, like the poaching and trading of pre-teen boys.

Michael Owen's amazing defence-defying dribble and shot against Argentina in France in 1998; being able to bend it like Beckham in the last gasp World Cup qualifier against Greece in 2001; Gazza's impudent lob and volley against the Scots in Euro 1996: these are the dreams of children – scoring vital goals in major matches.

Beckham, Owen and all of the current England team came through the old system, playing for their schools and attending centres of excellence two evenings a week at their professional clubs. That changed in 1999 with the introduction of the Charter for Quality, which had been drawn up two years earlier by the FA's technical director, Howard Wilkinson. It was a total revamp of elite youth development based on observations made in more successful continental countries.

Dave Richardson is the director of youth policy at the Premier League and he told *On The Line*:

> Over the years the English game has often said that the reason the continentals were technically better than us was because they got their players earlier and they didn't have the inhibitions or the prohibitions that were around us with schools football. The leading continental countries had access to children from a very early age, and they had unlimited coaching time with them. Now we've got a situation whereby we are no different to France, Germany, Holland or wherever – we have total access to children.

Football club academies can now sign players from the age of nine upwards. They are responsible for their football education and they can (and do) prevent players from over-playing by competing for schools and representative regional sides and in recreational matches. The academies are licensed by the Football Association and must meet stringent standards in order to keep their licence. They are compelled to employ specialist staff – not just coaches or medical staff but education and welfare officers to look after the players' non-sporting needs.

'It was finding the right age that children soak up information,' continues Richardson. 'It's recognized in educational circles that the golden ages of learning comes from about eight or nine through to about 12 or 13 where your body and brain are like a sponge – that's the best time to take things in.'

All of the top clubs have made major investments in the hunt to unearth the stars of the future. You have to delve deep in the Ribble Valley countryside to find Blackburn Rovers' academy. Despite being given detailed directions, I nearly missed the signs, confusing the entrance for a retirement village or lavish private hospital. Chalet blocks and neatly appointed gardens greet you along the drive. A huge photograph of Jack Walker gazes at you in the reception. It is an impressive place – new, clean, slightly antiseptic, with a hint of trading estate office neatness – but a world away from the grimy stands and introductions to mud-clogged boots and terraces in need of sweeping that would have greeted apprentices in the austere days of youth development.

Blackburn's academy director, Bobby Downes, explained the investment made here: £7 million on buildings and £2 million a year to operate the centre. 'We've been going five years now, so that's £17 million,' he said. At first sight this seems like an astronomical sum to pour into youth development but for Downes, a former player and coach at Watford, Aston Villa and Wolves, and his peers at Premiership clubs, the process has a clear bottom line. 'How much would Damian Duff be worth after his World Cup? £17 million, possibly?' asks Downes. 'How much is David Dunn worth? We don't have to have ten players a year. We have to find one or two.'

The hunt to find those rare players who might bring success, money or both has bred intense competition among the clubs. They aren't satisfied just to find and develop their own players, they also routinely look to sign players from other academies, with bigger clubs using their power and prestige to lure players from smaller ones. In an attempt to stem this flow, the Football League insist that what they describe as 'predator' clubs should pay compensation to the clubs losing the player. If the clubs can't agree a fee, a special body, chaired by a QC, called the Football League Appeals Committee (FLAC) sets the figure. These can be difficult decisions to make.

'We have to strike a balance whereby the club that originally unearths that talent is still incentivized to continue with youth development because otherwise there would be the tendency for them to take the view that it is no longer worthwhile,' explained Andy Williamson, director of operations at the Football League. The committee hears evidence from both clubs and then decides a level of compensation according to the time spent developing the player and the committee's view of his likely future in the game. 'A lot of these decisions are obviously based on potential, and nobody can be certain that potential will be realized in the longer term,' said Williamson, 'and so it's quite common for the Football League Appeals Committee to determine a compensation decision which builds up according to how much success that player has in future years.'

The committee also has to bear in mind that players and their parents have a right to choose who they want to play for and shouldn't be tied to clubs simply because it is too expensive for rivals to sign them. But this system has a curious effect: the club who have signed the player (and may have told the parents that he will benefit from joining them) then go to the committee and play down his chances of making it. 'The club losing the player say he's going to be a world beater, the club he's going to says he's only average,' says Dave Richardson.

On The Line obtained a list of the latest compensation rulings in June 2002. It made sobering reading. Players as young as nine years of age are effectively being transferred for a fee from one club to another, sometimes for tens of thousands of pounds. Usually there is an initial fee followed by amounts for signing on as a scholar, signing a professional contract, so many first team appearances and a percentage of any future sale of the player.

For older boys, in the 14–16-year-old age range, compensation can be set at millions of pounds, because they are closer to senior age and their potential progress is more certain. There were several players on the FLAC list in this category totalling hundreds of thousands of pounds, including an under-16-year-old moving from Swansea to Southampton for £500,000, and two under-16s signed by Aston Villa for fees which might reach £450,000 each.

In order to avoid paying these relatively large sums of money, clubs are now looking to recruit players at an ever younger age. The compensation payments are lower because their prospects are less predictable. Even so, there was an under-11-year-old who has moved to Manchester United from Preston North End for fees worth £136,000, and an under-ten-year-old player who joined Birmingham City from West Bromwich Albion for £35,000.

The view among the large Premier League clubs, who can afford to splash out this sort of money, was broadly summed up in the *On The Line* discussion following our programme by Aston Villa chairman, Doug Ellis who also chairs the FA's Technical Control Board, which has overseen the introduction of the academies. They are 'throwing lifelines' to smaller, often cash-strapped clubs, who are grateful for the money. But many of those same smaller clubs insist they would prefer to keep their players and are becoming dispirited by continually losing their brightest youngsters.

'It is frustrating, not just for me but for the staff involved,' said Andy Beaglehole, Oldham Athletic's academy director. Oldham have a reputation for producing good young players but they're a small, vulnerable club surrounded in the northwest of England by hungry, richer neighbours who know where to go looking for up and coming talent. Some clubs even reserve a kitty to shop for pre-teen talent.

'A friend of mine who is an academy director mentioned to me that as part of his budget he'd set aside £10,000 for compensation because they'd be looking at lads at nine or ten-years old from some of the smaller clubs round his region,' said Beaglehole. How many players might he get for that sort of money?

> On the present rate of £2,500 for a nine-year-old, he could get four under-nines or two under-12s, maybe at £5,000 apiece. There's more compensation to be paid but that's based on success and how well he does, and that's nothing to pay if you're getting a good player. We'd much rather have the player at Oldham Athletic than £5,000.

Unerringly, Beaglehole went on to explain that this expenditure is sanctioned by football club boardrooms: 'Our compensation claims go to the secretary of the club we're pursuing it from, so obviously that is discussed at boardroom level.'

Some people may find this legitimized trading of young boys a distasteful process. But it carries an even darker side – one which the game, despite the introduction of highly regulated multi-million pound academies, has failed to eradicate from youth development. Players can switch clubs at a certain point in the summer, during what is known as a window of opportunity, and compensation is payable. But some clubs commonly fail even to abide by this system. They break the code of conduct by approaching players directly and offering nothing to the club losing out. It's called poaching. The rumours are that it is rife. An exasperated Beaglehole explains:

> We've had an outstanding youngster in our under-nines

this year and when we've been playing other clubs in the northwest region we've had instances of him being approached by a scout from another club. In one case that scout was asked to leave and we reported these things, took it further with letters, tried to collect evidence, but the boy left us at the end of the year and now we're fighting to get some compensation for him.

Oldham also lost two 14-year-olds to Premier League clubs in the 2001–2 season.

Rumours of players being poached or parents being offered inducements are widespread but according to Richard Hodgson, the head of youth development at the Football League, illegal approaches are notoriously difficult to prove:

Allegations are really quite common but they can only be pursued by the leagues, whether it's the Premier or Football League, on the basis of evidence to corroborate those allegations. Flagrant breaches of the rules are where representatives of the clubs – scouts as they're commonly known – make direct approaches to the parents of players, or indeed even worse, to the players themselves, knowing that those players are at another club and so therefore they know that it is an illegal process. It's totally unacceptable and those sorts of situations put people under pressure and there are massive child protection implications when it's direct approaches to children. I'm afraid that's unacceptable.

Dave Richardson, Hodgson's opposite number at the Premier League, is troubled by the apparent scope of poaching, but he insists there is little he can do to curtail this activity among his member clubs:

There have always been clubs that have been accused of being pinchers or nickers. That's always happened and it always will happen. There'll always be some that have that reputation, by virtue of the people and how they operate that particular club. If a club has proof that they have illegally approached a boy, then as far as we are concerned, once we have the proof, we'll deal with it. We have, in certain cases, dealt with certain clubs.

Richardson says that heavy fines have been implemented and clubs have been threatened with losing their academy licence but he refused to name specific clubs, cases or players:

There have been instances whereby we have spoken to clubs at director and chairman level about the behaviour of their club and the threat of them losing an academy licence, and the opportunity for them to run their development process the way they're running it, if they didn't clean their act up. But we can only act on information received, very much like the police.

The illegal approaches are particularly galling for smaller clubs because it means they can end up with nothing after sometimes putting years of hard work into developing their players. Oldham's Andy Beaglehole said:

As a club we will accept that yes, we will lose one or two boys who see the stars in the Premier League and think that they've got a better chance of making it there, which I'd question. But if we are going to lose a boy we'd like it to be done up front and through the front door, and for a correct approach to be made for the boy and proper compensation to be coming in. That makes it worthwhile for us to continue to develop these youngsters from eight years upwards.

Richardson is a former schoolteacher from the North East who came into football, and the youth side of the game in particular, from an educational background. He is angry that big clubs are continuing to undermine this new system, which was introduced only three years ago to give them what they had wanted:

> I do get a little bit depressed, in the sense of upset, and concerned about the fact that here we are, we've changed everything to the way you want it. Now we've got a clean sheet. Whatever happened before, yes, the duckers and divers, everybody's done things and I would be the first to admit that in my career I don't think I'd be proud of certain things you do as a coach and as a developer. I'd be telling a lie and everybody would be telling a lie if they said they hadn't done things that way. We've now created a situation where we've said look, the slates are clean, let's get started again. Unfortunately, football is a selfish industry, you have to have a certain amount of selfishness in your nature because you've got to look after number one.

Richardson's call for honesty and integrity is likely to fall on deaf ears because of the desire to find the best young players. The pressure to discover those few rare gems and the potential sums of money that can be made from youth development are too high. Bobby Downes, Blackburn's academy director, says that the requirement to pay compensation does act as a deterrent to big clubs like his from signing other clubs' youngsters. But the effect is to increase competition to sign even younger boys and the clubs look to groom those players (the under-nine-year-olds) and link them to the club to prevent others in the area from signing them, as he explained to *On The Line*:

> As ridiculous as it sounds, with the compensation rulings and that, you would have to pay to get a 12-year-old boy, then obviously you've got to get it right at the very start. A lot of clubs have development centres now where they're starting with seven- and eight-year-old kids. There is so much competition for that best eight-year-old kid and in our region he would have quite a few to pick from, wouldn't he? It is vital to get those players at that age.

You might think it is nigh on impossible to decide whether a child as young as eight will make a good footballer. Perhaps inevitably, given the money at stake, the race has driven the scouting process down even lower, to children as young as five and six.

Clubs can't actually sign boys before they are eight, so they find other ways to tempt them, like using the community programme as a talent-spotting service. Beaglehole explained how the competition between the clubs at these age groups worked:

> When we start looking at boys at eight [years old] and we put money into a schools project where we invite boys in from primary schools at eight years old, the chances are they have already been in community programmes at Manchester City and Manchester United. It's phenomenal the amount of recruitment that's going on at earlier and earlier ages.
>
> Some of these community officers have big estate cars and it'll be laden with gear and club merchandise. So if a boy is identified, obviously they can't tie him to the club by registering him because they can't do so until he's nine but they will try to get him some affinity to that club and spoil him with goodies, this kind of thing. Then they keep tabs on him and invite him into the club and offer him a free place on one of the community schemes – try to get him attached to the club as much as they can so then they'll try to sign him as soon as they can.

On The Line discovered that one Premier League club actually employed three full-time coaches scouring their patch for players as young as five years of age. It seems amazing that youth development has come to this – professional clubs packing teams of coaches off to trawl primary schools to sign boys who have barely kicked a ball in anger let alone developed a love for the game or sport in general. The parents of players are all too often blamed for pushing their children forward, but with clubs behaving in this way at such early ages can anyone realistically blame them?

Not surprisingly, there are people among the UK sports coaching community who are appalled by the way some of Britain's biggest sporting clubs are behaving. John Stevens, chief executive of Sports Coach UK, formerly the National Coaching Foundation, told *On The Line* that football was flying in the face of the latest sports development theory:

> A nine-year-old just concentrating on football intensively to the detriment of any other sport, and to the detriment potentially of other aspects of their personal and social development at that age, I think, is very, very wrong. If you look at some of the academic research that has been done throughout the world now, they would advocate very strongly that probably even up to the age of 11 or 12 that a child's involvement in sport should focus on learning fundamentals – the ability to move, the ability to balance, to catch, to run, to jump. They should play lots of different sports and not start to specialize too soon. I think football needs to have a really long hard look at those concepts.

Most young players start their football education far away from the professional clubs, either in schools – where the sort of principles Stevens advocates are adhered to – or junior clubs.

On a wet Saturday morning the ever enthusiastic parents of Callowbrook Swifts, a junior community club in the Rubery area of south Birmingham, bring their children to a school playing field for their weekly training session. Callowbrook have 12 teams and over 150 members and they cater for players of all abilities from the age of six to 16. It is an FA Charter Standard club.

'We were one of the first in the Midlands to achieve the standard,' says club secretary Nigel Brindley. 'It's an FA approved kitemark for the club, the way it's set up and the way that it's run.'

All of Callowbrook's coaches are qualified, one even to UEFA 'A' standard (good enough to coach professional players) and the boys are proud to wear the club's green, black and white gear. 'The right standards of football are taught within the club,' says Brindley, 'and because of that, we're attracting a lot of interest from many other clubs.'

This is the sort of place where professional club scouts come hunting. Callowbrook's players are routinely invited to academies after being spotted playing for them. If they sign up it usually means they will be told they can no longer play for their community clubs. Yet despite the money swilling around youth development at the elite end, the clubs who start the players off, like Callowbrook, receive nothing for their efforts.

'We have no changing facilities, we have no car parking facilities, we have no toilets,' explains Brindley. 'If there is money floating around which League clubs are spending on young players, then surely that must come down to this level. There has to be some way whereby the money filters down.'

Football has its own value at this model FA junior club. It is a game to be enjoyed. Worth far more than just the ruthless pursuit of talent or success. The interests of the players are put first. 'I think it's a shame that so much pressure is put on players when they're so young,' says Brindley, who sometimes offers this stark message to parents: 'Don't let players leave to join League clubs until they're at least 13 or 14.' And his reason for saying this?

> Because the lads are just not mature enough to be able to cope with it. I think if you've got an eight-, nine- or ten-year-old player who thinks he can play for Manchester United, his entire life and perspective changes, his schoolwork suddenly goes downhill, he loses sight of perhaps some of the other things that he should be doing. If he makes it, fantastic, because the rewards are great, but if he doesn't make it, and out of probably every 100 kids who go forward only about five or ten actually do. So what happens to the rest of them? They're just thrown aside.

The popular public image of youth development is somewhat different. It is dominated by the spectacular success stories. Manchester United's Busby Babes of the 1950s, for instance; heart-warming tales of scouts coming across the likes of George Best and Alex Ferguson's 1993 crop; the Neville brothers, Nicky Butt, Paul Scholes; and, of course, old Goldenballs himself. But for every child prodigy like David Beckham, spotted and signed at a young age, who go all the way to fame and fortune, the reality is that, for all the huge investment in academies, the vast majority fall by the wayside.

David Brown was viewed as a wonderdkid centre forward when he was suddenly thrust into the public gaze in 1996. A schoolboy player with Oldham Athletic, he was controversially poached by Manchester United, who were fined £50,000 and ordered to pay Oldham £75,000 compensation by the Football Association for signing Brown as a trainee. Before they did this Manchester United gave Brown the red carpet treatment, as he recalls:

> When Manchester United beat Ipswich 9–0 they took me to the game and showed me round the ground. I met Alex Ferguson and Brian Kidd. They were very good to me and made me and my family feel very comfortable, so when they asked to me to sign it was a decision I made on the spot, really.

Once he had signed on the dotted line, despite the spotlight initially being turned on him, Brown slipped into anonymity at old Trafford. 'Nobody ever treated me any differently because I'd had this case and this, that and the other were being put in the paper,' he said. 'You just had to do the best that you could to improve yourself and improve your career.'

He was lost in United's embarrassment of forward riches. When Sir Alex decided to sign Dwight Yorke in 1998, Brown found himself tenth in line for a place in the first team:

> I went to Alex Ferguson and asked him what the situation was. He explained that they were trying to sign more forwards so I made my feelings known that if that was the case then I – not being funny with him or anybody else – wasn't looking to continue at Manchester United playing in the youth team and reserves. With the squad being

how big it is I may not have played many reserve games
so I just felt I needed to leave Manchester United to further my career.

Brown was sold to Hull, where he struggled and was released. He is
now playing for Telford United in the Nationwide Conference.

Brown's tale is all too familiar. Despite the huge investment
Premier League clubs have made in their academies, and the search
for boys at ever younger ages, the odds against these players breaking through are greater than ever. Less than half of the players in the
Premier League these days are British-born and FA figures for the
2001–2 season show that no 17- or 18-year-olds started matches in
the Premiership – and only eight 19-year-olds (of all nationalities). It
is a situation which leaves coaches working in youth development
extremely frustrated.

At Blackburn Rovers, Bobby Downes says the senior arm of the
clubs don't work well enough with their academies: 'I would say that
as a criticism of most clubs. There isn't enough longer term planning, which there has to be on the youth side, together with the
shorter term planning that has to be with the first team.' Although
the drip-feed of academy players into the senior squads is slow,
Downes believes the academies are proving financially viable: 'If you
come back in five years' time and ask what have we produced and
what money have we spent in terms of budget and buildings, I
would think we would be well in advance money-wise.'

But the human cost of this system, which can produce lucrative stars like Blackburn's Damian Duff, who can command millions
of pounds in the transfer market, is that it creates many more casu-
alties than successes. Richard Hodgson remembers the demoralizing
effect rejection had on a promising player at a club where he used to
coach, Manchester City:

There was one young man in the late 1980s called Peter
Bell, from Wigan, who was an international schoolboy
player. I thought he was a fabulous player, fantastic,
really skilful, quick, sharp, tight and intelligent and a
nice person as well. Everybody had very high hopes for

Peter, including himself and his family. When he wasn't offered a professional contract with Manchester City, Peter walked out of football. Such was his disappointment, he didn't continue playing football and I thought that was a sad thing, because it's a fantastic game and that was probably the first time that Peter had ever been disappointed. It was a huge body blow to him. That type of example is one I feel for almost as a dad would feel. It's a crushing disappointment to some of these young players whose hopes and expectations are sky-rocketed by all sorts of circumstances – not least the association with a major club.

Yet the emphasis on youth development in Britain is so often couched in terms of the club's needs rather than the player's. John Stevens of Sports Coach UK believes football has to change its priorities – to take adequate care of the children and young people it selects, now, from the age of seven upwards: 'There has to be much more thought put into managing the process, managing that player's development from the point of view that puts the player as the single most important person in that process. And I don't think football's got to grips with that yet.'

The academies employ education and welfare officers – qualified staff who can deal with all sorts of problems facing young people. Dave Richardson accepts they have created an undignified scramble to sign talent at the youngest possible age but, overall, he believes the club academy system is a vast improvement on the chaotic days when he worked in as a coach in the 1970s and 1980s:

There are still problems and there will always be problems whatever system we have in place. It's how we keep them to a bare minimum and keep them right at the periphery of the whole operation that is important. If you ask people, generally speaking, for all the warts, everybody says it's better than it was for young children.

This particular *On The Line* programme was compiled during the 2002 World Cup, when England were once again left nursing their wounded pride following their quarter-final exit to eventual champions Brazil. Their failure to mix it with the big boys of world football inevitably led to attention being thrown on the way we develop players, with specific concentration on the next crop of future stars. The clubs, it seems, are desperate to justify the money they have spent on their academies, and are chasing even harder to find the best young players to play in them. Nobody knows if it will work, but the danger is that in this rush for excellence and money, too high a price is being paid by too many boys, far too young.

CHAPTER FIFTEEN

Anyone for Prawns?

They Used to Be 'Boys in Boots' but Now They Are 'Men in Suits' and Can Be Found in the Ever-expanding Corporate Hospitality Areas of Football Grounds

After Hillsborough, the Taylor Report pinpointed alcohol and home and away fans mixing in stands as accelerators to the scourge of hooliganism. Touting tickets for football matches was subsequently made a criminal offence. Yet it is not the touts who are mostly responsible for boozed up home and away fans mixing in stands these days, but the clubs who flog thousands of hospitality packages week in, week out with little or no idea of who they are inviting into their ground.

Harvey Harris, it is fair to say, is not one for following the crowd. From his appearance, I'm guessing he was a rocker in his youth, when his Essex home was very much 'mods territory'. His DJ and entertainment act looks back to the rock and roll era of the 1950s, in preference to the more user-friendly 1960s. For years he used to live on Green Street, London E13, home to West Ham United, but he is an avid Spurs fan. Life has thrown the odd hurdle at Harvey, but despite that he comes across as personable, a happy-go-lucky fellow, even if the odd thing really gets his goat.

And of late, chief among the subjects for his ire has been the corporate hospitality arrangements at his beloved White Hart Lane, where he has hardly missed a match since 1959. Not that he has a problem with the principle of corporate hospitality. Not at all.

'I think it is a good idea,' he explains, as we meet outside the main gates of the ground. 'It earns money for the club. It means I pay less for my season ticket.'

The problem, says Harvey, is that at White Hart Lane corporate hospitality is impinging directly on his enjoyment of his football, for which, as a season ticket holder, he reckons he pays handsomely.

He's referring to a smart set of seats smack in the middle of what used to be the 'Shelf', the London club's equivalent of Liverpool's Kop or Manchester United's Stretford End. Harvey stood here as a boy, and now that it has been redeveloped he has a seat a few yards from this plush new open area:

> When it was first built I asked the stewards what it was. I was told it was called 'Legends'. The idea is you buy a meal before the game and sit with a Spurs legend. Brilliant! I would like to do it myself. Unfortunately, while the host may be a Spurs fan, evidently not all the guests are. I have even seen people wearing the away team colours, although that has been stopped recently and in some games, when the tension is naturally high – London derbies for example – the atmosphere has turned quite nasty when an away goal is scored.

Harvey does not blame the away fans for cheering their team and thinks they should be allowed to wear their colours, but only in their own section of the ground. He is even sympathetic to the fans who must feel pressured to sit on their hands during a game in these corporate areas.

> I can imagine it is sheer hell having to sit on your hands, especially when you have paid all that money but my point is that however gentrified football has become, however much money has been flowing into the game, however many fans swap their boots for suits, football runs on passion, and home and away fans should not mix, even in hospitality areas.
>
> It really does not matter to me what sort of bloke I sit next to at a match. I don't care if he has a criminal record as long as your arm, I don't care anything about him except the fact that when we score, we rise as one. It could be that the guy cheering in the corporate area when the opposition score is a fantastic guy but the reality is, for 90 minutes on a Saturday, he is not my friend.

And frankly, Harvey does not want such people sitting within earshot. Awkward? Maybe. Unreasonable? Well, it depends on your perspective.

As the ultimate paymasters, collectively fans do have power over their clubs, but typically the individual fan feels powerless in the face of his or her club when they take an executive decision, say, to move your seat, build a new stadium, or expand the hospitality business into open seating areas of their spanking new stands.

However the club dress it up, Harvey simply sees planting corporate seats in open areas of the stands as giving a green light for away fans to spread themselves in and among the home support. The club's perspective is that they are selling a premium product and the kind of people who will shell out for this do not cause trouble:

> I wonder what the reaction of the police would be,' he asks rhetorically, 'If the club decided that instead of a wedge of 200 or 300 fans behind the goal, they actually spread them out in blocks of three or four, all over the ground. I think there would be uproar, I think the police would object.

Clubs would like to think that the future of football lies in civilized bipartisanship, as would we all, but the reality is that we are a long way from that in England. Foreign players frequently say that the principal pleasure of playing the Premiership is the passion generated by the crowd.

It comes at a price. By its very nature, passion turns us into irrational beings. Fuelled with a pre-match drink, it does not take much to turn many reasonable people into unreasonable ones, who, at least for the duration of the match, actually loathe the opposition and all their works.

It is not just Harvey Harris who thinks along these lines. Lord Justice Taylor did when he wrote his famous report following the triple disasters of Bradford, Heysel and Hillsborough in the 1980s, football's 'dark ages'. He recognized that such was the nature of the English game and its highly-charged tribal histories, strict segregation was a key to a safer game for the spectator. He also recognized that alcohol at football was a key accelerator of trouble. The hospitality seat compromises the segregation principle and positively encourages drinking.

Some of the simmering resentment sections of support occasionaly feel towards their club is often embodied by the phenomenon of corporate hospitality. Possibly it is straight envy, or perhaps a more complex expression of the tribal emotion at the core of the committed football fan. As hospitality areas became more visible it seemed to some that rather than merely maximizing income, the club actually hankered after filling the stadium with these people at the expense of the long-suffering and loyal fan.

Even the dumbest football chairman could see that to do such a thing would kill the club dead because it would remove the crucial element in the equation that the corporate guest pays to experience: the atmosphere. Nonetheless, every now and then resentment towards the corporate entertainment phenomenon is refuelled, as when, after a listless United performance in the 2001–2 Champions League campaign had been booed, Roy Keane quipped that some fans were more interested in prawn sandwiches than appreciating what was going on in front of them on the pitch.

There is no doubt that it is boom time for hospitality at football clubs and there is a massive (and wholly understandable) temptation to sell more and more packages. At some clubs it is the difference between overall profit and loss. The problem is that corporate hospitality can only expand one way – into the open seating areas of the stands. Which in the last five years is what has happened at most clubs.

In the beginning it was a very expensive affair, limited to the people who could afford tens of thousands of pounds a season to buy a box behind plate glass. Today the majority of corporate seats are in special areas carved out of the existing stands, or even ordinary seats that have found their way to the tour operators who organize pre-match wining and dining away from the stadium.

It is assumed that the people who fill these seats and who are prepared to pay anything up to £500 for 'tucker' and a ticket will behave themselves. Furthermore, if they are away fans they will sit on their hands and stare at the floor if their team score. It is a denial of the social realities that have made watching the game in this country the greatest football spectacle in the world.

It is the appearance of neutrals and away fans in and around traditional home support areas of the stadium that has moved Harvey Harris to raise the issue whenever he can, in whatever forum he can. He sees it, at the very least, as the club simply being prepared to compromise his enjoyment of watching his team for the price of steak, chips and a bottle of wine. So how did it come to this and where is it leading?

It is true that violence is rarely seen at football grounds nowadays. But ask yourself why. Is it because hooligans in the 1990s suddenly repented and became pacifists? Unfortunately not. It was the orgy of stadium refurbishment and new buildings that started in the early 1990s and continues to this day that was largely responsible for the transformation.

Simon Inglis is an author and Britain's leading authority on football stadia, he told *On The Line*:

> Hooligans were designed out of the football stadium. For example, just look at the introduction of CCTV cameras into grounds. Twin this development with the all-seated stadium and the hooligan really has few places to hide. It is a lot harder to spot a troublemaker in among a seething mass of standing fans. However, give every fan their own space, that is a seat, and it becomes much easier to spot troublesome individuals and keep tabs on them.

The introduction of seating reduced the capacity at many grounds and left football clubs with a dilemma: how to increase the income from each seat without making the basic cost of entry to the ground more than the market could bear. One answer was to refine the concept of corporate hospitality.

In the early 1990s the 'open box' made its first appearance. With this design it was possible to move the glass doors to one side and step out into a seated area and therefore become part of the crowd. In the late 1990s what the Americans call a 'club seat' arrived in Britain. In aircraft parlance, it was a sort of business class in relation to the hospitality box's first class.

It was significant because, as already noted, these seats were commandeered from parts of the stadium that had traditionally accommodated home fans, with the best views in the ground. What makes these seats so attractive to both club and customer is the financial flexibility, as Simon Inglis explains:

> A lot of corporate clients did not just want 12 people in a box. They wanted the flexibility to invite 20 people one week and maybe 100 people the next. Equally, some supporters could not afford the corporate experience for a season but might like to splash out and celebrate an occasion or event with friends.

The club seat was a very clever innovation. At a stroke it enabled the club to take a bog standard seat and throw in the use of a lounge, with a drink, a meal and a programme. All this meant that a seat that used to earn you £30 now generated nearer £300.

It is the clubs' contention that they know everyone who takes up a corporate seat. There is intensive stewarding of the areas and if anyone steps out of line they are asked to leave.

Aled Williams has never been asked to leave a football match. It is doubtful whether he appears on the databases of many, if any, club marketing departments as a frequent user of club seats. But he is. Manchester United accounts for much of his disposable income. He travels to most away games and more often than not he sits in a corporate seat. 'It is not always easy to get tickets in the designated away area, which is obviously where I would like to be,' he explains, 'so I go on the internet and buy seats in other clubs' executive areas from local ticket agencies.'

Ever since ticketed events were invented it has been impossible to keep track and account for every ticket. If there was any possibility of such a system ever existing, dozens of businesses that advertise corporate knees-ups at everything from pop concerts to horse races would be living on borrowed time . Tickets find their way to touts, corporate marketing departments, tour operators and away fans every day of the week.

'You take a risk with your personal safety,' admits Williams, 'but generally I have been with sensible people. It is matter of judging the atmosphere, talking to people around you and getting a bit of banter going.'

It does not always work and sometimes he has just had to keep his mouth shut. Not everyone he knows has been so lucky: 'I know Manchester United fans who have been physically and verbally abused, you know, followed to the toilets and duffed up. Mostly it is verbal but sadly not always. It does not happen every game but neither is it a rare occurrence.'

It is entirely possible that Williams was one of those fans who irked Harvey Harris. In 1998 Harvey became so hacked off with the little 'islands' of interlopers around about his seat that he complained to Spurs. He says they ignored him. Then he got serious:

> First of all I applied through the local council to see if I could have the safety certificate removed from the ground on the basis that the club were failing to segregate but I was told that was a long and expensive thing to do. I just did not have the money. So I contacted the Premier League.

Having lobbied his local MP, the Football Association, the local council and the man in charge of policing White Hart Lane on match days and receiving no satisfaction, it is fair to say that when a letter from Premier League secretary Mike Foster dropped through Harvey Harris's letter box he did not hold out much hope for its contents. But he was wrong. Foster had enclosed a copy of a letter that he had sent to Spurs about the subject on 11 February 1999. Harvey's point about segregating or banning visiting corporate guests clearly touched a nerve with Mr Foster who wrote:

> I have recently had first-hand experience of the problems to which Mr Harris refers. I was present with my wife and daughter in the corner flag hospitality area on the occasion of your game with Chelsea recently. My daughter, who is 15, supports Chelsea and had her Chelsea scarf

on, and a steward requested that she remove it

When Chelsea scored I could understand the reason behind the request. A group of four people sat directly behind us jumped up to celebrate Chelsea's goal along with some other people. They did not celebrate excessively, nor did they taunt or do anything to aggravate anyone other than applauding the goal. The abuse directed at them by a large number of home supporters, had to be seen to be believed.

Harvey, as it happened, did see it and could quite easily believe it, having witnessed the same eruption, in the same areas, at the same fixture the year before: 'Our commercial manager at the time had to help escort some 30 Chelsea fans out of the same section because punches were being thrown in and out of that section. If that section had not been there no one would have been agitated in the first place.'

Mike Foster also felt there had to be a better way. He wrote:

The club, I feel, should decide if it is going to insist on no away supporters in corporate areas, in which case this policy should be made abundantly clear, or crack down on home supporters unable to tolerate away fans standing nearby and showing their colours.

The exiting policy of the club seems confused. On the one hand your match day programme contains a message saying corporate members have the right to invite guests of their choice, some of whom may support the visiting team, on the other hand the conditions of membership attached, for example to the corner flag club, stipulate that any person showing support for the visiting team risks being ejected.

In fact, back in 1998, Foster was not the only person who had noticed the occasional flare-up in and around some corporate areas at Spurs. Bob McIver is the head of building control at Haringey Council and he told *On The Line*: 'The big problem with football is that it is so territorial. No other sport comes close. Supporters regard anyone other than a home supporter in a home area as an infringement of their rights almost. They just don't like it.'

This is, of course, true at all football clubs and not just Spurs, as Foster had acknowledged at the end of his letter: 'I realise there are no easy solutions to this problem and that this type of difficulty is not confined to your club, however I do believe this is a serious issue which is worthy of your further attention.'

And ultimately the particular problem with the corner flag club at Spurs did receive some attention, not least because Haringey, who issue the licence for football matches, insisted on it.

Ever since all these troubles at Spurs, the club has passed into new ownership and has had a new marketing director, Scott Gardiner, who came to the club from Rangers in Scotland, where they know a thing or two about passion and violence in football. Gardiner believes that, even though it is impossible for a club to account for the destination of every ticket, this in itself is not sufficient justification to ban corporate hospitality from the open areas of the stands at football grounds:

> It is not in essence important for us to know who is occupying a seat; what is important is that whoever occupies it behaves in an appropriate manner or risks being thrown out. An away fan who takes up the offer of hospitality here must know that they are not sitting in a bubble, they must know they are in the home area and act accordingly.

Not good enough, according to Harvey Harris, who still insists, even though trouble has dwindled to nothing at White Hart Lane of late, that mixing home fans with away fans, be they corporate guests or not, is at the very least annoying and spoils his enjoyment of the game and at worst still remains a focus for trouble which, in his view, will surely one day erupt.

Simon Inglis, the stadium expert, sympathizes, and points out that while modern stadia have all but designed the hooligan out, they have produced an unexpected side effect:

No one predicted that, far from making people more tolerant of fellow supporters, you now have situations if an away fan pops up in a home stand, because they are now so much more readily identifiable and because the home stand is now modern and an object of pride among the home fans, it has merely served to ratchet up the territorial feelings of the local support.

Aled Williams knows just what he is on about. 'While often we have managed to establish a rapport with home fans in our immediate area,' he said, 'those a little bit further afield, who we haven't talked with and who see us supporting our team, have hurled abuse at us.'

And there is no doubt that corporate hospitality in stands does raise passions. *On The Line* witnessed what amounted to a siege of an open area of seating in front of a hospitality box while making a programme about Leeds United in 1999. It was a highly charged FA Cup tie against Tottenham – highly charged because it marked the first return to the stadium of George Graham weeks after he had walked out on the Yorkshire club in favour of the London one.

Shortly after Tim Sherwood scored the opener for Spurs, Leeds fans turned on an open area stuffed with Tottenham fans and started physically and verbally abusing them. Stewards relayed to the control box that matters were turning nasty and the group of Spurs fans in an open balcony in front of the box were frightened. We listened in to the police radio, as the law dived into the area to quell the unrest by evacuating some fans to another part of the ground. Altogether an unpleasant experience at a ground that was otherwise trouble free on that day.

It would seem that the nub of the issue is that clubs have to believe that fans can be persuaded to wine and dine and then not cheer if they support the visiting team. The clubs need the money from the corporate dining and they have confidence in the system of stewarding to snuff out any trouble.

But it is a fact that since the mid-1990s incidents of football related violence have been on the increase. Most of this is off-site, where both sets of knucklehead supporters, so minded, agree to meet up for a fight. There are no figures available for ejections from grounds, still less from corporate areas. When *On The Line* asked Ron Hogg, the deputy chief constable for Durham, who coordinates football matters, he turned down our request for an interview save to say, through his press office that: 'I am aware of the problem.'

Whatever the degree of danger in the continuing spread of corporate seats, one thing is clear: if anyone other than the club or authorized outlet is found selling a ticket then the authorities show no quarter in coming down like a ton of bricks. Football is alone among sports in that it is illegal to tout a football ticket. This legislation was brought in specifically to combat fans from either side mixing in the same stand, which, of course, as we have seen, is a phenomenon that the clubs freely abet in the sale of the hospitality packages.

The case of the Leicester players disposing of tickets to a Worthington Cup Final, which then ended up in the hands of thugs, has already been referred to elsewhere in this book but it bears repeating in relation to the hypocrisy and humbug surrounding the issue of corporate hospitality.

Nick Bitel was the lawyer who successfully defended Stephen Guppy against all charges of irresponsibly disposing of tickets. Tony Cottee, Andrew Impey and others were disciplined. Bitel told *On The Line*:

> Guppy, Cottee and all the others were being accused precisely of what the FA were doing at the FA Cup Final. That is, they were, without any regard to who was being supported, distributing tickets to an area, in that case a corporate hospitality area, so that fans were being mixed by their very actions.

The Leicester players were not accused of selling the tickets. They passed them without charge to friends. Soon after, it appears, a number of the friends had sold them onto agencies, who in turn sold the tickets in conjunction with an unofficial hospitality package. The resulting mayhem made the front pages the day after the match because a photographer captured the moment a hulking great brute of a man punched a woman in the face.

In defending Guppy, Bitel argued that the FA had created the same risk knowingly as they were accusing the players of having caused unwittingly:

> The FA's argument in the Guppy case was, yes, they were aware that home and away fans would be mixing in corporate areas and as a result had taken additional security measures to ensure that no trouble erupted. But that did not seem like a very satisfactory answer to me. If you are aware that a problem is caused by your actions, then surely you do not take those actions.

Left to their own devices, clubs will undoubtedly go on selling and expanding all manner of corporate entertainment within their stadia. Some clubs will push the envelope more than others and then everyone will profess shock and horror and, of course, a complete lack of culpability should anything serious and violent occur in the future.

They may not be left to their own devices for long, though. Ill thought out commercial practices with a public liability have a way of ending up in court. And indeed the club's right to sell a ticket to anyone it chooses has already been challenged in an English court.

In September 2000, at the height of the fuel crisis, Aled Williams sold a ticket outside Old Trafford. The ticket belonged to his friend with whom he usually attended all home matches. On this particular night, however, Williams's friend did not have and could not acquire the petrol to make it back from the Northeast where he had been working. It was a Champions League match against Dynamo Kiev.

It was Williams's misfortune that the man he sold the ticket to happened to be an undercover policeman, who promptly 'nicked' him. And he was prosecuted under the law referred to above, which means it is illegal to tout a football ticket, as he explained to *On The Line*:

> Well, I was amazed. I had offered it at half price and it was a European Champions League match. I knew from

his accent that he was not an away fan. The Crown Prosecution Service [CPS] would not drop the case, despite all the mitigating evidence. They decided it was in the public interest that I be prosecuted because I was endangering public safety.

The CPS told the magistrates how much danger I had caused, how the police tried to maintain segregation and how selling tickets had jeopardized that segregation. I had about 30 points of mitigation and one of those was a letter from a football club that accompanied some tickets he (Williams's friend) had purchased in the corporate area via the internet.

The letter pointed out that the tickets were in the home area and that the ticket holder should not wear away colours or do anything to provoke the home fans. Now this was a letter on a football club's headed newspaper. It was proof that the club accepted that the tickets may well end up in the hands of an away fan. And quite frankly a written disclaimer does not seem much of a deterrent or guarantee against an away fan with violent intent purchasing and mixing with home support.

'There is little or no difference between this arrangement and the transaction that had landed me in court.' complained Aled

The magistrate agreed with him and expressed amazement that clubs could be so lax and free about selling tickets over the internet. He was given an absolute discharge in mitigation of the double standards being operated by the clubs. In effect the magistrate found Williams guilty but blameless. Even so, it is still an interesting point for the football authorities to contemplate.

Corporate hospitality's spread into the open areas of a stadium was not a planned strategy but was rather the by-product of new and refurbished grounds. It was almost as if the clubs were taken aback by the number of fans prepared to cough up for the corporate experience.

With the reduction of tickets available for away fans to buy in most new stadia, a corporate seat has become an alternative way of following your team, albeit an expensive one. Those who are prepared to shell out so much are, one must assume, at the passionate end of the spectrum of support. The threat to public safety is inherent.

Some clubs are further down the road than others with the penetration of corporate seats in open seating areas. Manchester United are the brand leaders, while Tottenham, with 2,000 club seats, are at corporate capacity. Typically, most Premier clubs feature about 1,000 such hospitality seats in the open areas of their stands.

The clubs justify this by saying it is a financial revenue stream that they cannot afford to ignore and that with proper stewarding it represents low or no risk. The counter view is that it probably represents a greater risk than clubs are prepared to admit. It also demonstrates the stock in which most clubs hold their ordinary fans.

We'll let Harvey Harris have the last word: 'I think the motive of a club is to earn more money and if it meant it was annoying or inconvenient to other home fans, I think that is secondary to a club's policy of earning extra revenue.'

Index